# BORN TO MANAGE

# BORN TO MANAGE
## THE AUTOBIOGRAPHY

## Terry Venables

### with Alex Montgomery

### SIMON &
### SCHUSTER

London · New York · Sydney · Toronto · New Delhi

A CBS COMPANY

First published in Great Britain by Simon & Schuster UK Ltd, 2014
A CBS COMPANY

1 3 5 7 9 10 8 6 4 2

Simon & Schuster UK Ltd
1st Floor
222 Gray's Inn Road
London WC1X 8HB

www.simonandschuster.co.uk

Simon & Schuster Australia, Sydney
Simon & Schuster India, New Delhi

A CIP catalogue record for this book
is available from the British Library

Hardback ISBN: 978-1-47112-991-9
Trade Paperback ISBN: 978-1-47112-992-6
Ebook: 978-1-47112-994-0

Typeset in the UK by M Rules
Printed and bound by CPI Group (UK) Ltd, Croydon, CR0 4YY

To Yvette,
You've made me laugh through the good times
and even through the bad,

My wife, my best friend, my love

# CONTENTS

# FOREWORD

*6 January 2013, the Pacific coast off Valparaiso, Chile*
*My 70th birthday.*

WE ARE NEAR the end of 15 days of sailing on the southern oceans. The trip was organised to celebrate a milestone birthday but it also gave me the time to decide upon an outline for this memoir. This is our last night and we are on deck. The sun is setting. It is one of nature's grand gestures and we have witnessed a few since leaving Buenos Aires, hugging the Argentine coastline in the southern Atlantic before cutting through the Beagle Channel into a Pacific Ocean that is flat and calm for the time of year.

I had somehow missed out South America over the years, despite travelling extensively as a player and coach. On this occasion I had just enough time in Argentina to breathe the air that has produced so many great footballers, Alfredo Di Stefano – an early hero whom I eventually faced as an opposition coach in Spain and was as dignified as I imagined him to be – Diego Maradona, my player at Barcelona for far too short a time, and Lionel Messi the current star of Barça and a talent worthy of being considered alongside those two as the most outstanding the country has produced. The voyage has not been all straightforward. My wife Yvette and

I had planned to visit the British war cemetery and a battle zone in the Falklands, but the Argentines had warned they would refuse our ship access to ports further south on the mainland if we headed for Port Stanley. The trip to the islands was cancelled.

As the days grew longer, I reflected on times gone and a career in football which has occupied 90 per cent of my thinking. I always seem to have been told to slow down, take the pace out of my life, put down the phone and enjoy doing nothing. No way would I listen to that sort of advice, but during the length of this voyage, inspired by the scenery of the southern oceans, the distant mountainous shorelines, the sparkling blue of immense glaciers, the stark majesty of it all, I did just that. It is also a fact that getting reception on the mobile was virtually impossible, limiting calls in and out.

The plan is for this memoir to reflect on a career in football that stretches back to the late 1950s. My first autobiography was published 20 years ago in the belief that not much else was going to happen which would be of any interest to anyone. Therefore, I had never properly considered producing a follow-up, but an awful lot had happened to me in the interim.

There were aspects of my term as England manager I thought worth revealing, particularly memories of our Euro 96 victory against the Dutch and how much it meant to me. There were points I wanted to make about my early years, about FC Barcelona and the bitter-sweet years at Spurs. The sale of the book was actually halted by Alan Sugar, the one-time chairman of Spurs and my co-owner of the club who is now a well-known reality show host. It was argued I had been harsh in my assessment of him, the matter was settled: no more books could be sold.

Since then, the idea of putting more thoughts to paper had never been a consideration until I was convinced it could be done. We decided it would be worthwhile revisiting my life in football before

England, as well as what had happened since. So there are recollections of my childhood in Dagenham; my development as a player and as a manager; the 'miracle' of Barcelona; of winning an FA Cup at Spurs the season after we had finished third in the league, a position still not equalled. These are occasions I am happy to relive.

There are less comfortable moments when I was burdened with 'baggage' that made no sense to me. Is it water under the bridge? Definitely. I always tried to ensure, with the backing of Yvette, that my family was untouched by the controversies we confronted. We were not going to let my attackers get us down. More than anything, I want to explain why the great and beautiful game of football has had me in its grip for as long as I can remember. I want to explain my beliefs – philosophy seems a little high falutin – that had grown out of my desperation to learn, form my own opinions and then pass them on with relevant changes to the players in my charge. This memoir is about football and how I liked to play it and see it played. These are snapshots of my life as I remember them.

I

# PLANNING FOR THE PERFECT DAY

IT IS POSSIBLE THAT one match out of thousands can provide you with everything you believe in as a manager. You anticipate such a game, work for it and hope the expectation is fulfilled. For me, that match came on the particularly humid evening of 18 June 1996 when my England team surprised, subdued and overwhelmed the Netherlands at Wembley in the final group game of the European Championships. It was perfection: my most thrilling experience in football – more special than winning the Spanish title with Barcelona, or the FA Cup at Spurs, or the excitement of winning promotion.

As someone who prefers to look forward, not back, I have never spoken in depth and in public about an occasion, and the build-up to it, that meant so much to me as a manager. While there is always merit in quiet reflection, in this instance I am happy to relive what we achieved in that game. I feel privileged to have played my part in a match that actually galvanised the country. It gave me an enormous feeling of pride that the huge commitment of our staff and every member of the squad had received its justifiable reward.

It did not just happen. That performance was the culmination of two and a half years of preparation. In that time, I had convinced all the staff and players – not without being questioned – that we had the ability and character to change the style in which we played at international level. It was intended as a long-term strategy to take us on to the World Cup finals in France two years later, but sadly I would not be in position to see it through.

Going into that game, I was confident we would win and so emerge as group champions; I knew that it could even be achieved with a bit of swagger. For too long, too many had believed we had neither the skill nor the nous to beat the best in world football, in this case the stylish, elegant Dutch. We decisively proved that to be wrong, and I was jubilant, while the crowd at Wembley was in raptures at what they had seen.

I relished the chaotic scenes immediately after the match. I remember the looks of delight – I don't think relief came into it – on the faces of Don Howe, Bryan Robson, Mike Kelly, Ted Buxton, Dave Butler and our other physio Alan Smith, the backroom team who had worked with me for such an occasion. The whole bench was thrilled, shaking hands and embracing in the relative privacy of the tunnel. Dave Sexton, who was also part of the set-up, would have felt the same charge of excitement up in the stands. It wasn't as though we had won the World Cup, but we all recognised it was a breakthrough and a significant marker for the future. That was the moment I knew we would be ready for the World Cup in two years' time.

We had not just beaten one of the most sophisticated systems in world football, we had taken the Dutch apart. We did so by making them play the way we wanted them to play, not the way that suited de Boer, van der Sar, Bergkamp, Blind and Seedorf. The analysis of how we had done it could wait. For now, I just wanted to soak up the atmosphere; Wembley was rocking, celebrating like I'd never seen or heard it before. This was a moment to enjoy.

It had been 14 years and five attempts since we had last beaten the Dutch, and I was still struggling to take it all in when I had to head off to the first of the many press conferences I had to attend. As a manager – whatever the result – you try to be in full control, cool and ready for whatever is thrown at you. It is easy to be carried along with everybody else in a tidal wave of euphoria or depression, but I couldn't think like that. When I asked myself: 'What have we done?' I realised that there was so much more to do, starting by beating Spain in the quarter-finals. It was a fabulous performance against world-class opposition, but real glory comes from winning trophies.

What struck me about that press conference was the happiness we had produced. Too often England had had to suffer the serious disappointment of unexpected defeat when the stakes were high. Not tonight. As I walked to the banqueting hall where the team was waiting, I heard my fellow countrymen say it was the best performance ever. I enjoyed the exaggeration. Could it be the best ever? Or the best since England won the World Cup in 1966? Or our performances in the 1970 World Cup finals in Mexico, and the truly memorable defeat against Brazil?

When I got there, I was met by groups of England players, each surrounded by their wives and children and friends. There was a lot of back-slapping and high-fiving going on as everyone soaked in an atmosphere they were unused to, and surely wanted more of. My dad Fred was there, on the fringes of the hospitality area. What could he say? His presence was enough. My daughters Tracey and Nancy and grandson Sam were also there to greet me. My wife Yvette was at home, as she never attends matches, and has never felt the need to be part of the big-match bonhomie. Thinking of the passion generated that night, even now I find it to be highly emotional.

I was absorbed by what I had to do as I floated among the high and mighty, accepting handshake after handshake. Ah, the goodwill when you win! The players had been told this was a moment to have a beer, relax and enjoy their success, but tomorrow they knew we would talk, train and prepare for Spain in the quarter-finals. They had performed to the letter of their instructions, but we had to win three more matches against Europe's strongest countries before we could deliver to our supporters what they really wanted: the trophy.

On my way through the throng, I had heard someone say that Sir Stanley Matthews, one of English football's great figures, was purring at what he had seen. He was one of my boyhood heroes – in truth, he was everybody's hero and I had been thrilled to play against him at the beginning of my career. To those of us who grew up in the post-war era, we would read about players like him and occasionally be able to watch them live when they played in London, or just maybe see them on television. Now, if he was an admirer of the team's performance, it would be special.

I met Ted Buxton and we found a quiet spot where he told me the full story. Sir Stanley – who some months before had mistaken Ted for me – had stopped him as he walked along the side of the banqueting hall.

'He was very emotional,' Ted explained. 'He grabbed me and asked: "Where's Terry?" I told him you were in a press conference. So he continued: "I can't stay, I have a car waiting for me, but tell Terry that was the best England performance I have seen in years."'

Then, Ted added, Sir Stanley said the words that really got to me: 'I would have loved to have played in that team.'

My day was complete!

*

But I have jumped ahead of myself. First of all, I had to get the job as England's national coach, and that was out of my control. When the job became available, as a result of our depressing failure to qualify for the 1994 World Cup finals in the United States, I was embroiled in a legal action against Alan Sugar, having been sacked from Tottenham. Because of that, I did not think I had a chance to succeed Graham Taylor after he resigned on 23 November 1993. Certainly, there were some within the FA and elsewhere who were determined to dismiss me as someone with the wrong image for the job. Initially, FA chairman Sir Bert Millichip appeared to be one of them, which was not a good start, so I virtually gave up any chance of being invited for talks, let alone getting the job.

As a result of the fall-out from my departure from Spurs, there had been some horrendous newspaper headlines about me and my business affairs. Not only that, there had been TV documentaries made about me, and MP Kate Hoey had stated in Parliament that I was unfit for the job. The accusations hit me like a sledgehammer, and the often shocking criticism had an effect on my family, though they hid their concerns well. The general view was that I was burdened with too much 'baggage' from the court cases and the adverse publicity I had been receiving even to be considered for such a prestigious role as England's national coach.

My name had been linked with the position in the past. When Bobby Robson took over from Ron Greenwood after the 1982 World Cup, my name was floated, though I was never on the shortlist. When Bob stood down in 1990, I was mentioned by some in the press as a contender, but wasn't even interviewed by the FA. It was a fuzzy time for me, and a storm was gathering at Spurs, which clearly counted against me. If my situation had been deemed too complicated in 1990, it had hardly got any easier in the interim.

Immediately Graham resigned, the press was full of stories about who would be offered the job. My name was mentioned, but I remained pessimistic. I felt I had no chance at all, despite the fact my CV was good. I hoped it was more than that, and they might think it was bloody impressive: there were the successful years as Crystal Palace coach and at Queens Park Rangers, then I'd gone abroad to Barcelona and a La Liga title and the European Cup final. On my return to England with Spurs, we had won the FA Cup, taken the side to third in the league and played football the way it should be played.

The FA set up a sub-committee to find the new manager. On it were FA chairman Sir Bert Millichip, Noel White (chairman of the International Committee and a Liverpool director), Ian Stott of Oldham Athletic and FA chief executive Graham Kelly. I believe that Rick Parry, chief executive of the Premier League, was also consulted because of my dispute with Alan Sugar. Jimmy Armfield, the former England defender and manager of considerable experience, was appointed by Graham Kelly to take soundings as widely as possible from those in the game as to who they believed would be Taylor's most suitable successor.

Jimmy met managers, players, directors, supporters, and talked to everybody possible. He took his role very seriously, as he should have, and as you would expect of him. I knew him and we had meetings to discuss the position. Eventually, he reported to the FA that I had widespread support throughout the country. It would be untrue to say that the support was unanimous, but I heard of only one manager who spoke out against me, but that was largely because he believed the whole process was some sort of southern stitch-up.

Jimmy is not the type of person to fudge anything, and he took his time to reach his conclusions. I knew he would be cautious. I remember when he was managing Leeds United and he wanted to buy Peter Taylor from me at Crystal Palace. He offered less than the £200,000 I wanted, then asked me if I genuinely thought Peter was worth that (a lot of money then, to be fair). I asked him what he thought my reply would be. He thought so long and hard about meeting our valuation that we ended up selling Peter to Spurs for £200,000. He may be pedantic, but he had everyone's trust in this task, mine included. Believe me, if his research showed I would not have the support of the game, then that is what he would have reported.

I was in the race – as a front runner – and so I was invited for talks. Some questioned whether I might simply walk away from the whole process, but there was no way I was going to turn down the opportunity to manage my country. Especially now that I knew I had plenty of support, not just from outside the FA but also from within. I understood that Graham Kelly was a powerful voice in my defence at the FA's Lancaster Gate headquarters.

The first round of these interviews with the sub-committee was held in the Football League offices on the Old Marylebone Road, London. Unfortunately, the FA and I were well acquainted. Earlier that year, in March, the FA had demanded that Nicky Barmby should be made available for a youth tournament in Australia. I wanted him fit and well for an FA Cup quarter-final against Manchester City. Graham Kelly told me if we did not release him, Spurs would be sued. It was a very tetchy argument, as I remember it. I was left with no option; and Nick was immediately cleared to travel in the FA youth party.

Fortunately, there was no obvious hangover from that clash. I was relaxed, though I remember thinking Noel White looked tense. As chairman of the International Committee, he was never specific about what they would want from me if I was appointed. To me it was self-evident, but it would have been interesting to have White confirm it. The main concern was to develop a successful England team, particularly as we were hosting the Euro 96 finals in just two and a half years.

The interview was probing without being an inquisition. They wanted to know if there were any skeletons in the cupboard waiting to be discovered. Not as far as I was aware, I explained. I outlined some ideas I had about the structure of the game in England, talking about the need, as I saw it, for the two sections in the English game, the professional and the part-time, to be more closely aligned. They did not create any barrier between me and them by saying I would be unable to play certain players or that they expected certain players to be included. Despite a coolness from White, it was all very civilised, and I was told the decision would be relayed to me in good time.

It was during this initial interview that I noticed a mellowing in the attitude of Sir Bert towards me. His initially doubtful stance changed as time progressed and he was soon robustly championing my cause. I never could say that about White or Ian Stott. White appeared opposed to me from the very beginning, echoing the opinion of then Manchester City chairman Peter Swales. They were friends and had been business partners in a substantial electrical business in the North West. Swales considered me a close friend of Malcolm Allison, whom he detested when Mal was at City, so I was tarnished by association. Swales even phoned Graham to say I was not the sort for the job. But that did not stop him twice inviting me to join Manchester City as manager. Can you wonder at my confusion and why I still felt my chances of getting the job were slim.

Even on this very tense and important occasion, we soon discovered that there were far more important things going on elsewhere. During the interview, Graham Kelly went to look out of the office window and was horrified to see a woman threatening to commit suicide by throwing herself off the building directly in front of him. We watched the deeply upsetting scene as the police and the emergency services arrived. Thankfully, she was talked down from what, according to the concierge in our building, was a regular occurrence.

Just before I left I was told how high profile a job it was – as if I didn't know. Then they came to discuss the salary. I knew from the managerial grapevine that Graham Taylor had been on about £145,000 a year, so I wondered what I might be offered. I was told the figure would be £160,000.

'You might be surprised at that,' one voice, I think Stott, said. 'But that is what it is.'

'Well,' I said. 'I have a surprise for you – I'll take it.'

Graham laughed. He has a fine sense of humour, and I liked that in him. White and Stott looked taken aback, and more than a little surprised. I was then asked: 'Are you happy with that?'

'Yes,' I replied. 'Very happy, thank you.'

That was not what they were expecting. The salary was way below the rate the national coach of a country the size of England should have been offered. It was set low, I am sure, to put me off and leave them to negotiate with Gerry Francis and Glenn Hoddle – the two men reported to be my competitors – although it was becoming more and more obvious to me that I was on a shortlist of one. (For the record, Glenn succeeded me less than three years later, on just under £350,000.) What they had not considered was my determination to take the job without argument.

As I left the meeting, Jimmy Armfield took me to one side and told me on no account could I speak about this publicly and to remember the meeting was a secret. I picked up an *Evening Standard* on the way home and as I remember it the headline read: 'VENABLES IN SECRET MEETING WITH FA'. Some secret!

Having had my interview, I waited. And waited. A cartoon by Jak summed up the public impatience at what had turned into a saga.

He showed me with a long white beard and long white hair, sitting outside an interview room in one of the FA's corridors of power, being approached by a female member of the FA staff exclaiming that I would not have to wait for much longer and the delay was caused by the committee reminiscing.

While the FA took their time, I was contacted by Alan Evans of the Welsh FA, who offered me the chance to manage Wales. I had spent a lot of time in that fine country. My mother was staunchly Welsh and she would have been delighted if I had said yes to Alan. It would also have suited those members of the FA who didn't want me to take charge, but I was English, I had played for my country and I would manage them if I had a chance. I just had to sit tight in the hope the rest of the committee could be persuaded by Sir Bert and Graham to do what they didn't want to do: appoint me.

Surprisingly at that time, there was also interest from Nigeria which was looking for a national coach. It was an interesting proposition put to me by John Fashanu, the former Wimbledon striker and man of many clubs including Norwich (where he began his career with his late brother Justin), Millwall, Crystal Palace and Aston Villa. Both offers would have been financially better than the one England had put on the table. The difference was my desire to manage England, despite knowing I was unlikely ever to have my immediate boss's unstinting support. I felt that White could not have been more opposed to me had he been under orders. Because of all the bad publicity I had been receiving, he and Stott seemed to take it as read that I was all about money. The programmes and newspaper articles had damaged my reputation badly. They may like to know that I went into the FA interview prepared to do the job for nothing if there had been an argument about salary. They could ask me to prove that, and I could not other than through family and friends, but it's true.

The reality is that I have never been more money-conscious than you would consider normal. I was a friendly negotiator with England because I wanted the job; it would be the high point of my career; my ambition realised. I didn't bargain or go for the sort of massive money my successors were offered, climaxing with the over-the-top £6 million a year paid to Fabio Capello. When I took the job as national coach of Australia after finishing with England, I agreed a salary of A$200,000, even less than my FA pay. I accepted the appointment Down Under because, like the England role, I wanted it. I also felt there was no way at that time that I would be able to take a club job as manager in the Premiership, or anywhere else, despite offers of one sort or another, so soon after managing my country. It would be very difficult to step down a grade. So I decided to stick with international football for as long as possible, and that is why I headed for the southern hemisphere, though I would eventually return to the domestic scene to help out Bryan Robson at Middlesbrough.

Meanwhile, the wait dragged on. How long does it take to make a decision? Just when it looked like D-Day, another complication would cloud the water. It was all so frustrating, but worth the wait if the job was to be mine.

The call from Graham finally came through on 25 January 1994. One or two on the committee had actually proposed I be offered a six-month probationary contract. I didn't consider that as anything other than the insult it was. My title would be national coach not manager, but that suited me as it is what I was. I accepted immediately and we met with our lawyers to settle the contract at London's Royal Lancaster Hotel. My first official press conference as England national coach took place on 28 January, and I went into it with the extra confidence of knowing that Sir Bert and Graham were giving me their full support.

There is a difference between nationalism and patriotism.

Patriotism is about the way you are brought up. It came not just from my family, and what they felt about our country and how they instilled those feelings in me, but also from the community I grew up in. Strangely, for all that has been said about my time as England manager, and my career leading up to it, I cannot remember once being asked a question about what it was that brought about the deep emotion to support my country at all costs. Maybe my outward appearance did not attract that sort of question, but that loyalty was inbred: loyalty to family, friends and neighbours, to our area of East London, and to be passionately, emotionally, overwhelmingly loyal to England.

We didn't think twice about it. I was brought up in the post-war era to honour and respect those around us. The raw suffering of the Second World War was borne by the survivors in memory of those who did not make it through. We were that 'one nation' they have been striving for ever since, brought closer by the austerity of the times. When you understand that background, you will understand my feelings when I accepted the offer to manage England, having won honours as a player at every England level from schoolboy all the way through to senior, including amateur. I had also coached the England Under-21s when David Sexton was in charge, and now I was the national coach. That was the sort of 'baggage' I was very happy to carry around.

I knew exactly what I wanted to do, and how I wanted to do it. I had quietly prepared for the job before I was appointed. I was not being over-confident, far from it, as the wait seemed eternal. There were good days and bad ones, days when I felt confident I would be offered the job and others when I was less so. At least by working on an imaginary squad, I felt I was moving in the right direction. I began by sorting out the players I saw as certainties; men such as Tony Adams, David Platt, Alan Shearer, Teddy Sheringham and Gazza were at the forefront of my thinking. In all,

PLANNING FOR THE PERFECT DAY | 17

I listed a squad of 45, but I would have to find out more about the character of some of them before seeing if they were right, and that would come only from working with them.

Having selected a first squad on paper, I needed time to consider all the angles that I expected to confront, like answering the press, who I felt sure would not just be asking me about team issues. I would need to find out the working style of the people at the FA. It would be different, but I was confident it would work. I wanted to know as much as I could and be as well prepared for the job when I walked in to the FA office for the first time as national coach. I also knew how I wanted the team to play.

Ever since my youth team days, when we would go to the Netherlands and win 5-0 or even 10-0, I have had a strong interest in Dutch football. The games might have been walkovers, but I admired the determination of their little clubs to formulate a coaching strategy and stick with it, no matter how long it was going to take. Over the years, they emerged as the developers of what is recognised as 'Total Football', a label coined by the media not the coach, Rinus Michels. The tactic had grown from all those defeats. They developed a game based on attack, where defenders could be comfortable in attack and forwards could defend. It was almost as if their clubs would throw team shirts on the floor and ask the players to pick any number. They played without restrictions.

Since the emergence of Ajax under Rinus Michels in the 1960s, I have been strongly influenced by their extraordinary success at both club and international level. They were adventurous and inventive; they worked to be the opposite of obvious. They worked together to improve their game, and in the process made it great. I loved that, and decided it would be my way, or rather the best way, if we had the opportunity to express it. With exceptions, we English were terrible plodders. Even after we were brought to our senses, when the Hungarians made us look like pre-historic dinosaurs in football terms during the 1950s, we had been slow to react to new ideas, taking the best from what you admire, tweaking it, and seeing if it can work for you.

There are many qualities universally admired in our game: our never-say-die attitude is envied; we have managed to produce great and hugely successful club sides at European level – the most eminent being Liverpool, Manchester United and Nottingham Forest, all three with a high percentage of talent developed in these islands. We should also remember the success of Aston Villa. Sadly, only United (thanks to the persuasive power of Sir Alex Ferguson) and my former club Chelsea have maintained a strong European challenge into the new millennium, though both Liverpool and Arsenal have had their moments. But when it comes to the World Cup and the European Championships, we have failed lamentably to make any telling impact since winning the big prize in 1966. And remember, after 1970 it was 1982 before we next took part in the finals. That was a disgrace for a country of our size and footballing tradition, especially when Scotland, with far fewer resources than ourselves, qualified for five consecutive finals between 1974 and 1990.

Ron Greenwood's squad made a decent fist of the 1982 campaign in Spain, reaching the second round. Bobby Robson's England World Cup squad of 1990 was the most successful since Sir Alf Ramsey's teams. His team reached the semi-finals, only to lose its nerve in a catastrophic penalty shoot-out against Germany, when Stuart Pearce and Chris Waddle both missed from the spot. Two years earlier, we had been thrashed in the European Championships finals, losing all three group matches against the Republic of Ireland, Holland and Russia. The failure traumatised Bob to such an extent he isolated himself, to the concern of many, in a Munich hotel with no wish to show himself or speak to anyone. It took him time to recover from what he saw as a humiliation. He had already learned how to suffer. In the Mexico 1986 finals, it was Maradona's Hand of God goal and the overall power and skill of the Argentines that eliminated us in the quarter-finals. And to think those were the highlights!

I thought there had to be a reason for our lack of success and, once we worked out what it was, then we could begin to find an answer. I fervently believed I knew what it was. One of the main deficiencies in the English game was our players' failure to understand what was expected of them and what their role was in the team. This was not a case of a lack of individual ability, though that could be a factor, nor their fitness nor character. The Dutch, the Italians, the Germans, the Brazilians, the Argentines all know what they are, what they represent, what is expected of them. It appeared to me that we did not, certainly not in recent decades. That was what I planned to change. I wanted each player to have a specific role and to know exactly what it was in a system that was distinctly not what the world recognised as England's. Basically, we would surprise the opposition. We would be a team always in attack mode, but strong and ready to defend. Bravery would also be a constant theme of mine.

As an admirer of what was being taught and developed in Holland, even before my first sightings of Johan Cruyff and coach Michels's Ajax, there is no doubt the Dutch way influenced my thinking and how I would concentrate my work as a coach. I had used it successfully, with adjustments, at Crystal Palace, Queens Park Rangers, Barcelona and Spurs. Now I wanted to do the same with England, though I knew I would have to persuade the coaching staff and my players that it would work for us.

I tried to explain some of my vision for the team at my first press conference, and was surprised by the interpretation by one newspaper of what I had said. The headline claimed my plan was to have England playing like Brazil, even though I never mentioned that as a possibility. It turned out that the reporter's editor had not felt my description was clear enough and insisted that the comparison should be with Brazil. Had I been asked the question, I might have given the idea a little backing. Who wouldn't love to play like Brazil? It served only to remind me of the cavalier attitude among a few, who think they can make it up as they go along. In fairness, it takes a strong-willed reporter to tell his sports editor that he is wrong, and they should stick to what was actually said.

My first task was to recruit my backroom staff. I had a 'plan B' prepared, in case it was impossible to appoint those who were at the very top of the list, but I got all those I approached. I wanted football men of the right stuff, not men who would agree with every word I said, but people who would argue like hell if they thought I was wrong. They had to be the type who would put me under pressure when I proposed my Dutch plan. I said to them when we met that they had to tell me what they felt was right and what was wrong. I believe you have to keep stretching yourself, and if you stand still you cannot possibly go forward. You must always ask questions and, as Malcolm Allison used to say to me, we have to listen to other opinions and ideas, because if you work only with your own, then that is what you end up with: your knowledge and yours alone.

I took my lesson from Ron Greenwood when he was appointed England manager in 1977, after England had failed to qualify for a second successive World Cup. It was the make-up of his backroom staff that was so important, as he brought in people who would challenge him. And I am not saying that because he brought me into the set-up to listen and learn – and, with respect, ask questions. I worked with him at the European Championships in Italy in 1980 and then the World Cup finals in Spain two years later.

He named Bill Taylor, a Scot, as his coach, along with Don Howe and Bobby Robson. Dave Sexton would look after the Under-21s, with me and then Howard Wilkinson to help him. But it was Ron's appointment of Brian Clough and Peter Taylor as England's youth team coaches that attracted the headlines and created so much excitement and anticipation. It frightened the hell out of the FA, as Brian was seen as a divisive figure, but can you imagine young kids having such a pair to learn from? That was smart thinking by Ron, even if he and Clough eventually fell out. He wasn't afraid to appoint people who would challenge him.

Some managers and coaches are scared to bring in people they fear might try to grab their job. If that is how they think, maybe it will happen because they are not good enough. What you do not need is inferior quality. It has been a persistent problem for the Football Association. If they had been clever, they could have given Brian Clough the job as national manager, because the country wanted him and he achieved so much in the role at club level, but they have this ridiculously cautious attitude. I suspect if they thought someone swore too much or didn't dress or speak properly, they would rather appoint a lesser person than go for the best man. And we wonder why we are always asking: 'Why doesn't the England team improve?' It didn't matter how Brian Clough came across to the international committee, it only mattered that he could produce results for England. If he did that, he could behave as he damn well liked. The FA should understand they are employing someone because he possesses the qualities that will allow England's national team to improve, nothing else.

Because of all that, Don Howe's status as an outstanding coach, plus his vast experience gained over many years at the top, made him a premier choice, which was essential if I was to get the best out of my squad. Meanwhile, I wanted Dave Sexton to look after the Under-21s. When I said I was keen to appoint Dave, I was asked by a committee man if I knew Dave was 64. 'I want him as a coach,' I replied. 'Not a player.'

These two would be a vital part of my think tank. Don knew the game better than anybody at club level, having been coach of the Arsenal Double team of 1971. He also had vast knowledge of the international scene, having worked with both Ron and Bobby Robson. Dave was always a pleasure to be with, an astute and inspirational coach. I had known him since my early years at Chelsea, and had learned so much from him then and when we worked together during Ron's tenure. He had a way with him that could be beguiling, unless you riled him. His input was going to be invaluable, and he would develop the players I saw as essential for the next stage, the World Cup finals of 1998 in France.

I wanted to bring in Bryan Robson – a wonderful player at the highest level with England and Manchester United – to liaise between the squad and us. He was younger and closer in age to the players. The FA was also very keen for someone to be groomed as a future England manager. I had discussed it with Sir Bert and Graham, and that was the extra value of having Bryan on the staff. All the major countries, without exception, had a plan of succession, apart from the FA. Unfortunately, it was not followed through with Bryan after I left.

Mike Kelly was appointed technical goalkeeping coach. He was also an acknowledged motivator – a great man to have as part of the inner circle. Dave Butler was on the team as physiotherapist. I had worked with Dave over the years and knew his capabilities. Ted Buxton would scout for me, always happy to move at short notice when required. Ted, and I make no excuses for this, was my extra pair of eyes and ears. It took a month or two of extra negotiation to clear his appointment, because of opposition from the committee, but I got him in the end. They would all have their say, and nothing would be held back. Having these men around me – people who could be propagandists for the new way – was crucial. With them in place, I was surprised how confident I was. I didn't feel the pressure that I had expected might dog me at the outset.

With my back-up team in place, I knew what the press expected from me: they wanted England not only to win, but to win with style. I shared that feeling as I believe how you win is the whole point of the operation; it is a beautiful game and I wanted my teams to recognise that.

Dealing with the media is always a tricky part of any England manager's job. With a few exceptions, I didn't see the press as a problem on purely football matters. All England managers, from Sir Alf right the way through to Roy Hodgson today, get bowled a few googlies from time to time, and you must be able to deal with them, but most of the time they're asking about the team: how would they play? How did they play? Who played well? Which players are under pressure? Are you going to qualify for the finals? Those sorts of questions go with the job. The press should never be considered a major problem.

When I outlined to my coaching team how I wanted England to play, there was some opposition from Don Howe and the rest, but they took on board what I wanted. Don was concerned that we had too little time to make such a big change in the way we played. I always knew this would be the biggest worry for Don, which was fine. It wasn't that he and the others were against the Dutch system, or a fusion of the best of English traditions with a strong Dutch influence: attack first, be ready to defend. But they worried a new system of play would not be understood by the players in time for Euro 96. I agreed it was not like a club set-up, where you train every day and have freedom to explain what you want, but I believed we could do it.

I did not feel I was being overly optimistic. We were taking over a squad that had failed to qualify for the World Cup 1994 finals, so I knew I would be making changes to the line-up. It would take time to work out the right 22 players we would need for the finals, irrespective of what had happened to Graham Taylor. I understood just how traumatic it would have been to him and his assistant

Lawrie McMenemy to have missed out on qualification, but I wanted to do things in a different way.

Graham chose to play a long-ball or direct system – call it what you wish – which I have never really liked. It had not worked for England, because they failed to qualify, but it was his prerogative to try that approach. Bad luck and misfortune tripped them at crucial times, as in the decisive qualifying group match against the Netherlands. A poor referee or poor decisions can be as fatal as the wrong system of play. Maybe Graham was not totally true to a set-up that earned him so much success with his club sides, particularly at Watford and Aston Villa; only he knows.

However, I saw how the country reacted with deep disappointment to yet another failure at the highest level of our game. It was my aim to ensure that did not happen again. As hosts of Euro 96, we did not have the problem of qualifying, but it was still important that we built up a winning habit. It allowed me to be single-minded about my selections and the way we would play.

The debate over whether or not we had the time to make it work perfectly was exactly why I had chosen this group of coaches. They pointed out that Ajax was a unique club, and by 1994 they had been teaching their special way of playing for decades. Time, or lack of it, did not stop them integrating signed players such as Kanu, Finidi George and Jari Litmanen. We looked at every angle of the game. It wasn't just a question of how the team would be set out, but how they would use possession to their advantage. It is not all about systems but about common sense. For instance, I had noticed that our teams tended to tire in the final ten minutes, but if they kept the ball and passed it, they would conserve their energy right through to the end, while the opposition would tire having to chase around to try to recover possession.

The players had to be on my side, and I worked from the principle of picking those I saw as best for the job, which isn't the same thing as saying they were simply the best players. There were some, as already mentioned, that I wanted to build my team around, while others were left out. For example, although Gary Lineker was a top goalscorer, he had retired from international football and his career was winding down, so there was no way I was going to bring him back and anyway he would not be around for Euro 96. Others, such as Carlton Palmer and Des Walker, did not fit in with my plans. In truth, the choice of players is totally subjective and only matters when you lose matches and the critics use a non-selection as the stick to beat you with.

It was essential the players agreed that what I had in mind was workable. I could not force something on them that they felt was unworkable, which is why I flew immediately to Italy to have talks with David Platt, the then England captain and a senior and well-respected professional with Sampdoria in Italy. Tony Adams was another key player on my list. I was the salesman: it was up to me to persuade those who I considered essential to the future to take on board what I wanted. I had to ascertain from two of the strongest in a strong squad whether or not they possessed the nerve to do what I wanted them to do.

Tony and David were full of enthusiasm. They were convinced England had the players with the quality and the intelligence to understand my plan. I met Tony at Scott's, the London restaurant with a reputation for excellent seafood. I did not realise he had a serious drink problem when I offered him a glass of wine as he arrived. Tony recalled this meeting in his autobiography – albeit from a different perspective. He explained how what we had said was very exciting, but that he then set off on a four-day bender because of that glass of wine.

Tony and David were both highly successful players and key figures in the side, so their backing set my mind at rest. There was the possibility of failure, but we would have a chance if the others were as positive as these two. If they had not been convinced, then there would have been no point in carrying on with it.

It was one thing to win the somewhat grudging backing of the FA, but now that I was installed, the important factor was winning the support of the players and the public. I was delighted by the reaction of the two senior players to my proposal to radically change the way we were going to play. I knew they would carry the rest of the team. I had fretted a little that they might have thought it was too much, too complicated. But no, as forward thinkers they were for it. We would work match by match, piece by interlocking piece until everyone knew their lines.

We had to get our ideas across to the players quicker than we would have liked. It was no good being wordy. The message was simple enough: we would present the system then explain to each player what his role would be within it. Each member of my staff had to constantly spread the word, not just in meetings but as they came across players, reinforcing the same things, again and again. We were determined to make it work, but it was also so much fun trying something new. We knew there would be setbacks along the way, but you have to get players to give 100 per cent and shut out any external criticism when things are not going well for them, as a team and as individuals.

I would constantly repeat my mantra: 'All our life from when we were learning to kick a ball as kids, we have dreamt of playing for England at Wembley in a major tournament; that, and playing in an FA Cup final, were the two things at the top of the dream list. If you have the chance to do it, you can't waste it. If you do, you have wasted your life, because this is what everyone, and I mean everyone, would love to do – and get paid to do it.' For all that people criticise the wealth footballers earn, in truth the real motivation for the majority is fulfilling that childhood dream, not in earning the big pay packet. The key thing, I told my players, was that they shouldn't end up looking back when they'd finished saying: 'If only I'd given more, if only ...' They had to understand this was their time, and to go for it. That was my message to them. It was all done to ensure there was no negativity in the camp.

I knew there would be setbacks along the way, times when we might not play to the plan and mistakes would be made, but when a game goes wrong and fans start to boo, players need to be strong and take no notice. That's not always easy, as the crowd can diminish a player's bravery. The bravery I am talking about doesn't come from sticking your head in or tackling, however tough the opposition. Bravery is about wanting the ball when the crowd is getting onto you; wanting the ball under all circumstances. If you pass badly, go and look for it again. From the outset, I said that fear was our enemy, not necessarily the opposition. I told them that if they felt fear they should tell me. None did.

Bravery is particularly important for the strikers. The fearful ones try not to get in the position of having to take a chance on their own, in case they put it over the bar again. By contrast, we all know players who go for it every time; they go in and they might miss it, but you know they're going to score in the end, because their persistence will ensure that. It is what the great goalscorers do. A striker like Gary Lineker in his pomp was never beaten. He knew that if he kept trying, kept going for it, the goal would come. That sort of bravery is about playing on when you are struggling. It is the least a manager should expect.

I wanted captains everywhere, players who would not be frightened to make a mistake, but if they did they could recover from it and shrug it off. And I wanted commitment. There's always the temptation to say you can give ten per cent more. If there is any more to give, fine, but if you are truly giving 100 per cent, don't try to do more.

When you pick a squad, everyone is involved during training, but you can get dissatisfaction from those players not being selected, which can affect everyone. I never once sensed that with my group in over two years. That was the extraordinary thing about them: every player was happy to be part of it. The ones not involved in every match played a crucial part in keeping everything together. They worked, anticipating they could receive the call at some stage. And because they gave everything in preparation, it meant they were ready if called. When things looked a bit bad, they were still supporting each other. I know that international team coaches can have desperate problems massaging the egos of their stars, but I had nothing like that to distract me. In their own right they were all leaders.

When I saw the squad train and play, it gave me a feeling of excitement knowing that with every training session we had they were getting closer and closer to my ideal. We believed these players would never give in, even if they had to face hostile crowds home or away. But it is so much easier to play when you feel that surge of encouragement and optimism sweeping from the stands towards you and the team, and if we played the way I wanted us to play, I was sure we would get that. I took on the job believing we could actually win the title at Wembley in the summer of 1996. I told the players that they must feel it, too. Once they understood the target, and believed in it, then was the time to go into details about how we were going to achieve it.

Furthermore, I was comforted by the public welcome I received more or less wherever I went. I had considered the possibility that all the adverse publicity would have had me ostracised, but the public ignored the headlines, so wherever I went I was asked for autographs or photographs. I saw England as my mission, and was immensely proud to have the opportunity to lead my country into a major tournament, and maybe they recognised that. Certainly, the support we received was always excellent, and the fact we played good football helped the fans give us their hearts.

Happily, the FA soon became very supportive. They also wanted to watch a winning England side, one they could be impressed by and be proud of. It was what I wanted. They supported me as a manager of the country. I felt good and confident about the future. Was I ever apprehensive? I'm not sure. Had I been, it would not have lasted long. If the team performed as I knew they could, then all would be well.

From the start, as a group we did not involve ourselves with imaginary problems. The vibrations were not just good but great. All we wanted was an improvement every day. Initially, it can be hard for players, being asked to do something new, but the squad were hungry to just get out there each time there was a game. If that happens, you see the full force of it in tournaments, as by then they know exactly what is expected of them.

The correspondence I received on taking charge was considerable and the message was clear: people backed the England team, and they would be quite happy if it was my regime that brought the country success. They weren't worried by the criticisms I'd had from some in the press. They wanted to be proud of the team and the way we played. I was delighted that people thought that way – now it was up to me and the team to give them what they wanted.

When I took charge, there were a couple of issues that I'd long thought needed to be resolved. Now that I was in a position close to the power base at the FA and with daily access, it was a chance to make my move, so I spoke to Graham Kelly about both. The first concerned players' suspensions. The way it had previously worked, if you were suspended from club football you were also unavailable for England. These rules were a historical absurdity, something that happened nowhere else. I told Graham it did not make sense to ban a man playing for his country because of onfield offences committed while playing for his club. He should be suspended for his country only if he had committed an offence while playing for England. The ruling was changed, which made good common sense to me.

My second request was that I wanted us to be the Auld Enemy again. However, the return of an international match against the Scots was more problematic. The Scottish Football Association was as sickened as the rest of us by the aggression and disruption caused when Scottish fans invaded the pitch at Wembley in 1977, but why end a great tradition because an admittedly substantial minority were prepared to go on the rampage? Attack them, not the fixture, which had eventually been abandoned in 1989. To me, we had to bring back one of the great international dates. After all, it was the original international match, the forerunner for World Cups and the other international championships. It was the one that pumped the blood of fans and players, like no other match at the end of every season.

It was never my privilege to play in one of these fixtures as a senior, but I would have loved to. One of my great early memories was representing England's youth side against Scotland at Ibrox in Glasgow, when I was up against Billy Bremner, who I would face on many later occasions. Billy, no longer with us, epitomised the spirit of the game. It was one personal reason why I wanted it back. Graham was a strong supporter of the idea and talks went ahead with the Scots, but Jim Farry (their then chief administrator) was totally opposed. I have never been able to understand his reticence, so turning it down after we had put so much work into reinstating it was a big disappointment.

Happily, we were to play the Scots in major competition at Wembley during the Euro 96 finals and then a two-leg European Championship qualifier which we also won when Kevin Keegan was in charge. It returned as a friendly at Wembley in the summer of 2013 and I was delighted that such a major fixture – so engrossing, so exciting – was back on the calendar. It had been absent for too long, and it all went off without a problem. I hope to see the fixture taking place more regularly again in the future.

But now, with my vision for the side in place, it was time to start putting it all into practice.

# 2

# PUTTING THE PIECES TOGETHER

HAVING PREPARED EVERYONE for what I wanted to do, now was the time to put my England plan into operation. We would discover which ideas worked and what would be discarded. As hosts of Euro 96, we knew we would be playing all our matches on home territory, and after the draw ceremony on 17 December 1995, we knew we would be playing at Wembley. If you consider England's home record, we rarely lose, so if we played what we know best, 4-4-2, the chances were that we would win a high percentage of matches, and hopefully all of them.

But this was the European Championship finals, with England hosting a tournament second only to the World Cup. I wanted us to go for it, to shock our rivals and do something different, but still win and entertain our public. I had almost two and a half years to find the players to fit the new system I wanted to present to the country. In the process, I knew I would be criticised for selecting some good-quality Premier League footballers, and then discarding them too quickly.

I knew exactly what was required of my squad and could quickly tell that Andrew Cole, a first-rate goalscorer for Newcastle United and then Manchester United (who signed him for a record transfer fee), was not going to be better for me than Alan Shearer, Les Ferdinand or Robbie Fowler. Matthew Le Tissier was brilliantly talented, but he did not fit the bill for my team. By the time of Euro 96, who would I leave out to let Matt in – Sheringham, Gascoigne, Anderton, McManaman? Dennis Wise is another I had a high regard for, but at the last minute I decided not to include him in my squad for the finals. He wanted to be successful with the team, and possibly tried too hard so did not look like the same accomplished player he would become at Chelsea.

Decisions had to be made quickly, as I ended up having fewer than 20 games before the tournament started. In those circumstances, with so many contenders, it is not always possible to give people several opportunities, especially when you are also trying to build a settled side who are used to playing together. Despite that, Paul Parker, Graeme Le Saux, Gary Pallister, Peter Beardsley, Steve Bould, David Batty, Kevin Richardson, Paul Merson, Ian Wright, Barry Venison, John Barnes, Robert Lee, Neil Ruddock, Warren Barton, John Scales, Stan Collymore, David Unsworth, Colin Cooper and Jason Wilcox were all tested. It was a close call for them and players like Ugo Ehiogu and defender Rob Jones, who was a certainty until ruled out through injury. Rob's departure, sad as it was, opened the door for the prodigious talent of Gary Neville to flourish. The loss of Le Saux to injury was another blow that had to be countered.

Although we had so little time, the plan was to build the team in stages, gradually introducing what I saw as the final squad, working from the front backwards. First I wanted to find our strikers, then our wide players, midfielders and finally the defenders. Before I knew we would be facing the Dutch; I had studied them intensely to see what I could learn that could help us. I did not copy their style slavishly, but I was attracted to parts of it that I thought I could develop.

Graham Taylor, my predecessor, had agreed a number of friendly games for England before he left the post. The first of them couldn't have been much tougher: we were due to take on the current European champions, Denmark, at Wembley, on 9 March 1994. The one thing I was anxious to avoid was a losing start. It would have undermined confidence not just among the players but among the supporters, who might think 'here we go again' after missing out on the World Cup finals.

Happily, a David Platt goal meant an honourable start as we won 1-0 using the 4-3-2-1 system that became known as the 'Christmas Tree'. It was a compact system where Peter Beardsley and Darren Anderton (making his debut) supported striker Alan Shearer, with Paul Gascoigne, Paul Ince and David Platt in midfield. The strength of the Christmas Tree system was in restricting the opportunities of the opposition to unsettle you. It worked on that occasion, so I am glad we used it. Commentators kept saying it was a regular system of ours, when it was not. In fact, I cannot remember exactly when we used it again, as I had other things to try.

There were numerous ways I could shape the team. What I was working to achieve was to convince them to play with fewer defenders. You could line up with eight behind two attackers, but I didn't think that was good enough. What about three attackers and seven behind them? Or could we even have four in front of six? I didn't want us to park the bus in front of goal, so three and seven was the target. I wanted movement and flexibility from defence through midfield to attack. So there were three basic tactical systems I wanted us to be proficient in using: 4-3-2-1 (the Christmas Tree), 3-5-2 (which could revert to 5-3-2 if we needed to) and 4-3-3. I was prepared for us to take a risk, without us actually taking too much of one.

Our second match was against Greece, who arrived in May. They would go on to surprise everyone when they became European champions in 2004, but we beat them comfortably 5-0. Having played an experimental side, where six of the starting line-up had three or fewer caps, I was delighted by this. Five days later, Norway had every reason to be confident as our opponents, having played so successfully against Graham's team in the World Cup qualifiers, winning 2-0 in Oslo. They were held to a goalless draw before we went on our summer break and watched Brazil beat Italy on penalties in the World Cup final.

Once the 1994-95 season got under way, we had three autumn friendlies at Wembley in quick succession: we beat the USA 2-0, drew 1-1 with Romania and beat Nigeria 1-0 in mid-November, thanks to another Platt strike. The performance against Romania exposed a flaw we had to repair. The Romanians were adept at the possession game and we had given them far too much room, so despite making progress there was plenty for me and Don and the staff to work on. I recognised we needed to have midfield players who would themselves keep possession. Looking at who was available, I eventually decided that Jamie Redknapp and Gazza would be the best for that role. Gazza had the strength of two men as an extra to go with the skill that so often astonished me, but unfortunately he was injured for most of the 1994-95 season with a broken leg, while Redknapp was still only 21 and not yet quite ready for the step up, though I would give him his chance within the year. I was full of admiration for the commitment the players were prepared to give, as they coped with the mental demands required.

As I mentioned, I wanted to develop my strike partnership first, and that autumn was the first time I partnered Alan Shearer and Teddy Sheringham up front. Shearer had suffered a cruciate ligament injury in December 1992 that had kept him out of much of England's World Cup qualifying campaign. As he battled to recover, perhaps he thought he might never play again on the international stage, but when he returned to club action, it was clear to me that he was still a force to be reckoned with. All he needed was a goal to set him off on a run, and I just knew it would come. Instantly, there was a special rapport between him and Teddy and it was shown by the fact that Alan scored both the goals against the USA, the first time the pair started together. Sadly, those would be the last goals he scored for me until Euro 96 got under way. I never doubted my man's ability to rediscover that powerful touch in front of goal, and he was strong enough to know that the goals would return, even if some in the media began to question his place in the side – especially as we had so many options up front.

I was not looking for problems but was prepared to face any that confronted me. When one did rear up in my next game, it was so unexpected I was doubly shocked. The riot caused by people who called themselves England fans took place during our friendly against the Republic of Ireland in Dublin on 15 February 1995. That game marked the beginning of my second year in charge and should have allowed me another opportunity to watch players whose club form deserved England recognition.

Shamefully, the match had to be abandoned after 27 minutes because of the appalling crowd trouble. The fact the Irish were leading 1-0 was an irrelevance. All that mattered was the safety of the fans, Irish and English, in the firing line of the violent minority. I don't know how many trouble-makers there were, but the FA had received only 4,000 tickets to make up ten per cent of a 46,000 crowd inside Lansdowne Road. The minority chose to rubbish our game and our reputation. I don't know the reasons behind their actions, whether it was political or sectarian or a challenge to the

IRA, only that the rioting – for it was bad enough to be described as that – turned horribly into violence, with seats and all sorts thrown from the top of one stand to the tier below.

I never suspected such a thing could happen, something I had not experienced before or since. It was a friendly match, and the first time we had played in Dublin since a November 1990 qualifier for the 1992 European Championships. As most teams are pre-match, we were cloistered away beforehand, so I have no idea if there was some sort of undercurrent building up. When the Republic scored and then we were disallowed a 'goal', the violence erupted and the referee called the teams off. Jack Charlton, the Republic's hugely popular and highly successful manager, was as distraught as I was. We were two Englishmen ashamed of what was going on above us. It became so bad there was no question that the game could continue. I don't know who or what infects the minds of these people, but apart from the damage to our reputation there was for a short time a concern that UEFA might reconsider the suitability of England as the venue for Euro 96, some 16 months away. A violent few had dragged us into the gutter.

By now, I was having much greater input into who we were meeting, and I wanted to make sure we had fixtures that would test us because we didn't have any qualifiers to provide that additional intensity and pressure. Our next match was against Uruguay in March 1995, when Nick Barmby and Andy Cole made their debuts; the game finished goalless.

The Umbro Cup was an important tournament scheduled for the summer before the finals. Unfortunately, too many players found reasons not to report for duty. I was upset to say the least that Paul Ince could not make it. That is not the attitude I wanted from a man I considered a key player. He was being transferred to Inter Milan at the time, which was important to him and his family. He was also a witness in the Eric Cantona court case, following the

Frenchman kung-fu kicking a spectator at Crystal Palace. I was so unimpressed I kept him out of the side after we lost our last Umbro Cup match to Brazil. I eventually selected him again nine months later, by which time he had missed eight caps. To be fair to him, his attitude was good on his return against Bulgaria at the end of March 1996. I never could understand players being reticent about playing for England. If there are genuine reasons for withdrawing, you can have no argument but two other players, whom I will not name, were reluctant to join the squad and they had no reasonable excuse. To miss the chance of playing against the Brazilians, which Ince did, is incomprehensible to me.

The Umbro had us face Japan (whom we beat 2-1), Sweden (an amazing 3-3 draw) and world champions Brazil (who beat us 3-1 – the only defeat in open play I suffered in my time in charge). During the tournament, I was able to ease Gazza back into the set-up for the first time since my first game in charge. He came off the bench in all three matches as part of his recuperation from his broken leg. I continued to experiment with the line-up during that tournament, with five more players making their debuts, including Gary Neville. He was the first of that marvellous crop of youngsters that were coming through the United ranks to make it into the England side and I believed they would play a key role for me in the 1998 World Cup. They made it, tragically for me I didn't. Gary was the pathfinder followed by his brother Phil, David Beckham, Nicky Butt and Paul Scholes.

As we moved into the final season before Euro 96, we began with another goalless match against Colombia in September. The South Americans, like the Romanians, were ultra-clever in possession. This time we had our own possession men ready for the challenge of upstaging them – Jamie and Gazza. We had also been working on producing width to our attack for Shearer and Sheringham to profit from. Good, positive wing play would stretch the opposing defence to our advantage, but I would ask for more from them when the time was right.

We increased the frequency of games that autumn, playing once a month before Christmas, starting with the Colombians. We went on to draw 0-0 against Norway in Oslo and then beat Switzerland 3-1 in November, with Jamie and Gazza back together. It was an excellent score against a Swiss side who had made it to the States for the World Cup finals and comprehensive enough to worry them should we meet in Euro 96. We then drew 1-1 with Portugal a couple of weeks before Christmas.

It offered another chance to learn about players, their attitude, commitment, bravery, their general suitability for the final squad and whether they could cope with what they were being asked to do. The Newcastle defender Steve Howey played and Nottingham Forest's Steve Stone came in and scored our goal; he looked good and comfortable. He would do for me, maybe not as a first choice but an excellent man to have available as back-up.

By now I was confident I had players that combined well together and who joined me in wanting to play entertaining, winning football. The matches were enabling us to test our systems and the best use of our players within those systems. I was delighted with what they were producing and our results ensured that the nation was behind us. They were beginning to see the possibilities, and as we became more confident so did they.

It was at this time the FA would have been expected to offer me an extension of my contract to continue through to the World Cup finals in France in 1998. Unfortunately, the qualifiers would begin immediately after the Euros, and clearly we needed to start planning for that tournament soon. Sir Bert Millichip stated unequivocally that he wanted me to be given an extension until 1998. Others in the FA saw it differently. On the morning I was due to travel to Birmingham for the draw for Euro 96, Yvette showed me an article in the *Daily Mail* which stated that the International Committee, headed by Noel White, was adamant I would not be given an extension to my contract. It was not what I wanted to hear or what I should have heard. I felt that my record showed that an extension should have been automatic.

I was seething when I read it, and that was the mood I was still in when I arrived at my hotel. I had virtually decided I had no option but to leave after Euro 96, unless, and this is important, I was given the support of White. It would have been encouraging also to receive the backing of his International Committee pal, Ian Stott. I met Graham Kelly who said he had seen the article. I then told him I had discussed the situation with Yvette and that I could not see how I could continue. It was now important that I had a face-to-face meeting with White, with Sir Bert and Graham also present.

When I met White, he said he was backing me and would continue to do so – but only up to the end of the Euro finals. Inwardly I was incensed by this, but managed not to show it. He reiterated there should be no new contract until after the committee had assessed England's performances in competitive matches. How offensive could the man be? Precedent alone should have given me the opportunity to take England into the World Cup. I told him I was no longer prepared to accept what I considered to be sniping from insiders. I do not know what his problem was with me, but I believe Noel was listening to nonsense being spouted about me by others, such as Peter Swales, though why he was hostile to me is a mystery. It was clear from Graham Kelly's published recollections that Swales was out to get me, and that White was the person to put an end to my chances.

Graham was aware of the situation between me and the cabal from the North West. He backed Sir Bert's demand to White that I be offered what all England managers receive: a fair and reasonable contract extension. Sir Bert actually named the date – 1998. But White was adamant: he wanted to see what my team would do during the finals. He was also concerned about possible court cases that I might be caught up in. I said there was no chance of that, and our lawyers agreed, but if by some mischance there was a case to answer then I would walk out and quit without a fuss. Sir Bert said directly to White: 'It's not fair what you are saying.'

What the hell had White and his committee been doing for the previous two years? I felt we had played well and were making great progress; we were introducing young players while keeping a settled squad; and we had lost just one match so far and that against the Brazilians. These amateurs work in strange ways. Still, that was it; I felt I had no option but to confirm I would stand down at the end of my contract. Maybe that was what they wanted me to do. Who knows? But if so they got their wish. I would be out of a job as soon as England was eliminated from the Euros.

I believe White seriously damaged my England career. He undermined my long-held ambition to manage England into a World Cup campaign. The emotion I still feel about that remains as intense now as it was then, and my feelings towards White will never change. I am told by friends that I should have accepted his terms, as it was a certainty I would have been offered a new contract after Euro 96, because of how well the side performed. My concern was that White would find another reason to prevent me from continuing in the role.

I felt that White did not like me and didn't want me in the job. It was obvious he was uncomfortable in my company on the rare occasions that happened, yet I never treated him with anything other than respect, a respect which I felt was not returned. This was about politics not football. Let me clarify the situation: information about my position as national coach was reaching the media before I was aware of what they had planned for me.

I made my decision to step down in December 1995 and I stand by it. It was not made in a fit of pique but astonishment at the way I was being treated and in my fury that White could effectively countermand the wishes of Sir Bert and Graham Kelly. That is how I felt then and how I feel now. That morning the Sunday newspapers carried quotes from Sir Bert confirming his support for me. He said he wanted me to carry on after Euro 96 and encouragingly that I had the team playing the way he wanted to see England play.

Not a word passed between White and me after we lost to Germany. There was all the incredible passion that we had generated and suddenly it hit the wall. We were deflated and down, yet the man who was in charge of the International Committee did not express the disappointment I am sure he felt or thank the squad for their efforts.

There were 16 national coaches involved in the tournament, and I was the only one who had not a clue what his future held when the championships ended. However, if I needed any additional motivation to try to take England to victory, that was it. Graham searched for a compromise and came up with one he thought might suffice. Would I consider a new one-year contract? That would take me to the first stage of England's World Cup qualification for the 98 finals. I thought that was ridiculous, so the answer was no. Would I go through it again? Yes, without a moment's hesitation. It was an honour and a privilege to manage my country, and to have worked with such a great group of people. It was without a doubt the highlight of my career.

We didn't have a game in 1996 until we beat Bulgaria 1-0 in March, a match that saw the return of Ince. With Shearer injured, Les Ferdinand scored the only goal of the match. Croatia were next, and provided a good test, and defensively we stood up well to their probing to finish goalless. It was disappointing not to score then, but there were two more friendlies before the finals, and we dominated Hungary at Wembley in the first of them with a 3-0 win. Anderton scored twice, which was encouraging, and Platt got the other. Alan Shearer had been injured, and continued to receive criticism from the press for his England goal drought. I had to find a way of helping him recover his confidence and his touch. He was only semi-fit before the game, but I decided we would play him for part of the match and told him he would be coming on in the second half. That one act took a massive amount of pressure off him. I knew his goals were going to be vital for us, and I was confident Alan had plenty in reserve, as he had continued to be in prolific form in the Premier League.

Doing that, I was putting into practice what I had learned from experience and what my mentor Ron Greenwood had shown me. Ron was one of the finest coaches I ever worked with. He saw things others did not and trusted his players, which meant he almost invariably got the very best from them. He did not rely on the obvious or what is accepted as the way to do things. For example, the received wisdom has always been that you must have pace as a player at domestic level, and even more so at international level, but at West Ham he developed Geoff Hurst, Bobby Moore and Martin Peters, none of whom had speed going for them. What Ron recognised was that they were three bright, intelligent footballers, who saw what was happening in advance, which compensated for their lack of pace. Alf Ramsey was clever enough to bring them into his England squad as a group and play them as such, which made his job easier.

Barring injury problems, we were ready for the long march to Beijing and the Workers' Stadium. China would be our last match before our opening tie against Switzerland on 8 June. I selected Anderton and McManaman to start together for the first time in Beijing. I had asked so much from them in the past and now I wanted more by way of a super-human contribution. They were both tall and slim, and they could run all day and certainly over 90 minutes. Their workrate and enthusiasm were phenomenal, which was invaluable, but I had something extra planned for them.

It is normal for wingers to attack the full-back, but then pass them on to their own defender should the opposition full-back surge forward. What we asked was for Steve and Darren to run all the way with the full-back, as this was a crucial part of my plan, so they could protect a three-man defence. With most Premier League teams playing four at the back, this idea had been received with some concern, but it was quickly resolved when it was shown to work. However, if Steve and Darren could not go all the way, a tight three-man defence would be stretched, possibly fatally. Fortunately, they both believed they had the stamina for the job and would prove it. This meant I could be flexible about the number of defenders I would play, depending entirely on the number of forwards we would face. This was the final piece of the jigsaw I had been building since I took charge.

The experience of playing in Beijing's Workers' Stadium just a couple of weeks before our opening Euro 96 match against the Swiss was quite something. The crowd of 65,000 saw two goals from Nicky Barmby and a third from Paul Gascoigne. The pitch didn't make it easy, nor did the general conditions, which were hot and extremely humid, but we coped brilliantly. I was able to use 16 players during the game and had the effort I was looking for from them all.

With the announcement of the final squad due to be made only a few days later, it was a last chance for some of the players to impress. Gareth Southgate was superb, as were the Neville brothers. It was such a challenge for Phil, who was making his international debut on his 19th birthday. He coped magnificently playing at left-back alongside brother Gary in what is normally a terrifying experience. The Neville family radiate a confidence and belief that is in their genes. They excel in a number of sports, with their sister Tracey a former England netball player.

There were some critics who felt it was too long a haul, flying all the way out to China, but that was the point – it meant we missed quite a lot of the build-up shenanigans. It was planned to take some pressure off the players, and I thought the trip was more than worthwhile. It's fair to say that the travelling contingent of FA executives also enjoyed the journey, as not only did they have the opportunity to see Beijing, but also the Great Wall of China.

We were due to fly from Beijing to Hong Kong, a two-hour trip, before we journeyed home. The FA had booked 24 seats in upper class, which were allocated to FA officials and the executive party. The players were to sit behind in economy. I thought it would be a good idea to reverse the roles, so the players could sit in upper class. Denying the top men their position at the front of the plane was audacious and cheeky of me, but why the hell not? I felt that the officials were essentially having a jolly-up while the players had been training and playing in stifling heat, so they deserved the treat.

I was speaking with David Dein, then an Arsenal director, when we got to the departure lounge, telling him how the players were in good spirits and ready for the tournament. The conversation turned to the question of the tickets, so I suggested: 'Well, we've got twenty-three players plus our doctor, John Crane, and there are twenty-four tickets up front. Why don't we give them to the players? They rarely have the chance and I think it would be good for them and good for morale. They can have a laugh together and I also think it would make them feel special if you all said: "Go on, you go up front for this one."'

I added: 'But you, you recommend it, not me.'

I heard someone in the background say: 'Oh, I don't know about that.'

Another added graciously: 'It is a fine opportunity. Everyone says there's always that distance between us and the players. We are not going on holiday.'

They decided to do it, and so all the players turned left on entering the plane. Noel White, who had not heard my discussion with David Dein, said to me: 'There were twenty-four tickets for upper class and twenty-three players.'

'Yes?'

So he added: 'Well, I want to ask you something.'

'Yes.'

'I suppose I know who's got the twenty-fourth ticket.'

'Who?'

'You!'

'Wrong! I've given it to the doctor. He works hard and I think he should be up there as well.'

The players thought the change of roles and seating was hysterical, while the officials took it in good part. Mostly. Doug Ellis, the Aston Villa director who could be a bit grumpy, didn't care one way or the other. Meanwhile, Bryan Robson, Don Howe and I sat together, watching those who moaned a bit and those who didn't give a damn. One of the malcontents said loudly: 'It's not right, you know, it's not right. We'd just be on our port now, with cheese and biscuits.' Port! Not on a domestic flight, I don't think so!

We had a stay in Hong Kong, played a training match against a local select team, won that and then the players were entitled to a night out. Unfortunately, what should have been a chance for the players to let their hair down and relax before flying home to the serious business of Euro 96, earned us some terrible headlines when it ended with three of them – Gazza, Teddy Sheringham and Steve McManaman – being photographed in a nightclub with Paul on the now-infamous dentist's chair gurgling drink.

I had told the players who left our hotel to be careful about what they did. I believe in treating my players like men, not boys. They knew, as I had explained to them that this was too big to screw up. At the same time, I had no wish to demand my players be confined to barracks. All that leads to is them becoming stir crazy. The ones who wanted to leave the hotel and go into Hong Kong city had my permission to do so. Of the total squad, only six or seven went out, leaving the rest to have a beer and an early night.

What happened then should not have happened. They were caught out not because of the police, the press, tabloid or otherwise, but because of fans who had followed them, from a distance, photographed the scenes in the club and then alerted the media. I was furious that they should expose themselves to ridicule. In any incident like this, there are degrees of culpability, and I will always deal with them appropriately, but I should point out that these players returned to their hotel before the curfew I'd given them. If there was a punishment, it was the picture. They looked ridiculous, to me, to the rest of the squad and to their families back home.

It was to become even more perplexing. The Cathay Pacific flight from Hong Kong to London also created problems when it was alleged there was damage done to the seats and television screens in the area where players had been sitting. Some media accounts suggested that what went on in the upper section of the jumbo occupied by the players was some sort of sordid Sodom and Gomorrah party. I have never seen or been given evidence of that, quite the reverse.

Firstly, it is worth explaining the relationship between a coach and his players. It is never less than strong, and never stronger than prior to a tournament. I am not talking about a cosy world, where all is sweetness and light and you can afford to be righteous, but when you are heading for an extraordinary event there is a special relationship. So, even when some overstep the mark, occasionally in a way others say is outrageous, I believe we should band together unless the 'crime' demands severe punishment. We have all heard the phrase: 'What happens in the dressing room, stays there.' There were plenty of moments in my career where I have applied that rule, and we have sorted out problems quietly and away from the limelight.

This wasn't one of those moments. I can now confirm nothing happened on that damned flight. I say 'nothing happened' because no evidence was submitted at the time, or has been submitted since, to convince me otherwise. All I heard suggested the opposite. The man in charge of our travel arrangements told me there was no trouble, and he was seated in the upper section with the players. Two reporters on the flight seated just below the upper deck have subsequently told me there was no excess noise and no trouble. Ted Buxton reported that Gazza had annoyed a female flight attendant with his language, for which there was an apology. That's it. If something happened that I had to deal with, why was I not presented with the facts? I was not because there were none to give. No one came to me during the flight, no one said anything to me about trouble.

I am a players' man and always will be, but I am also aware of my responsibilities. You react when you have the facts to react to. I have been a director and a half-shareholder of a major club. I know these jobs and have never been disrespectful to anybody in doing them. But to win games you need players. Why do people pontificate about matters they have no real knowledge of and that would apply to some of the less enlightened FA gang, always ready to stir the pot?

When we returned to our Bisham hotel, we had no idea what was going on or the media storm that was coming our way.

It was Paul Gascoigne who initially took the full brunt of the media fury at what had been turned into a scandal. Steve McManaman and Robbie Fowler were also named. They were angry enough to take legal advice against one newspaper, but that eventually came to nothing. The tabloids went to town with polls of their readership asking what should be done about Gazza. It was judge, jury and executioner in one, as you might expect. The polls in the *Sun* and *Mirror* gave Gazza the thumbs down. 'Throw him out,' was the cry. There may have been other newspapers also calling for his head. To my dismay, I was told that Sir Alf Ramsey had jumped on the bandwagon, even threatening to stay away from Wembley if Gascoigne was selected.

I accept the media made it look very bad, but I was outraged by their outrage. The message would have been passed on to me if Graham Kelly expected action from me to punish anyone, but it wasn't. I have never been anti-media; I understand what they are here to do. I have learned, contrary to the views of some of my compatriots, that newspapers far prefer to write about success than failure; they would rather have a good straight story to write about than one that is angled and is nonsense. I saw it as part of my job as England's national coach to rise above it all and help provide the media with information, so I usually knew what to expect.

The complaint I have against Cathay Pacific and one of their employees is that they chose to leak a party story – it was Gazza's 29th birthday – into something it was not. It was in the hands of newspapers before we knew of any alleged problem. It could have really affected us as a group, but we were able to turn it round, and use it to draw strength from adversity. One of the theme songs for the finals was Mick Hucknall and Simply Red's 'We're In This Together'. We decided to adopt that motto for ourselves after our trip to China, agreeing on 'collective responsibility'. When Gazza scored his 'wonder goal' against the Scots shortly afterwards the mood towards him changed, and he was now a hero. The *Sun* even ran a piece under the headline: 'Paul Gascoigne – An Apology'.

I have mentioned the benefit we gained from travelling to Beijing and Hong Kong, but there were two other factors that had helped build my confidence about the future. These were a series of get-togethers, which I found almost more useful than friendly matches, and the help I had received from the Premier League managers. The first of these Premier League meetings was held in the north. Alex Ferguson, now Sir Alex, went out of his way to help me with preparations for England. When I took charge, he made it easy for me to add Bryan Robson (still then a United player) to my staff. He also offered me facilities at the United training ground as a meeting place. Nothing was too much trouble for him or his staff. The other managers wanted to hear what my plans were and to a man they offered any help they could regarding player release to develop the system we wanted to imprint on the minds of the players.

We had three sessions in all, lasting three days each, when we could concentrate on team shape, team play and the role of each player in the system. It gave us the opportunity to try things, to feel relaxed and be able to talk to the players without the pressure of preparing for a match. If what we were doing worked then we could use it, but if it did not then it might be honed until it was acceptable or simply forgotten.

We were able to squeeze in six two-hour sessions over three days. The players loved it, as did their clubs, as the managers knew their men would be returning to them without any injuries. In each of these sessions, we would concentrate on two or three aspects of the game, such as good defensive attitude, good attacking attitude or passing. We packed in more during these sessions than we would in the build-up to a friendly match. The trouble with friendly matches is that they are far from that. With England, you are always expected to win them, and that adds pressure to a situation where there should not really be much, and so there is a danger you might unravel the players' confidence.

By now, I was convinced we had the balance right, and that our players were strong in body and mind. They wouldn't be the type to wilt, and they were able to take on board exactly what I wanted from them. They had done that without moaning, in fact with an eagerness that excited me as their coach.

As we flew home from the Far East, I had to reduce my squad from 27 to 22 for Euro 96, and I was spoilt for choice. These are good problems to have, but in truth they are lousy ones to resolve. I had been left in the cold, when Alf Ramsey thought better of including me in his final squad for the 1966 World Cup, so I knew exactly how gutted my five would be. For example, when it came to choosing my strikers, I had six to choose between. I'd decided that I wanted to pair Teddy Sheringham and Alan Shearer as my front two. It meant I had to tell a superb pro such as Peter Beardsley there was no place for him in the squad; that a class player such as Robbie Fowler could expect only moments as a sub, even though he was one of the finest young goalscorers we have produced. He would have to wait for his chance, as would Les Ferdinand, another quality player who was going to struggle to get much game time. Nicky Barmby offered something different up front, but was also aware that he wasn't going to play much. Despite that knowledge, all of these players were so committed to the team and strongly behind it. When you have players like that, you have a chance.

It is so easy when someone is not actively involved in the team for them to mope around, and that can cause problems. I just could not afford to have anyone around who didn't have the right attitude, who hadn't caught the spirit of the squad and what we were trying to do. I wanted nothing to detract from our target, and that was to win the European Championships.

Along with Peter Beardsley, Jason Wilcox, Ugo Ehiogu, Dennis Wise and Robert Lee also missed out on being a part of Euro 96. Wilcox and Ehiogu had both won just one cap, so perhaps the decision wasn't too unexpected, but the other two had been more regular, while for Beardsley it was to mean the end of his England career.

One of the benefits of being an Englishman, managing in England, was my familiarity with the players available for selection. I pride myself in knowing the style and character of the players who play in England – in all of the leagues. I had always studied them, from when I was a kid. I knew who my XI were going to be, but also how I was able to strengthen that team with the right back-up. In the end, I went with this squad of 22:

Goalkeepers: David Seaman (Arsenal), Tim Flowers (Blackburn Rovers), Ian Walker (Tottenham Hotspur).

Defenders: Gary Neville (Manchester United), Tony Adams (Arsenal), Gareth Southgate (Aston Villa), Steve Howey (Newcastle United), Stuart Pearce (Nottingham Forest), Sol Campbell (Tottenham Hotspur), Phil Neville (Manchester United).

Midfield: Darren Anderton (Tottenham Hotspur), Paul Ince (Inter Milan), Paul Gascoigne (Glasgow Rangers), David Platt (Arsenal), Steve McManaman (Liverpool), Steve Stone (Nottingham Forest), Jamie Redknapp (Liverpool).

Forwards: Alan Shearer (Blackburn Rovers), Teddy Sheringham (Tottenham Hotspur), Les Ferdinand (Newcastle United), Nicky Barmby (Middlesbrough), Robbie Fowler (Liverpool).

I had no sooner named the squad than Steve Howey was forced

out through injury. We immediately called our friends at UEFA to explain the situation, in full expectation of being allowed to call in a replacement, but they refused to allow it. I think it was relayed to me by a member of the FA staff that some gentle soul at UEFA had told them they would consider a switch only if Howey had been hit by a car. It was ironic that this should happen to us, as I was the coach who led the argument to have the squads for this tournament increased from 20 to 22. Suddenly we were back to having 21 to choose from.

I knew this was going to be my one chance to bring success to England, as I was standing down after the tournament. Now it was our moment to achieve our dreams.

# THREE LIONS
# COME SO CLOSE

As we drew ever closer to our first game on 8 June 1996, the focus in our build-up was to maintain a positive attitude. We had done the work; the players knew their role exactly. We knew how our opponents in the group – Switzerland, Scotland and the Netherlands – would play. We had home advantage, so we certainly didn't have any major concerns, other than the perfectly natural ones you face before confronting the opposition. After all, how many teams come to Wembley and put us to the sword? The odds would be in our favour, but it would be suicidal and unprofessional to think like that. We had all worked to produce a team that would entertain, be different and win. Our moment of truth was on us and we had to make sure we produced our best. It had worked in practice and looked good, but we needed to think game by game and if we kept on getting it right, it would take us to the final.

I'd had a big decision to make ahead of the tournament: who

should captain the side? It was between Tony Adams and David Platt, who had been my skipper up to that point. I felt that Tony's stature within the Arsenal set-up was a big plus in his favour and so decided that he should lead us into battle. It was a decision that David surprised me by taking badly. I left him out of the opening match, but that appeared to be less troubling to him than losing the skipper's armband.

'Why are you taking it off me?' he asked. To me it was simple – Tony was the dominant figure in the squad and, as I reminded him, his captain at Arsenal; why could he accept it in one situation and not the other? There was no answer to that. David was an outstanding player for me and for the country, and a vitally important part of the squad, but Tony was the right man to be our captain for the tournament. I saw him as a natural skipper from the age of 17 when I first took notice of him. I was always envious that he played for Arsenal and not at Spurs. I watched him all the way through his career and recommended him for a coaching job, in Azerbaijan, when he stopped playing. I simply thought Adams was the better captain, otherwise I would not have changed things. David was a well-educated young man who knew his football and had a superb career as a player and latterly as a coach, but Tony Adams was the captain I wanted.

Perhaps the only surprise for the opener in my team selection was the fact that David Platt, who had not played in China, was on the bench. The team therefore lined up as: Seaman; G.Neville, Adams, Southgate, Pearce; Anderton, Ince, Gascoigne, McManaman; Sheringham, Shearer. They had never played together before as a unit. It was a major day for all the players, but particularly for Gary Neville, who was the youngest in the team. I knew he had the intelligence not to be daunted. He may have been inexperienced but he was also marvellously talented. I trusted all my players, which gave me the confidence to pick my team according to the opposition we faced, and to know that if there was an injury, suspension or some matter out of my control that we could cope.

Our first hurdle was Switzerland, but the best-laid plans … Sadly, our opening match – the first of the tournament – was a duffer. Perhaps some of the players were nervous. It was the first opportunity we had to savour the real passion and excitement of our supporters, who were completely caught up in the whole experience. On the coach to the stadium, I phoned a friend I knew was already at Wembley to ask if there was a buzz there and whether the atmosphere was building up. I was told we would be stunned by the support we would receive. He had seen nothing like it, that he could remember, for an England match. He said there was a feeling of excitement and belief that this would be our competition. Our approach to Wembley confirmed everything he said. It was an emotional journey that became more and more exciting for us as we neared the stadium. If we could be willed to victory, then the fans would do it. Our job now was to inspire them.

It is often the case that the opening steps in major competitions can be more difficult than they should be. We have seen world champions stumble in their first defence of the cup and that was our fate as chasers of a title. We took the lead after 23 minutes through a welcome Alan Shearer strike, perfectly timed after all the media comment about his goal drought. I believed he was the best goalscorer in these championships, though I was as relieved as he was to see that first goal go in. It was an excellent finish to a first-class build-up involving Gazza and Paul Ince. At that moment, everyone would have anticipated a victorious start to our campaign against a Swiss side that were no more than competent, especially after their manager Artur Jorge had surprised us all by axing Alain Sutter and Adrian Knup, two of their most highly rated players, from his squad. They were considered a work in progress when coached by Roy Hodgson, who had handed over to his Portuguese successor for these championships.

We played well enough for an hour on the back of Alan's goal, but then it was as if our legs had been drained of energy. This was so frustrating, as it had been one of the issues I had identified right at the start of my tenure, and here we were falling to the same problem. The Swiss equalised with less than ten minutes of the match remaining when Stuart Pearce conceded a penalty and Turkyilmaz scored. Was it a penalty? For me, no, as the ball was shot into Pearce's arm. These are the irritations you have to accept as graciously as possible. We wanted a win but a draw, considering the occasion, was acceptable.

Scotland were next, a week later on 15 June. Because of the gap between matches, I gave the squad 48 hours of R and R. They had two days to do what they wanted to, to visit their families or just relax. There were no restrictions on them – other than their own good, common sense. Three of them, Teddy, Sol Campbell and Jamie Redknapp, quite reasonably decided to end their evening of relaxation in a nightclub. This, as we know, is a hanging offence for English sportsmen, particularly footballers. Their presence was reported by the usual bar sneaks hoping to make a few quid from the media, and once again we had to go through the inquisition of explaining the actions of these 'bad boys'. It is the price you have to pay.

If I had thought they had broken rules laid down by me, then I would have been less than happy with them. But I knew that having a few drinks, even at 2.30 in the morning, would have no effect on their fitness to play six days and numerous training sessions later. The war, and it can feel like one, between the England squad and the media switched to overdrive after the disappointment of only drawing against the Swiss. The nightclub incident intensified the criticism of the players. I was incensed by what I considered to be outrageously over-the-top reporting, I described the action of some reporters as the work of traitors. I meant it then. Not only was so much of the criticism shocking and abusive, it was wrong. Traitors! Why not call them that when they dragged every minor incident on to the front pages of their newspapers, on to every radio and TV bulletin? The press had turned it into a huge scandal and witch-hunt in the middle of a major competition. You cannot condemn players for enjoying themselves when they have every right to do so and had been cleared to rest and relax.

As we prepared for the next game, at least one writer offered the advice that Gazza should be dropped for the Scotland match. That was not a clever shout. As England manager I get to listen to it all, but it is not mandatory that I agree with any of it – and I certainly didn't in this case.

When we met up again as a squad, we analysed the Swiss result and our performance and worked out what I felt we had to do to defeat Scotland. We knew the Scots would be highly motivated. We had to fend that off, let the game unravel and then go for them. There was no rush for us. I anticipated it would be tough and messy, but basically it was about us sticking to our plan, so I decided to play the same starting XI as before. As the game progressed in a brilliantly charged atmosphere, it became clear we could do with just a little bit more creativity, and so I knew I had to make a change at half time.

All managers have to be ready to make relevant points at the interval – some are good at it, some not. The half-time break is when you earn the right to call yourself a manager. In the first 45 minutes, you assess how your plan is working, but this is the time when you can most easily make changes to improve things. You have 15 minutes to sit the players down and calmly tell them what you have seen and the things you want covered. Sometimes I would ask the players what their thoughts were, and whether they had anything to add, but the final decisions were always my responsibility

Even if the first half has gone well, it is vital never to assume the game is won. I knew I would be asking for trouble if I ever praised the team to the heavens during the interval. If they've gained the edge, I would keep them guessing. I would not say: 'Great! You're winning! Terrific, you've done it! Same again, please!' It would be like paying someone to do something for you before he has even started the work. If you pay him in advance, you have taken away his incentive. It is the same with players, including the best in the business. I always preferred to emphasise the things they could be doing better, so they could sense I wasn't entirely happy. That should drive them on if they have anything about them, and they will react. If they got complacent, they might start playing sloppy by over-indulging, taking an extra touch that would allow the opposition to make a tackle. If you keep moving the ball, and they can't get it, that frustrates them.

The other important aspect of a half-time talk is not to bombard the team with words. If you do, you are overdoing it. You can make two or three points, if addressed to five players or the team as a whole, but if I was talking to an individual, the chances are there would be just one point I would drum in to him. The less I say, the easier it is for them to take it in and for me to explain. Words must always be rationed, and I would not speak to everyone individually. The other thing I thought important during half-time talks was to have a bit of a laugh and a joke to keep it light. The players usually know that if they have let themselves down they have also let down the team, so there's no great point in yelling at them; you want to raise their spirits.

On this occasion, with Scotland's Gordon Durie sharp, incisive and potentially dangerous, I decided to replace Stuart Pearce and move Gareth Southgate to the left of Tony Adams as a back three.

I moved Paul Ince to become a deep-lying central midfielder, and brought on Jamie Redknapp, which I thought would give us a little extra creativity that we needed. Sadly, he did not last the game. He always seemed to be the victim of an injury that stopped him playing for country as well as club. It was bad luck, not just for the player but for what I had wanted from him in a crucial match. I had made a change I felt was necessary and he eventually had to come off with five minutes remaining, which was so disappointing and frustrating. I had always appreciated the football Jamie played. I had known about him from his young days, when his dad Harry was manager at Bournemouth, and I'd tried to sign him for Tottenham and thought we were going to do the deal, but they were more impressed with Liverpool.

Despite the misfortune with Jamie's injury late on, we were excellent in the second half. The Scots will always make you fight with a workrate that is truly exceptional. So I could be nothing other than satisfied at the way our attacking system put pressure on them. And the goals! Stunning! Alan scored his second of the tournament in the 53rd minute as proof that his touch was in great working order. It was a classic finish to a great passing move, with Gary Neville showing the quality that would be the hallmark of his game after a mesmerising series of passes ended with Gary laying the ball in for Alan to connect.

Gazza's temperament can reach a high pitch prior to any match, especially the biggest ones. He was hyped up for this one, but nicely so, in control. There have been many occasions when I have watched his genius. You don't explain it – it happens. We needed another goal as Scotland tried to recover lost ground and were lucky when Gary McAllister had a penalty saved, thanks to the judgement of our keeper David Seaman.

But it was what happened next that everyone remembers from that game. Gazza's goal was testimony to his quality as one of the

great talents we have produced. Colin Hendry must have wondered why he had been singled out to be the victim of our man's
moment of consummate skill. There was no time for him to think,
as Gazza's brain operated a second before Hendry's. Darren
Anderton received the ball out wide on the left after a long clearance. We were screaming at him to hit it first time or it would be too
late to find Gazza, who had made a great burst forward in the
inside-left position and was heading in the direction of the corner
flag. Darren struck the ball forward to Paul, who saw that Hendry
was sprinting across to cover him. With his left foot, he flicked it
over Hendry, who was left sprawling as he tried to recover, and as
the ball fell to earth Paul volleyed it into the net and away from
Andy Goram. It was fast, incisive and brilliant. Pelé at his best
would not have bettered that movement and finish. The
cognoscenti drooled, as we all did. It was a goal of unimpeachable
quality, world-class, extraordinary, a wonder to behold. To have the
confidence, the skill, the balletic ability, the sheer nerve and bravery to do that only comes to the blessed.

I thought back to the time when we were at Spurs together, and
how I'd talked to Paul about the importance for a midfielder of
keeping the forward run going, over the 18-yard line, and how by
going those extra few yards he would be in front of goal and in a
position to nick a chance, which might come to him from a rico-
chet off a player or off the woodwork. I wanted him to extend his
runs. He had got to grips with the possibilities of that concept and,
given that he could do what he did with a ball better than anybody
else, it made him a formidably complete attacking midfielder. I
believed it was important he should never feel restricted and
under pressure, as too many midfield players are, by coaches who
demand they go so far and then stop their runs in case they have
to track back.

Paul's goal was a classic example of one of the things I wanted my players to do: staying cool under pressure. I did not want casual. Casual and they'll make mistakes. Cool and they'll be sharp and flow to the rhythm of the game. Speed of thought and accuracy of passing were what we were trying to achieve. That goal – just five touches from one end to the other – was a perfect example of what we were trying to achieve.

There is a marvellous video on YouTube that shows not only Paul's goal but also every move, pass, tackle and run made by him against Scotland. It shows how Gazza at his best was unplayable. He had mastered every aspect of the game, both as an extraordinarily gifted individual and as a sharing team player. It is a must-watch.

You couldn't envisage two more brilliant strikes in a match so crucial. I could feel the crowd responding to what they were watching. This was what it had all been about. Would it get better? It is a corny phrase, but I wanted a feast of football and I think it was at that moment that I thought we could possibly provide it. Our performances were beginning to match the country's expectations. The fans who actually had tickets for Wembley were behind us as never before. The noise level was deafening – you could sense the depth of the empathy they had with the team. It was particularly obvious against the Scottish supporters, who themselves never leave any doubt about their presence on the terraces. As I've said, we hadn't been out and about on the streets. We knew there was a groundswell of goodwill for us, but it was only when we met it full on in the stadium that we realised the country was preparing for a great big party. I cannot emphasise enough how important it was to have this relationship with the supporters. The Scotland game was everything I wanted; the wonderful football and us matching the passion of the Scots.

My confidence, never low, was increasing. Immediately after the game I had to attend the usual series of press conferences. When

I'd finished them, I was walking with David Davies of the FA through what was now a completely empty stadium. All the fans had gone. The only people left were those working, delivering goods, tidying up, restocking, and so on. In one area I noticed a group of police officers. They saw me and David walking across and to my astonishment they began shouting their support for England. They were jumping up and down and then flung their helmets in the air. I thought: 'Christ Almighty! Even the coppers are going potty.' It was a wonderful feeling.

Going into the final round of matches, which took place just three days later, we needed a point to qualify for the knockout stages, and we had to find it against the Dutch. I can still hear the unimaginative and the overcautious warning me to beware of being overwhelmed by the intensity of support throughout the country. If that was a concern, I cannot think of a better one. We stayed on our own as a group in our hotel, interested only in what happened within the group and focused on the next match. I was actually holding them back every training day, as they were so clearly up for it. It is hard to imagine the level of anticipation within the squad.

I felt sure that the build-up and the game itself would be amazing – although we did not know how remarkable the day would be when we awoke that June morning. Before the match I kept it simple: I didn't want to say too much, or clutter up their thinking. Players should be free on the day of the match. All the 'clutter' must come in training, not when they are getting ready to play. You work hard, but in the final 24 hours, you just top and tail things.

There was an exuberance I could sense in the air at our Bisham base. My job was to make sure it was maintained at the right level. Even though in many ways we were cut off from the excitement we had created, the FA told me good luck messages were flooding in and I immediately spread the word among the players, who were as delighted as me at the positive response to our performances. There has to be a link between the supporters and the players, and there certainly was here. You may think professionals should operate in a vacuum. We can, but it is easier when you know you are appreciated.

There was nothing grand or tub-thumping about my pre-match routines. If the players did not know what was expected of them in the days preceding a match, I would be the person asking questions of my team selection. When I had chosen my group, or the one that would be the basis of our England campaign, I told them what they needed to give: not to me, but to the country. I told them what I would tolerate and what I would not condone. By far the most important quality was bravery. You must never be frightened of losing. It is so important. Too often, players of great ability have under-performed for England, stricken by tension, paralysed by the fear of failure, resulting in nationwide disappointment.

The players I had assembled were exactly what I wanted in terms of ability, experience and mental strength, and I knew they would not weaken at the first sign of pressure. They were just happy and content to be with each other, because they knew they were on the verge of something that was potentially very special indeed, possibly life-changing. Sometimes players can get too intense ahead of a big game, and in those circumstances you may have to find a way of dragging players out of their deepest thoughts. But if you know they're up for it, why put pressure on pressure? It's like training a horse: you always hear trainers talk about the right timing, holding the horse back, and then just letting it go. That was us, collectively on hold but geared to go when the moment came.

We had to amuse ourselves within the confines of the hotel – which was no great hardship. We watched videos, films and listened to music. There were those who read, or played cards, all sorts of games. That sort of interaction is vital. When a player is playing cards he will talk football; as he feels relaxed he will go over what his role will be and how it will dovetail with others. This is what I meant about passing on my plans: the staff would tell the players and the players would then discuss it among themselves.

Occasionally we would involve ourselves in some practical jokes to keep us active. One of the best was played on David Davies. David can appear to be quite pompous, fussing and fretting about something going wrong that the media would then find out about. It was a natural fear in his position, especially after some of the stories we had had in the build-up. We spoke to the security officers and explained we needed their help to make our joke work. As they stood by, late one evening I went up to David's room and knocked on the door. He was in his dressing gown and pyjama top, just about ready to go to bed, so the last thing he wanted to hear was that the police were there.

'The police! What's happened?'

'You'd better come down and see.'

He sighed and we walked down together to meet the police, who told us a neighbour had complained that his daughters were shocked to see a naked man running about in the grounds of our hotel. The officer in charge began to question David and me, and we asked what the hell they were talking about.

'Well,' the officer in charge confirmed, 'the colonel who owns the property next to the hotel has made a serious complaint. His daughters looked out of their window overlooking the grounds of the hotel where a naked man was cavorting.'

David, who can be quite high handed, dismissed the claim out of hand: 'That has got nothing to do with us,' he said, adding: 'It could be anybody coming in here doing that, you know, doing a streak and having some fun. That's ridiculous.'

The copper said: 'Colonel Saunders told us his daughters said it was a man with white hair.'

Silence from David. White hair. That pointed the finger directly at Gazza, who'd had his hair dyed for the competition. The officer said we couldn't leave it at that, and there would have to be a line-up and Colonel Saunders' daughters would have to attend to identify or clear the possible culprit. Davies had by now worked himself up into a state, and I shouted at him: 'It's your fault, David. You should have spoken to him about this sort of thing.'

David turned on me: 'How the hell . . .?'

Then the penny dropped! 'You effing bastard!' he roared.

The players weren't in on it, but Gazza soon heard about it, and that kept him occupied for a spell. The following morning, I had to do some television interviews at the bottom of the hotel gardens. The camera was on me, but I asked the cameraman to stop filming for a minute. I could see reflected in the camera lens what was happening behind me: Gazza was dancing about, making a fool of himself in a way which could easily be seen in the shot. He was dancing in his pyjamas, not naked, thank God. I think, if my memory is correct, Steve McManaman and Robbie Fowler were with him as two of the other dancing culprits. Everybody was laughing when I was trying to be serious. Interludes like that can do wonders to break up any tension that may be building up with some players.

It was all so normal on the morning of the match, as the minutes ticked down to what was the biggest professional challenge any one of us had faced. If I could sum up the atmosphere, it would be tranquil, nicely relaxed and cool. We conserved our mental and physical energy. I cut myself off, took no calls and made none, not even to Yvette or my dad or the rest of the family. I didn't take any calls unless I was told it was absolutely crucial. I tried not to read the papers, but did, or to watch much on the box, but did, though with little interest. I do not believe total isolation is generally beneficial, but there are occasions when it is unavoidable, and this was one of those moments when the squad needed to shut itself away. It is a good thing for each individual player to prepare their mind as they want to, without having to be sociable.

I noticed a stillness had descended on our camp. I liked that. When you work for as long as we had, preparing for a good, old-fashioned decider, then you are entitled to feel you can do the business, produce the performance that will not only see you through conclusively but electrify Wembley and thrill the rest of the country. As always, I tried to keep the pre-match routine simple, ensuring that the players were thinking only of the game immediately ahead, not about what a win would do for us. We knew we were not unstoppable, but equally we were gathering momentum like a snowball rolling down a hill.

I knew that too often players of great ability have under-performed for England, resulting in nationwide disappointment. My job was to make sure we didn't repeat that error. The fact that we were up against the Dutch, whose style of football I had admired so much, made it particularly special. Now I had a plan to outmanoeuvre them, using their own strengths. I had set out saying that I wanted us to play like the Dutch – now we were going to have to do just that, and do it better than the Dutch themselves. I could not wait.

As we were on the coach to Wembley, I made my usual call to my friend at the stadium to ask him what the atmosphere was like, and what our fans were doing. He set the scene for me. The crowd are very much part of it, so it was important to know their mood and feel their excitement. I was told we would be in no doubt how much support we had, and that everyone gave the impression of believing, as we did, that we could do it. The clincher wasn't that we had beaten Scotland, but the class we had shown in doing so. It had been a performance to be proud of. Previously, we as a nation have tended to take a win over Scotland as something that was expected of us. This time it had been different. These were our finals and we wanted to win and win with style.

I cannot imagine ever feeling as emotional as I was when we emerged from the Wembley tunnel to a reception much greater than any of us could have expected. The feeling of sheer wonder and well-being and optimism will never be bettered in my professional life. It confirmed what I had always believed: that the English are unbeatable as a nation when they have a common cause. I have found anticipation can be as exhilarating as the event itself – even a victory. This was the moment I felt I had been born for. It would be my defining moment as a coach and the opportunity for my players to show we could produce a style that entertains and wins. I had been thinking about this game ever since the draw had been made six months before, at Birmingham's National Exhibition Centre in mid-December 1995.

The Swiss had been difficult – first matches always are. The Scottish hordes had come at us waving their imaginary claymores and demanding our blood. Craig Brown's side had been formidable opposition. But the Dutch were the recognised class act in the group. They had finished second to the Czech Republic in their qualifying group, which was a surprise. They then had to face a tough play-off against the Republic of Ireland at Anfield.

The Irish were right to fancy their chances of making the finals. Instead, the Republic went down far more comprehensively than the 2-0 scoreline suggested. They were not used to being dominated and had not been since Jack Charlton took over as manager. Jack, as you would expect, sorted them out as a defensive unit and that commitment to give little or nothing away was his legacy. The result and performance confirmed what we could expect. It was the clearest indicator that, even though the Dutch had taken the long way to Wembley, they were ready for the fight. Here was a team, with striker Patrick Kluivert in dangerous mood – he scored both goals against the Irish – who not only could play but mix it. When we had been drawn against them I was delighted, because I honestly felt we could take them on and beat them. If there is such a thing as a perfect storm, when everything collides, for good or ill, then in football terms that for us was now. If we could now provide a performance and a victory this would be a perfect moment.

I had studied all our opponents for Euro 96, thanks to my connections with ITV, who provided me with lots of extra footage. Despite rumblings that they were being torn apart by rows in the camp, the Dutch appeared to be in good form, and after drawing 0-0 with Scotland they had beaten Switzerland 2-0. Ajax, their leading club side, had featured in the two European Cup finals immediately prior to Euro 96. A year before, coached by the brilliant Louis van Gaal, they had beaten AC Milan 1-0 in Vienna. Van Gaal is an amazing mixture of arrogance, straight talking, kindness and good fun. Ajax then lost on penalties to Juventus in Rome's Olympic Stadium a few short weeks before we were due to meet the Dutch at Wembley. I knew they could out-think and out-perform opponents, and their great players had an expansive vocabulary of expression on the field.

I had prepared for this moment, and believed that the key to our success would come if we were able to attack them but not be over-run if they were able to counter-attack. This is what they had always been so good at doing to the opposition. It was also vital that we broke up their combination play, so they couldn't get into their usual rhythms. I felt we had the players who could fulfil these things.

Although I kept the same starting XI for the third successive game, I made a tactical alteration to counteract the way I knew they would want to play, which would force them to play the way we wanted. I'd had six months to prepare for this game, and to make sure the players knew what was expected of each of them, and what their role was within the system. The Dutch were expecting us to play with two up front, with Sheringham just behind Shearer, and four in midfield, as we had done in the previous two games. They liked to play with three at the back, with Winston Bogarde and Michael Reiziger lining up quite narrowly either side of skipper Danny Blind in the centre. In this way they would have been able to stifle our front men.

What we had worked on since the moment we knew we would face Holland was this: we would play a basic 4-3-3, with three attackers – Shearer in the middle, with Sheringham to the left and McManaman to the right. The midfield three were Anderton on the left, Ince in the middle and Gazza on the right. By doing this, I believed the Dutch plan to stifle our attack would be in trouble, and I was sure they would then be forced to play an extra defender, which would reduce their attacking threat. Until they adjusted, the Dutch defence was left with a dilemma, as defences hate it if they don't have a numerical advantage. By playing Teddy up against Reiziger but inside him, it meant that if Darren then came down the outside, Reiziger had two men to deal with. If Teddy stayed more central, then Reiziger would have to follow him, leaving acres of space outside for Anderton to run into.

When they changed to play an extra man at the back, we were able to outnumber them in midfield, especially as Sheringham could now drop deeper to find space just behind our front line. It was almost as if Teddy were saying to the defender: 'Well then, are you coming?' If the defender stayed where he was, then Teddy had time to play a pass either to Alan or out wide. If the defender came with him, it left more room for Alan and the wide men to run into.

For all the influence Teddy had, with his intelligent movement, use of space and distribution, it was McManaman who was the key in this system. He had much more of an attacking role than in the other matches. He played up and down that right side and tormented Bogarde so often that the Dutchman had to stay back in defence, and was unable to move forward as he usually did. With Gazza also playing more on the right, rather than centrally, they both had the space to cause trouble.

It worked superbly and we took the Dutch apart. Our goals were beautifully constructed – two each for Alan and Teddy, including a Shearer penalty. We could have scored before we did, but Richard Witschge adeptly (if a little luckily) diverted a chance from Shearer. Our first goal came from a corner we had conceded: after the clearance, Sheringham and McManaman worked the ball forward. Steve found Paul Ince who went past Blind like an express only to be tripped. It was a clear penalty. Shearer slammed the kick away from Edwin van der Sar.

The Dutch played football that was dangerous enough to confirm to me they were neither mentally nor physically broken, but I was sure we would break them having gone in to the interval just 1-0 up. We settled into the second half, and in the 51st minute Teddy powered a header from a Gazza corner past van der Sar. If that was a set piece, our third goal six minutes later came straight from the plan we had worked on. The build-up was inspired by Gazza and Sheringham who laid it off with the gentlest of touches for Alan to drive in his second goal of the night and his fourth in three matches.

I had spent two and a half years saying how it could be done; now we were proving it. The fourth, after 62 minutes, left the Dutch chasing a cause that had long been lost. Anderton had played at his peak and deserved a goal, only for his shot to crash off van der Sar into the path of Teddy, who touched it over. I would have been utterly content if we had not conceded a late goal to their substitute Kluivert, which allowed them to qualify for the quarter-finals and sent Scotland on their way home. The victory also meant we would continue to play at Wembley, which was a great incentive to us knowing we were being backed by such passion and an inspiring optimism from our fans.

Despite the goal from Holland that meant the Scots missed out on qualifying, nothing can spoil the memory of the occasion for me. However, I was furious with Paul Ince's show of petulance when I replaced him with David Platt midway through the second half. I hate to see players give it the big 'how dare you?' to the bench when they come off. He wanted to be there at the end, and I don't blame him, but I was looking ahead to our future matches. He was the best central midfield player we had and I therefore wanted him fit and available. When you are four goals in front, it is the best time to give a hard-working player some respite. Ince always had the capacity to be a nightmare. When we returned to the dressing room, I gave him full vent to my anger at his behaviour. He came and sat next to me on the coach back to Bisham and we sorted out our differences. Paul was going to miss the Spain match anyway, as he had received his second yellow card of the tournament against the Dutch.

I was disappointed when I saw some reports blaming the Dutch for how badly they played, rather than crediting us with playing well. They argued the Dutch were inexperienced and in some disarray, riven by dissent and generally way below their best. In my opinion, that argument missed the point. I can always take criticism if it is well informed, but I do not think saying the Dutch weren't up for it is the best basis for an argument. How do you know who is and who is not up for it? After all, we are talking about a team here, not an individual. There had been reports of unrest and fighting in Dutch squads at previous tournaments, yet they had still gone on to do very well. And how inexperienced were they? Well, there were inexperienced players in the team, but quite a few of them had played in two European Cup finals and World Club Championships. I thought the reports should have focused more on what we had done, rather than concentrating on what the Dutch supposedly hadn't done.

With the Dutch out of the way, Spain were next in the quarter-finals. They were a very good Spanish team. They had gone 20 matches without defeat since their World Cup quarter-final in the USA. They were up there with the best of the Europeans and they would test us to the limit. Spain would have to wait a little longer for their matadors to win both the World Cup and European Championship, but that should not diminish the excellence of the team we faced. Having managed Barcelona in the mid-1980s, this was a special occasion for me, as I had continued to follow football in that country, which all added to what was an increasingly emotional campaign for me. Spain's national coach, Javier Clemente, would have anticipated victory from a squad hardly lacking in outstanding players. They had made it into the quarter-finals with draws against Bulgaria and France before a 2-1 victory over Romania at Elland Road, thanks to an 84th-minute winner from substitute Guillermo Amor.

We prepared as normal, but for me it could hardly be that. I had been so engrossed in team affairs up until now I had chosen to ignore the fact I had no work lined up after Euro 96. It dawned on me that this tie against Spain could very easily be my last in charge. I would be unemployed whenever we exited the competition, and there were no guarantees of work after that, though I was never depressed enough to believe my coaching career would end with England.

There had been so many positive signs in our games. What I was most pleased about was our power; physically we were in prime condition. We were good with the ball, so that helped confidence, and we were playing well. If there was extra time against Spain, I was confident we would see it through – even with the prospect of a golden goal decider to stop the real lottery of penalties. For the first time, because of Ince's ban, I was forced to make a change to the starting line-up, with Platt coming in to replace him. You have to accept this sort of setback philosophically, but if we survived he would be back for the semi-final.

After all the excitement of the game against the Dutch, this one turned out to be a dramatic, one-slip-and-you-are-gone encounter. It was goalless over 90 minutes, and still goalless after extra time and then we had penalties. Although Spain played well – and there were those who felt we were lucky – I thought we were the better side, and should have won in extra time.

Spain had only two real scoring chances that I can remember, though Clemente took me by surprise with his defensive line-up. I knew the man and the way he worked as a coach from years of us being rivals in Spain. He would often tinker with his team, but rarely his defence – until we faced his side at Wembley. He had gone from a four- to a three-man defence, which meant Sergi had the freedom to attack us with his runs. It was sorted at half time when we decided to push Gary up on him to keep Sergi wide. If we did that we would restrict him to crosses and there were none better at dealing with that than Tony and the rest of our defence. That allowed Teddy to concentrate on playing up front, while Steve would operate in the hole.

Having expressed my confidence, Spain had a goal disallowed early in the match. It certainly looked like a clear goal, but had it stood I believe we had enough about us to win through to the semi-finals. For us, Shearer could have scored midway through the second half, when Gazza set him up, but Alan spun the ball over. There had to be an end to a gripping a match of high quality and entertainment. Whatever the outcome, nobody could say it was boring.

Penalties: on the bench we were helpless – we could do nothing. Shearer made it 1-0 with a confident and powerful right-foot shot to the left of Andoni Zubizarreta. Fernando Hierro then stepped up to take Spain's first kick, and hit the bar with his shot. David Platt made it 2-0 with a right-foot shot to the right corner. Amor made it 2-1. Then it was Stuart Pearce's turn. He had famously failed in Italy against Germany in the World Cup semi-final in 1990. He did not duck out of the responsibility of stepping up again, but went for it, showing the bravery that made this side so strong while laying his demons to rest. When I asked him later what kept him together, he said typically that he had to score, there was no alternative. He shot left-footed to the bottom right corner. It was 3-1, and the whole of Wembley joined him in roaring with relief. Alberto Belsué made it 3-2.

Gazza was next. If he scored then whoever was to take Spain's kick would need to beat Seaman to keep them in the tournament. Paul didn't let us down, so now Miguel Nadal, aka The Beast, had all the pressure on him. It was a right-foot shot hit to the right of centre. Seaman guessed the direction correctly and turned it round. We were through! It was a match as intense as can be imagined. The players were brave, they never considered failure.

The reaction nationally was extraordinary. They replayed David's save on the big screen at Lord's during the Test there, and that somehow summed up the effect our campaign was having on so many others. We were being acknowledged, not just among followers of our great game, but by the country as a whole. That had been what I wanted from the very start: for everyone to feel part of it, and proud to be so. We showed a level of performance by an England side that has maybe not been witnessed at that level and in a game of that importance since.

The Germans loomed, ready to spoil the party. We met at Wembley on 26 June, and I saw no reason to fear them, or anybody else, after our performances so far. If we had carried a little luck to get to this stage, that in no way detracted from our excellent football. We knew we were taking on the most difficult and competent of rivals. There was nothing different about our build-up; the moments before kick-off were calm, the players were ready. We walked out to another extraordinary welcome. Oh, how much I wanted us to win! The team I chose was: Seaman; Southgate, Adams, Pearce; Ince; McManaman, Gascoigne, Platt, Anderton; Sheringham, Shearer.

The only player missing was Gary Neville through suspension; he had such a fine Championship for a young man, albeit a young man with an old head. He was replaced by the returning Paul Ince, though not directly, but there was no change in our approach which had taken us this far. The Germans also chose to continue as they were.

Our system was flexible. If they played two up we would play three at the back, but if they had gone with three then we would have had four in defence. I knew I could respond at any stage if there was an injury to deal with or I wanted to change the shape. It was not about changing the personnel but getting them to switch positions. Gazza, Anderton and Sheringham had all been with me at Spurs, so they knew what I wanted and would help the others to pick it up from them. Sheringham knew how to confuse the opposition by walking, not running, into position and would stand waiting for the ball.

On the day, we played as well as we played against Holland without being able to score. And we didn't score because of a lack of opportunities. It was a high-pressure game and goals were missed. I thought we were fantastic but it was not enough to see us through. The way we played and the way we set the team out were faultless. Our elimination had nothing to do with the content of the game but missing penalties.

Alan Shearer scored so early I had hardly taken my seat. The goal in just three minutes is clear enough: Gazza's corner was flicked on by Tony Adams and Shearer went for it – 1-0. Sadly, the Germans retaliated soon after, with Stefan Kuntz scoring on 16 minutes, and the battle continued through 90 minutes without further goals, so once more we were going to have extra time.

We had two clear chances to win and score the golden goal. I thought Gazza was certain to score when he went to reach a cross from Darren Anderton. As the ball came across, the German keeper Andreas Köpke was in front and looked favourite to get it, so Paul slowed down slightly, but when Köpke missed it Paul couldn't stretch the extra few inches in time. That was bad luck, not misjudgement. Moments like that are difficult to accept, but you do because the game goes on. Even after that, we still had another chance to clinch it when Anderton shot against the inside of the post and the ball came back to the goalkeeper. That was shocking bad luck, especially when you consider that in the final Oliver Bierhoff hit a shot off the inside of the same post. Instead of going straight to the keeper, it went in.

All of a sudden, it was penalties, and we knew of Germany's uncanny knack of not losing shoot-outs, with the memory still vivid of Turin six years earlier. We began in the same order as we had used against Spain, with Shearer, Platt, Pearce and Gascoigne all scoring, as did the Germans. Sheringham came next, and it was now effectively sudden death. He scored, but so did Kuntz: 5-5, and I had to find someone else to take the sixth, a penalty that had even greater pressure on it.

I understand how difficult it is for any player, and the pressure was massive – after all, a place in the final was at stake. In those circumstances, there is no point in arguing. If I'd said to a player that he was the best penalty-taker in the squad, and he said he was unsure or he had lost his strength, how could I force him? Impossible! If I did so and he missed, then he would say he had told me he wasn't right. I cannot criticise anyone for not taking a penalty, because everyone had performed so well throughout the tournament.

In the end, Gareth Southgate volunteered, and a volunteer is worth ten men pressed. I thought then, by volunteering, he had it in him, but I wonder if Ince or Anderton or McManaman, who would be considered by most to be the better shot-takers, might have done so instead. The point was, Gareth stepped forward without argument.

The strongest and best players have all missed penalties, and poor Gareth was to be the latest. The moment is clear in my mind: he placed the ball and stepped back. When he hit it, it was all wrong – a low shot, saved by Köpke. There were so many heads in hands at Wembley, and I am sure among the millions around England watching on television. My first reaction was the same as theirs: first disbelief, then sympathy. I knew how Gareth would be feeling, but I had to stay focused, for the Germans still had to score to win. It was left to their skipper Andreas Möller. Seaman could not stop it – the end. Gareth was inconsolable, but at least he had the guts to take it.

The result was a disappointment that dug so deep it made me feel sick. I carried on without expression, like a robot. There was no one to blame, and it took time for the depression to set in. We had achieved so much in a short time, it was surely not going to be considered a catastrophe to go out in the semi-finals. At the very end of the match, I looked behind me to see Graham Kelly on the track. The chief executive of the FA was 'gone', wrapped up in the occasion. I would have expected him to be despondent, maybe even displeased, but no way: 'Fantastic, wonderful, magnificent!' he said, if I remember his exact words. He was reacting like the fan he was at heart. I have often wondered why he was so quickly by my side. He could have stayed with the UEFA people and made a fuss of them, but that was not his way of working. I have never asked him, but knowing him he would have wanted to show me support in public when he knew I would be devastated. Graham was one of the good administrators who had to suffer the fools at FA

HQ. My admiration for him grew in the time I was in the job. He backed the national manager and was one of the few you actually believed meant it.

As for Gareth, he was shattered and very emotional, concerned that he had let everyone down. It would take him a long time to get over it, to recover his confidence and pride. All these years on, he will still be embarrassed, because it meant so much to so many people. He shouldn't be. Gareth wanted to take it, and if you are faced with someone who accepts the responsibility, you let him see it through.

I told Gareth that if he wanted to leave immediately to meet up with his family that was fine by me. It was the same for all the players, who would usually head off home after a game. This time they stayed. What they had all accomplished was exceptional, so I think they got together and decided: 'Come on, let's stay over. We'll go off in the morning.' We had a few drinks with the squad, some of whom saw it through the night. Some went to bed and got a few hours' sleep, felt a bit better for it, had a shower and were off.

There have been reports some FA insiders tried to have me reinstated as England manager after Euro 96. That may be true, but I certainly know nothing about it, and nothing was ever said to me. In any case, how could they change Glenn Hoddle's appointment anyway? The Chelsea manager had been appointed at the beginning of May, because I was stepping down. He was lucky to be inheriting a team full of strong characters who knew what they were doing, and he would go on to do well with them. His England side qualified for the 1998 World Cup finals in France, and he was able to call upon a new group of players, who I'd been looking forward to working with and who we had been developing through Dave Sexton's Under-21s. He would be the one to benefit from the skills of Paul Scholes, David Beckham and Michael Owen among others.

Having Hoddle already lined up as my successor before the tournament did not work out well, and the FA was partly to blame for this when they asked that I include him in a press conference. I agreed only so as to stop the situation developing into a major media row, but I was not happy. Glenn infuriated me after I opened the door for him to see the squad in action. We looked after him, he met the players, watched us train and had lunch with us.

I was stunned when he phoned and asked when he could arrange for further visits, basically wanting an observer's role for the tournament. To me that was so damned arrogant. 'Glenn,' I said to him, 'these are my finals; you get yours next time.' Until then, he was to stay away from my squad. It seemed so unprofessional of him, and it carried the danger that it could distract and confuse the players, if they began to wonder whether I was still the one in charge, or should they be trying to impress him instead. He should have known better.

Glenn was also fortunate that my team and I had fixed the broken link between the national side and the country after the disappointments of the previous failed qualification campaign. Some years later, I was even more infuriated when Glenn accused me of endangering England's chances with my choice of match dates. As national coach, it had been my duty to organise England's schedule in the period up to the 1998 World Cup finals, which at the time I had hoped would be mine. The word got back to me that I had deliberately chosen the matches to sabotage the team's chances; essentially that I was working against my country. That is as bad as it gets with me.

The draw had taken place in the Louvre in Paris in December 1995, where we found ourselves in a group with Italy, Poland, Georgia and Moldova, but after that there was a second meeting, in Poland, to decide the playing schedule, and this was as complex as can be imagined. It got to the point where indecision could have left us drawing lots for dates to play our games, which would have left us at the mercy of fate, so I thought it best to get on with it. My strategy was based on my belief that England would win enough points against the rest to ensure that our trip to face Italy in the last match (it was eventually scheduled for the Olympic Stadium in Rome on 11 October 1997) would not matter. I thought that at the very worst, we would have second place and a play-off to qualify.

As it turned out, Glenn led England there needing no more than a draw (which they achieved) to qualify for the finals. He has my admiration as a player, and I have no doubts about his quality as a manager/coach, but his great error was to drag his personal life and beliefs into the England camp, and then talk about subjects such as healing and reincarnation when he must have known that sooner or later it would make unfortunate headlines.

Noel White was conspicuous by his absence when it was all over. From the moment he asked me to 'audition' for the job to the day I left, I cannot remember a constructive word between us. As chairman of the International Committee, you would have thought he would have offered his thanks, or said something to the players by way of gratitude for their efforts. I am unaware of him making any direct contact with the players post-Euro 96. If he did, I apologise. White eventually met up with me when I was working with England as Steve McClaren's assistant.

When I reflect on what happened in Euro 96, I still think we played as well against Germany as we did against Holland, but just could not get the ball in the net. I thought what we gave the game was outstanding, and we did not make the final because we lost a shoot-out. I would argue that, if fate had been on our side, we should have won on the balance of chances created.

When I look back now, I remember how my squad sweated blood for the honour of playing for their country. They were all heroic, all main contributors, and they all had particular gifts; the camaraderie and team spirit were superb. McManaman and Anderton were the pathfinders of my team, illuminating the way. Their workrate down the flanks was phenomenal. They were built like hairpins and could run all day, with the strength and lung capacity of marathon runners.

McManaman was one of the 'lads', alongside his Liverpool colleague and mate Robbie Fowler. I really grew to relate to them both. On the first day they joined us before the tournament got under way, there was a bit of a fracas in their hotel bedroom. I called them down for a chat and to give them some advice. I said all I wanted was to treat the players as men, not like kids. I explained they were making a lot of noise and that all I expected to hear from them was for them to say they wouldn't do it again. They said they wouldn't and they didn't. They were absolutely brilliant.

At the end of the tournament, Robbie came to see me, shook my hand and said that, despite his lack of action, he had enjoyed every minute of the experience of being with England. You know with players they will sometimes say something and not mean it, but not these two. They were funny and mischievous, but they weren't malicious and they were fantastic members of a memorable squad.

It is easy for a manager at the end of a tournament, when asked to name his star player, to reply that they all contributed in a way, so it is impossible to select one as being unarguably special. However, I can say that in all honesty about Euro 96. Not one of the players who represented England fell below a very high standard. Shearer's goals were crucial. He was the top scorer in the tournament, with five, in front of great talents such as Denmark's Brian Laudrup, Germany's former Spurs striker Jürgen Klinsmann, Hristo Stoichkov of Bulgaria and the Croat Davor Šuker.

There were other spectacularly magical moments from individuals: Gazza's stunning strike against Scotland was one of the best I can think of at this level of competition, and Seaman's penalty save in the same group game, plus the one he stopped against Spain, were masterly. Our defence was solid throughout. I could make a case for Southgate being the tournament's outstanding defender, and yet he suffered as the player history will claim as the culprit when he missed that penalty. The bravery of Pearce, taking his spot kick and scoring against Spain, was a personal triumph for a man who at that moment had in his own mind repaid the country for missing against Germany in Italy.

We went into this together and all of my players, without exception, found a peak of performance and held it. Not making the final and losing out to Germany the way we did would have been a greater disappointment had the defeat not been balanced by these performances. My career disappointment was not having the chance of developing this squad further, and hopefully taking them on to qualify for the World Cup finals. I was excited by the quality of the players, not just the ones with the experience I used, but the others coming through the system. Alas, they were no longer mine but Glenn's.

Sometimes you can look too far forward, though that is not a crime. I am always optimistic and what I had to consider was that so many of the squad, when I took over in 1994, were relatively inexperienced themselves. I was convinced that with the Euro squad, plus Beckham and the rest of the young talent, we would – not could – have won the World Cup in France. It is easy to say that, but that is what we were preparing for and I still feel entitled to be so confident about that team's potential.

As it worked out, I was in charge for a total of 24 games, with 11 wins, 11 draws, the abandoned match in Dublin and just that one defeat against Brazil in that time, plus losing to the Germans on penalties. My time with England will remain a secure and lasting memory. I loved it. The players were magnificent, they listened, they took on board the plan and they came so desperately close to us reaching a major final for the only time since 1966, a 48-year span of disappointment and, occasionally, humiliation. I was able to work with a support staff who, like the players, were of the highest quality, equal to the very best I have been associated with. Their attention to detail, the way they worked on behalf of the international set-up, was driven by their desire to see a successful national side. As for the support we received from the public, not just the regular football follower, but the millions who let their national pride inspire us, it was . . . I was going to say overwhelming, but no, we wallowed in it, loved it, needed it and wished we could have won the title for them as much as ourselves.

For me, having grown up in Dagenham and been brought up to have a great pride in my country, it was an honour to have been a part of it – something I could never have imagined when I started out. But that pride made me feel even more that I'd been denied the fulfilment of my dream. Even now, nearly 20 years on, never a week goes by (and I'm not exaggerating) without someone, somewhere coming up to me and mentioning Euro 96. It fills me with happiness to know that even though we failed, people still appreciate the football we created. The words 'beautiful but so brief' were spoken about it once and to me they say it all.

# 4

# THE BOY FROM CORNED BEEF CITY

MENTION DAGENHAM AND most people think of Ford, car production lines, strikes and Mondeo Man. But for me it was home. It was where I grew up, was educated in life, developed my love for football and my ability to play it professionally. My memories are of good neighbours, families who cared about what went on around them. There were rows and fall-outs, but mainly of friendships that have lasted a lifetime. I am not claiming it was some sort of urban paradise; it was a hard, working-class community and a fine place in which to be brought up.

In the 1940s and 1950s, Dagenham might have been a big town, but it felt like living in a village or at least what I imagined village life to be like. At the time, Dagenham was seen as a place of opportunity, after Ford had opened their factory there in 1931. Many of our neighbours had moved there to get away from the restrictions of living in the claustrophobic East End of London or to escape the

Blitz during the war, often arriving with their only possessions piled high in a push-cart or a pram. Dagenham still had its rough edges, but these rarely approached the mindless violence that is a distressing fact of life today everywhere.

I was born on 6 January 1943, more than halfway through the war, so I missed the worst of the Blitz and have no real memories of that time. Even then, there was still a danger to your home and your life from bombings. We were lucky as our original house was bombed just after my mum and dad had moved out. My parents had got married when they were still young, my dad, Fred, was just 20 at the time, while my mum, Myrtle, was even younger at 18. Dad was serving as a petty officer in the Royal Navy based in Halifax, Nova Scotia, at the time I was born, so he had to wait some months before he was granted leave and could come home to see his son.

Mum had been born in Wales and was staunchly Welsh. She had moved to London with her parents and sister as a 15-year-old. Her parents, my granddad Ossie and Milly, my grandmother, were to be big influences in my life. My dad came from a large family of six brothers and three sisters, having made the much shorter move from Barking; which meant I was never short of uncles and aunts. I was surrounded by relatives. It seemed like bliss to me. As I grew up, I have happy memories of visiting Dad's family on Sundays, where the table in the front room would be stacked with food: mussels, whelks, bread, butter, cold meats, salads. These were memorable get-togethers. There was a lot of love around me.

My mum's family were different; there were fewer of them for a start, and they were quieter, but just as kind. Mum and I stayed with some of her family in Clydach Vale in the Rhondda when we were evacuated soon after I was born, and I would often go back there for long periods after the war had ended.

For a while, my mum and dad were very busy running a pub, which meant I spent a great deal of time with my granddad Ossie. He was a strong man physically and mentally, having left the pits behind as a young man and opened a general store before heading for the capital. It was the same road taken much earlier by his friend Jimmy Seed, who became a national name as an inside-forward with Spurs, Sheffield Wednesday and England, then latterly as a long-serving manager of Charlton Athletic. Jimmy actually came from a pit village in the North East and played for Sunderland before moving to Wales to sign for Mid Rhondda. One of Granddad's delivery boys had been Tommy Farr, the Welsh heavyweight, who in 1937 fought the great Joe Louis over 15 rounds in New York, but lost – I kept being told – to a controversial points decision.

Mum always talked with passion about her life in Clydach Vale. The village, like so many others, endured disasters and the terrible loss of life in the mines, with two horrific tragedies happening in the years before I was born that cost the lives of 40 miners. My mum was so committed to Wales that she wanted me to play for the country when she realised I maybe had it in me to be a professional footballer. In those days, however, you could play only for the country where you were born, though that has been amended since then.

Football was my obsession from as early as I can remember. It was much the same for the other lads around me, and there certainly was not a second from the age of 11 when I did not believe it would be my life. In one sense in particular, I was fortunate to have been growing up in the 1950s, because today's kids, if they want to play outside, have to worry about all the traffic, and in some rougher parts of our cities, they may have to look out for criminal gangs, stabbings and drugs.

For us, the worst that could happen was that we might be

confronted by the Grange and Heathway gangs. They were pussy-cats compared with the ones we read about in today's press, but they tried to act far harder than they really were. However, it taught me to look after myself as well as I could, though such problems rarely arose in actual fact. The worst I can remember was a scary night when I was surrounded by a group of boys. I would have been 14 at the time, not big and burly and not even very fast. They didn't touch me, but as there had been a recent newspaper survey claiming that Dagenham was the second worst place in the country for crime, behind Liverpool, I felt very uneasy. That survey didn't reflect my impression of the area. There might have been the occasional domestic rumble, but I wasn't scared to walk the streets at night, and I can't remember anyone else feeling too worried at the time.

In truth, I was far more likely to get injured or badly hurt playing football beside the Bandstand and the Ten Tall Trees, features of Valence Park, where I played so often. A group of us would turn up there with our hefty football boots, with their heavy leather toe-caps so tough you could smash your foot and still not break a toe.

The downside of such solid protection was that you didn't want to be on the receiving end from one. I remember how in one game I accidentally took one full in the face when I went to head a ball. There was not a lot of blood, but my face ballooned and when I returned home my parents were worried about the possible long-term damage. I went straight to bed and got up early the next morning to have a look. My face was like a watermelon. There was not a crease in it; no nose, no eyes, no mouth. I could see through the swelling only when I used my fingers to prise open my eyelids. It took ten days to make any real improvement. The only other time I received a similar heavy blow to the head, it was self-inflicted when I ran into a post box and needed 20 stitches round my nose and forehead. I still have the scar.

My memories of those days are mainly about playing football in parks, backyards, streets and school playing fields. If there was a flat bit of ground, we would get a game going. Dagenham was extraordinary for the number of footballers it produced. We all know the stories about the Geordies and Scots shouting down a mine shaft and calling up another Jackie Milburn or Alan Morton. It was the same in Dagenham: there may not have been any coal mines, but we still produced a lot of class footballers. England's 1966 World Cup-winning squad featured three players from the area: Jimmy Greaves, Martin Peters and Bobby Moore. Ronnie Boyce, who played for and then coached at West Ham, was another local lad. Ken Brown had a successful career as a player for West Ham and manager of Norwich, and in his young days lived about eight gates from our house.

But if there was one family that personified Dagenham's footballing heritage it was the Allen clan, who lived a few doors from us. Les Allen was six years older than me and like his son Clive played for Spurs and QPR. Les was also on Chelsea's books, managed at Queens Park Rangers when I was at the club and at Swindon Town. Les's younger brother Dennis, who died a relatively young man, played professionally, as did his son Martin. Les and Dennis had another brother, Ron, who didn't make it as a professional, but his son Paul kept up the family tradition. In more modern times, England internationals Tony Adams, Paul Ince and Paul Parker were all Dagenham or relatively local products.

But for me probably the most influential footballing product of Dagenham at that time was a player you almost certainly will never have heard of. His name was Dave Coney and I looked up to him because he was captain of the Tottenham youth team – and he was just an amazing, forceful personality. I was always quizzing him about the set-up at White Hart Lane. Lads like Dave were inspirational characters, even though his career never took off as expected. His presence at a big club showed me the route forward and pushed me to work hard at my game. You read of the hungry fighters who punch their way out of slums and poverty. We thought football could be the way to a new life for us, too, if we were good enough.

There were no slums in our area and I cannot remember grinding poverty, though I can recall families who had very little. Dagenham was known as Corned Beef City to us kids. We didn't know why it had such an extraordinary name, but to our young ears it was different enough to be interesting. My mum used to hate it when she heard the name. 'Call it that and people will think we are poor,' she said. A few were very poor indeed when they arrived between the wars, and corned beef was just about all they could afford, which we later learned was how the place had earned the nickname.

You could say we were 'working-class prosperous', eventually able to afford tellies and cars. But when I was a kid we could still play football in the street without worrying about being hit by one. As I grew up and the country recovered from the aftermath of the war, more and more people were able to afford cars. This meant that Ford transformed Dagenham with the money that was earned from working on the production line. The 1950s were a great time for the town, with rapidly improving job prospects and pay packets, before the industrial strife that would follow in later years.

One of my proudest early memories was when I represented Dagenham Under-11s against Paddington, from across London. We played in maroon and amber hooped jerseys and won 12-0 on Dagenham and Redbridge's Victoria Ground. Although I was still young, I felt it was an experience that drew me closer to my ambition of being a professional footballer, and as a consequence I began to give less attention than I should have to my studies.

By the time I moved up to Lymington Secondary Modern, I was

sure my future lay on the football field. The teachers explained to me the dangers of neglecting my education on the off chance I would be one of the lucky few who would not only play professional football but make enough to live on. I wouldn't say I saw my education as a waste of time, but it took me some years, and one or two patient friends, to show me I could both seek knowledge and play football. I have always been inquisitive and keen to ask questions, but I couldn't see the point of studying grammar or reading books, unless they were about football. My maths was adequate, and I enjoyed woodwork and metalwork; I still have a coffee table I made at school, but that was about the sum of it. To the utter despair of my teachers, I had a one-track mind: football.

What they did not understand was my inner confidence. They could tell I was smart enough academically, and so they were frustrated that I did not choose to apply myself, because I knew what I was going to do with my life. One teacher, Mr Warren, told me that in 30 years of experience many youngsters had passed through his classes determined to make football their career. No matter how talented they thought they were, he explained that in the end they had all fallen short. He asked me what made me think I could succeed where so many had failed. It was a belief, I told him. I would not be happy unless I tried. He argued that there was only a one in a million chance, and I replied that in that case I would be the one, because I was unswerving in what I wanted to do.

I didn't miss any opportunity to improve my game. I would carry a tennis ball in my pocket as I went to school and in time I learned how to control it and make it do what I wanted it to. I would play football every day in the school playground, after school, in the street, in our local park, with lads my age or considerably older. It was wonderful. These games taught me so much: about comradeship, the team ethic, defending myself, the excitement when you score and not being prepared to lose. As we played, more and more lads would turn up and be told which side to play in, so a five-a-side game would develop into one where each team might have 16 players. You might not know some of the boys on your team, and we didn't have any team kits, but automatically you worked out how to pick him out and find him with a pass. Learning to find a team-mate that way was to be a great asset in my professional career. That technique became second nature to me in the shadow of the Ten Tall Trees.

It is a genuine comfort to look back and recall being happy with my family and friends in those early days. Granddad Ossie would push and encourage me in whatever I was doing, particularly sport. He had been a professional sprinter in his younger days, so he knew all about the competitive instinct. He and my grandmother were a major influence during my upbringing when my mum and dad were busy running a pub.

I often look back and smile at the regular banter which went on between us. I would come home from school in time for tea, having stayed behind to have a kickabout with my friends before doing so. On the days where I'd been in a match at school, I would walk through the front door and my grandmother would come out to the passage, wiping her hands on a tea towel with a big smile on her face: 'So you played well today, then?' she'd say in her soft Welsh accent.

I'd grin: 'Not bad.'

'Not bad! By all accounts you were the best!' she would add, flicking the tea towel at me.

Then Ossie's Welsh tones could be heard from the living room: 'Milly, will you stop getting his hopes up. The boy will have such a big head if you carry on like that. He's good but not that bloody good!'

She'd then raise her eyes and we would smile at one another. 'I'm only telling him what I've heard,' she'd say as we headed into the living room, where he would be sitting at the dining table fin-ishing his tea.

'Come over here,' he'd say, calling me to his side. 'Now don't you start thinking you're as good as she says, Terry, because you're not and you've got a lot more work to do before you are.'

'I know, Granddad,' I'd say as he ruffled my hair. As Granddad was bald, I'd trace my fingers over the blue lines which marked his head, caused by the many bangs he took on it over the years when working down the mines, which would make him laugh.

'Right,' he would say. 'I'm off to the club for a pint. I'll leave you two to it.' And then he'd be off to the Winding Way social club, where he would spend the evening playing snooker with his mates.

As the door shut, I would turn to Grandmum: 'So who saw me?' I'd ask excitedly.

'Sit down, sit down,' she'd say, as she pulled up a chair opposite me. 'It was Mrs Jenkins. She said you were marvellous and had a sweet left foot. May I never move from here, these were her exact words. I don't know how she knows these things, Terry, but that's what she said.' She'd then lower her voice as if she could be over-heard: 'Between you and me, I think she's got connections in the football world.'

'Really?' I said.

'Apparently, but you know me, I don't like to pry.'

'But how did she see me playing? We were in the fields behind the school,' I'd say.

Her lovely face would then go all serious: 'See. You're just like your grandfather; you think I'm making this up, don't you?'

'No, of course not, but it's just that we don't normally see people watching us when we play at the fields,' I explained.

'Well, there's a lot you don't know. Mrs Jenkins' sister was poorly, she was visiting her and she saw you from her back window that looks out over the fields. Now, enough of this. Let me go and get your tea, and you can then have a slice of the rhubarb pie I made specially for your afters.' She'd then get up and go to the scullery.

I'd sit there feeling really pleased with myself, whether Mrs Jenkins had seen me or not didn't really matter. My grandmother always made me feel ten feet tall, but then in my sensible ear I had Ossie bringing my feet firmly down on the ground. They played the 'good cop, bad cop' routine perfectly. Whether it was planned between them I'll never know, but it certainly worked. The truth is nobody – not even Mrs Jenkins – could have seen me.

West Ham United were our local team, and so they were the ones everyone hoped to impress. If you were any good as a player at school, the chances were the Hammers would be looking and invite you to their coaching courses. That is the way it was before clubs developed their academies. They represented the big time for me and my mates, Peter Augur, Ronnie Hanley and Jimmy Hazell, whose surname I used years later when I worked with Gordon Williams on the Hazell books that were subsequently developed into a television series. We all knew lads who had become part of the set-up at West Ham, which made us want to emulate them.

Despite this, I have to admit that from an early age I was a Spurs fan, because I just loved watching them. The main focus of my attention was on two of their greatest players: first Danny Blanchflower, and then, quite some time later, Dave Mackay when he arrived from Scotland in March 1959. As a partnership they were magnificent. There were others I could name and whom I looked on as gods, like Cliff Jones. I would read everything I could about them and, as I have mentioned, football news and match reports were about the only thing I did read in those distant days that live on in the memory with a clarity that surprises me. I can still vividly recall the atmospheres, attitudes and goals scored and passes made back then.

I was simply mad about Spurs and collecting autographs. Just being near enough for a player to sign my book was wonderful for someone like me. I don't claim this as one of the great forecasts, but I signed my own autograph book 'Terry Venables Manager of Tottenham' as a youngster. It took time, but I made it.

As I got older, my football career was developing nicely. I began by representing my school, then moved on to county level, and England Schoolboys were the next target. I had a very specific reason for wanting to play for England Schoolboys. For ages, I had pestered mum and dad with non-stop talk about joining a professional club. But Mum was a disciplinarian, much stricter than my dad, who laughed and joked a lot. She would take no nonsense from me. When I was playing, even in the street as a kid, she would shout out: 'Terence! Shoulders back, stand up straight!'

It was embarrassing in front of my mates, but that didn't stop her. Perhaps it was something to do with my being an only child. She lived through me, but wasn't happy at the idea of me being a pro footballer with no alternative employment. That did not suit her celtic mind-set, which demanded everything had to be just right for her. I may not have thought so at the time, but her influence taught me about respect for others and how to behave. She was aware that I was beginning to get interest from various clubs, but she also worried it might come to nothing, as it has for countless youths who have over the decades been sucked into the system then discarded. So she told me she would agree to my trying out as a professional footballer only when I had been selected for England Schoolboys.

By the time I did eventually receive my England call-up, Chelsea had been chasing me after being told of my potential by Jimmy Thompson, a very eccentric scout. I'll say more in the next chapter about the influence he had, not only on me but on so many others who turned their back on the bigger clubs to head west to Stamford Bridge.

They weren't the only ones interested in signing me. Both West Ham and Spurs were keen, too. They would both offer me and Dad, an Arsenal fan, free tickets to come and watch them in action – clubs often did this for youngsters they considered good enough to be possible future signings. The seats were usually at the very front, virtually on the track. And this led to my first – and very embarrassing – appearance on the pitch at White Hart Lane.

I had turned up at Tottenham wearing a gaudy Donegal tweed suit my parents had saved up to buy for me. On this day, we were watching a cup match against Chelsea, so it was quite an occasion. George Robb, an England international, was playing on the left wing for Spurs and, as the ball went out of play, I leapt out of my seat so that I could throw it back to him, only for my shoes to slip on the wet grass, sending me flying, with the crowd jeering at my misfortune. My lovely suit was caked in mud.

For all that I dismissed my teachers' concerns and my mum's worries about my future, I now understand they had my best interests at heart – in those days in particular, when medical knowledge was so much worse than it is today, it would have been easy for an injury to rob me of my chance to make it. Had that happened, or had I fallen short, I have no idea what I would have done about making a living, though I feel confident I would have given my new career all I had. If I had been a waiter, I would have dealt with the customer so well he would have had to leave a tip. I was brought up to be a hard worker in the belief other people would recognise that quality in me.

I might not have been a great academic, but I loved asking questions. Maybe this was my way of compensating for my lack of reading. If you don't read about history or literature, then you can enquire about these subjects. I asked questions at school, but mainly I asked coaches and trainers and scouts about football. I've always sought knowledge, and I would recommend to any young player reading this book that they should adopt the same policy: the more you ask, the more you have a chance to learn and improve.

My mother was convinced my constant questioning and thirst for analysis of the game suggested that I was perhaps best equipped to coach and manage. She had recognised something in me she felt I could develop.

In fact, there was one other way in which I chose to learn more about the world: I was a film buff from an early age. It was a regular treat and a great educator. I would be taken to the pictures, as we called them, every Friday. I can still visualise the films. There would be double features and mysteries, like the Edgar Lustgarten films which always began, it seemed to me, shrouded in fog with a cat jumping over dustbins and screeching. It helped that my mum was for a time the manageress of a cinema in Romford. To watch the great stars of the time added dollops of colour to our lives, and I seem to remember we would always have a meal out before or after we went to the cinema, which made the whole experience even more special. You have to remember that in those days television was only just beginning to infiltrate our lives as the wonder of the modern age. Very few could afford one, so they were very much for special events when we would pile into a TV-owning neighbour's house to watch the FA Cup final or something of national importance, such as the Queen's Coronation in 1953.

In those austere times, no one was brought up to worship money as there was none to worship. What we had we would spend, or else we would save up for a good holiday or a car or telly. I'll admit I wanted to be successful, but money was not the be-all and end-all for me at that time – after all, in those days footballers were still on a maximum wage, so it wasn't the case that people went into the game expecting to make their fortunes, as they might nowadays.

My Dagenham upbringing left me with an outlook on life that I am very proud of. I know very wealthy people who wouldn't give a beggar a quid, or who wake every morning worrying about the person they think is going to try to nick a pound off them. I have never felt that mean or cynical. I was blessed with a good family and good friends, lads like myself, who wanted to play football and who, perhaps, weren't all successful in life, but weren't jealous if you were. It might surprise you how many of these friends of mine went on to be successful in all types of business. They weren't vicious or ruthless. They certainly enjoyed life, they enjoyed being your pal and you were happy to be theirs. When I have heard of someone from my street or area who has been successful in business, I have never been less than delighted – proud, actually. I am thinking of lads like Joey Jennings, who was a runner for his dad and is now a very wealthy man with a string of bookmaker's shops.

Those lads I grew up with stayed together as a group even after Chelsea had signed me as an apprentice. Many of us are still in touch all these years later. It was our environment which made me realise the importance of friendship and trust. When you have these qualities in a football team, you win things. I was brought up in a real community, but knew I would soon be entering an entirely different one.

You may think that I am viewing the post-war years, which were hard and difficult, through rose-tinted glasses, but those lucky enough to survive the war were different, and more appreciative of what they had. When I think of them all and what they did for me and what I learned from them, I realise what special people they were. These were the good people that drove me on, made me committed to success. When it came good for me, I knew they would be pleased for me; equally, when I faced up to my critics, I knew they would be suffering on my behalf, too. When I walked out with England, I carried their values with me, for Dagenham had prepared me for life. It was just as well, for I was soon to face a new challenge as I sought to fulfil my dreams.

# 5

# CHELSEA – ALL FOR ONE

WHEN I JOINED Chelsea, they paid me £5 a week as a 15-year-old apprentice. I was still officially an amateur. Most of that money was spent on tube and bus fares from our home in Dagenham to either Fulham Broadway (the nearest station to Stamford Bridge) or Hendon (when we trained out there). I would catch a bus from Becontree to Barking and then take the District Line. Sometimes I would get off at South Kensington and catch the number 14 bus to the Bridge. Training at Hendon meant first the bus, then a tube to Mile End where I'd have to change on my way to Brent, which was renamed Brent Cross long after I used it, and finally a bus to the Welsh Harp. I was always dressed in suit, collar and tie for a journey that would take a minimum of two hours each way. I never thought it was a waste of time or boring as it took me to where I had always dreamed of going. I was now officially a footballer, and nothing was going to stop me from reaching the top.

There were little financial extras. The seniors would give me or one of the other youth team lads, such as Johnny Hollins or Barry

Bridges, a couple of bob – 10p in new money – for cleaning their boots. We were also very generously handed out luncheon vouchers, worth about half a crown (12.5p) to make sure we ate well in Aunties café, which was left out of the stadium, over the hump-backed bridge and then left again. If we didn't go there, we would be in the café between the stadium and Fulham Broadway, which was owned by a Polish family. They had a very pretty daughter, Irena, and Barry fell for her. They eventually got married when he was earning a bit more, though still not a lot. He had a terrific career as a player, winning four caps for England. Afterwards, he managed St Pat's in Dublin for a season and coached at other clubs, but I don't think it was for him. They went on to own a hotel in Eastbourne before returning to Barry's native Norfolk, where he ran his granddad's farm and had other business interests.

We were not offered scientific advice about what to eat, as players are now. Be sensible, we'd be told, and that was about as far as the nutritional advice went. We took it to mean that we should eat as much as we could in the Welsh Harp! They served some great, traditional English food: steak and kidney pudding, shepherd's pie, sausage and mash. The vouchers gave us enough money to have a pudding as well, so we'd normally have jam roly-poly with custard. We called ourselves the luncheon vultures. Admittedly, I was more careful on match days when I would have toast and some fish or chicken, but today's nutritionists would have been horrified.

When we were training, we had to report in by nine o'clock, but despite the early start this was no trouble at all. Indeed, I recall those days as among the happiest of my life. Sure, we had to clean up, sweep the rubbish down from the top of what appeared to be sky-high terraces on the Monday after Saturday matches, but each and every one of us was also being given the chance to prove we could eventually make it in the professional ranks. If the system meant we had to help out with the cleaning, it was part of the deal.

We would train every day. Dick Foss, a great football man, looked after the apprentices with help from Jimmy Thompson, who had shadowed me on behalf of Chelsea for years. The training was basic by modern standards, and focused on track work. Dick, whose knowledge of the game and his love of passing it on to youngsters like us was gratefully received, would split us into small groups then think of a number. 'Six,' he would shout, and that meant we had to endure six laps of the stadium. Sometimes it would be eight or four laps that we had to do. There was a lot of running. The Bridge had a huge athletics track round the pitch plus a dog track. After we'd done our running exercises, we would have five-a-sides on an asphalt pitch. It could often be painful if you slipped on that surface or slid in to make a tackle, but despite any such discomforts, I knew that this was what I wanted and where I wanted to be thanks to men like Dick and Jimmy.

It hadn't been inevitable that I would join Chelsea, as a number of clubs had been interested in signing me. My local team West Ham had been keen to sign me up, and many expected I would join them; Tottenham Hotspur, whose style of football I adored to watch, were also keen to bring me in. From further afield, Manchester United made inquiries. They were all enthusiastic and full of promises.

The Hammers were particularly keen. Malcolm Allison, who was club skipper and even then a larger-than-life character, and the old chairman, Reg Pratt, came round to our house, Malcolm wearing a garish check jacket that I can still picture to this day. I trained with them and was as mesmerised as all the other kids by this charismatic footballer we could talk to and discuss things with. His outward appearance might have been stylish and a bit gaudy, but it was his knowledge of the game and his desire to learn more that interested me. Malcolm was part of the new movement who believed you could change systems and develop strategies that could give you a greater chance of success. He wasn't scared to try something new; he talked football incessantly and was always looking to try out things. Malcolm was a positive influence in the game and would be one of my teachers.

By that stage I had been contacted by all sorts of clubs. Jimmy Murphy, Matt Busby's assistant, tried to sell me the advantages of joining him at Old Trafford. I would have loved to have had the opportunity to meet Duncan Edwards, one of that era's great players. I was impressed with his style and his power, and Dad took me to watch United when he was playing at Arsenal – just to study him. I remember the date clearly, it was Saturday 1 February 1958, and United won a thrilling game 5-4; but a few days later Duncan was dead, one of the victims of the Munich air disaster. I was on the bus in Dagenham when I read the news on a poster about the tragedy. It was hard to believe that so many of United's great players plus staff and media were dead. It made a huge impact on the whole country, and I have to agree with those who say that England would have been stronger challengers for the World Cup in 1958 and 1962 (let alone 1966, when he would still have been only 29) had he still been playing.

In those days, it wasn't easy to watch sporting heroes such as Duncan Edwards in action. I might see snippets of him on newsreels at the cinema if I was lucky, and even more occasionally on television. So the only way to fully understand what all the fuss was about meant you had to wait until United were in your area and then hope you would be able to grab a ticket. At least I can say I did see him in the flesh, and was as impressed as everyone else inside Highbury that day.

In a strange way, the tragedy made United the club most youngsters wanted to sign for, but I was determined to stay in London and forge a career in the capital. Arthur Rowe, the great man of 'push and run', invited me to join Spurs, and as they were my boyhood team many would think it would seem to be a natural choice for me. But I do not remember there being much of a dilemma in my own mind when it came to making my decision. I felt that if I went to Spurs I would have to wait several years before I pulled on the white jersey, and I was impatient to progress.

With Tottenham out of the picture, that meant I had two clubs to choose between: the Hammers and Chelsea. West Ham was close and supported by most of the families in our area. Maybe that was the reason I thought Chelsea would be the more exciting club to join. It would be different: different attitudes, new faces. When I decided to head for Stamford Bridge, Malcolm reckoned we had simply taken the Chelsea shilling. He said he could give 10,000 reasons why I decided to join them. He was meaning pound notes. That was Malcolm being a bad loser. He was wrong. I wanted to join Chelsea and they had also offered my dad a part-time job scouting. I think my dad received a fiver for each of his reports. For that he found them a keeper in John Dunn who made the first team before moving on to Torquay, Aston Villa and Charlton.

So it was decided: I was to be an apprentice footballer at Chelsea, signed on amateur terms. Not everyone agreed with my choice, including my dad, who couldn't understand why I had ignored Arsenal, the club he supported. But I never trained with them, though I had invitations to attend Highbury. Dad just could not work out my thinking. The fact was I chose Chelsea because I had worked out that, being hard up, they would give me the best chance of making their first team at an early age. With the major clubs, I knew I would have to wait much longer for an opportunity to break into the senior squad. I was only too aware it might never happen in a game that would covet you if you sparkled like a new star but ignore you if you had holes in your boots.

In those days, of course, Chelsea were nothing like the all-powerful, hugely wealthy outfit of today, run on a Russian's cash reserves. But there were other aspects of life with Chelsea that appealed to me, not least that it had a certain glamour. It could not have been Stamford Bridge's closeness to the Kings Road, as that scene was very much in its infancy in the late 1950s, but there was still an aura about the area that contrasted with the modest family-friendly lifestyle out east. The swinging West End, with its theatres and new working-class celebrities, appealed to me. In time it allowed me to meet and enjoy the company of society photographers, musicians, songwriters and film stars, as well as the characters who owned local market stalls. It was they who got me started on doing business deals, such as producing Thingummywigs – hatwigs – for women to wear over their curlers. We sold a few but not enough to keep the business going.

Chelsea never let me down. They signed me in my mid-teens, looked after me, helped me develop as a footballer, presented me with my senior debut at 17 and made me club captain at 19. Because they were a relatively modest club, they had to produce their own and they did: Jimmy Greaves, Bobby Tambling, Johnny Hollins, Bert Murray, Ron and Alan Harris and Peter Bonetti were just some of those who came up through the ranks there.

I admired the way the seniors conducted themselves, the way they dressed like men ready to walk into jobs as bankers in the City or have lunch in one of London's finer restaurants. This stemmed, I believe, from manager Ted Drake, who always had an air of sophistication about him. He was erudite and trustworthy, a man of great charm. Chelsea had been champions in 1955 under Ted, and it was he who signed me on amateur forms. In all the time I played for him, we had only one mild difference of opinion, but nothing that would alter my view on him as a man of impeccable behaviour.

That argument came when I turned down his offer to turn professional. Ted had called me into his office and said: 'Terry, you are seventeen and I want to offer you professional terms. You deserve it.'

When I asked if he would mind if I waited a little longer, he became upset, accusing me of being tapped up by another club, which wasn't the case. I simply wanted to take part in the 1960 Olympics as I had been told there was a good chance of being selected. I wanted to be an Olympian. I was selected and played for the England amateur team against West Germany at Dulwich Hamlet, but disappointingly failed to make the final squad for the Rome Olympics. As soon as I knew that my amateur career was over, I signed for Chelsea.

That stint with the England amateurs meant I eventually made a unique piece of history by becoming the only person to represent his country at Schoolboy, Youth, Under-23, amateur, Football League and full international level. The subsequent decision by the FA in 1974 to abolish the amateur set-up meant my record will never be beaten.

Jimmy Thompson was Ted Drake's confidant as well as scout. Jimmy could not have treated the role of being a scout with more subterfuge had he been an MI5 officer. Unfortunately, he was over six foot tall, and stomped about suited and booted, his outfit topped off with a bowler hat. Even in those days, there weren't many bowler hats to be seen in Dagenham! So his efforts to conceal who were his targets were often doomed to failure.

I have to admit that on one occasion, I didn't help him. He'd been visiting me at home when Reg Pratt and Malcolm Allison turned up to try to persuade me to sign for the Hammers. When he saw them approaching, he immediately hid away in another room, so he wouldn't be found out. But I wasn't having any of that and shopped him, much to his embarrassment. An amazing character and an eccentric personality, Jimmy had been determined that I would sign for Chelsea through him and spent a lot of time at our home, ludicrously believing he was inconspicuous. He was a good man and his advice was sincere. Jimmy always sold me and my folks the line that at Chelsea the door of opportunity was open for young players. He would have known, as he had brought some of the best to the club.

I doubt if there are scouts like Jimmy around anymore as I can't imagine anyone in that role being as devoted to the job as he was. Once he had spotted your talent, he made sure that no other club was going to muscle in on his find. Of course, he was paid on results, but the money would not have been life-changing for him – he just loved his job.

Occasionally, he went a bit further than his role might have allowed for. One time when I injured my foot just when I was preparing for a trial for an England Schoolboys game. Jimmy was confident he could solve the problem and turned up at my house with an ointment he assured me was safe, but not something we should talk about. At that, he spread the unction over my damaged foot. I have no idea where it came from or what it was, but within a minute my foot had turned as black as pitch. I shouted at him, demanding to know what he had done.

'No worries. That is the treatment working, Terry,' he tried to reassure me. 'Have you got a ball handy? Grab it, and we will go out in the back garden.'

Our back garden was tiny. We went outside with me hobbling on one white foot and one black. He ordered me to kick the ball at him. 'My foot is killing me,' I protested.

'Hit the ball as hard as you can.'

I did, straight at him with all my force from the bad foot. I cracked him hard and he went down. At the same time, I collapsed in agony from the pain in my foot. Whatever he had done, it was certainly no miracle quick cure. You can't imagine anything like that happening today.

I was lucky that a wonderfully talented bunch of youngsters were gathered together when I started at Chelsea. Many of us made it into the first team by the age of 17 or 18, which was something the Hammers were also doing, as Bobby Moore, Martin Peters, Geoff Hurst, Johnny Sissons and Ronnie Boyce all had early opportunities there. It was an era when young players were given the hope that hard work allied to ability would be rewarded. Nowadays, with Roman Abramovich buying the very best players from around the world for Chelsea, and other foreign owners doing the same for their clubs, the supply line of youngsters into the top flight has been seriously reduced. It is easier for managers to buy the best ready-made. It cuts out coaching time when you are buying in the quality others have produced.

But in those days, financial necessity made the development of young players a vital part of every club's strategy. The success of the Busby Babes, who won the competition for its first five years, meant the FA Youth Cup attracted great interest and big crowds, as it was seen as a sign of what was to come, with all clubs anxious to maintain the production line. Like United, Chelsea took the competition very seriously indeed.

We were lucky enough to win the FA Youth Cup two years in a row during my time. In 1960, we beat Preston 5-2 on aggregate and a year later Everton were defeated 5-3 on aggregate. In my first season, Peter Bonetti and Bobby Tambling were in the side, while a year later Ron Harris was promoted. Jimmy Greaves had been in the Chelsea team that lost the final to Wolves in 1958, falling by 7-6 over the two legs. It was a great achievement for the club to keep on finding so many talented young players.

The difference between the modern game and ours in the 1950s and 1960s was the willingness of managers and coaches to work with us and invest time in us, in the belief that we would become first-team players further down the line. Of course, it helped that managers then could think in the longer term, whereas few now have that luxury. The Youth Cup was the first real step on the road to a senior career. It was where they sorted out those that could play from those that might not have the talent to make the reserves. Our victories in successive seasons meant we were in line for promotion to the first team. The world of football was opening up to us and we would either grab the chance or fall below the radar.

Life for me had become a series of magical occasions, the sort I dreamed about when I played football as a boy in Valence Park. The players, thanks to the strong youth system, were like a band of brothers. We would have our dicey moments but we were there for each other, working for each other, which is why as I developed as a player I was often more interested in producing a goal than scoring one.

Of course, there is no comparison between the life we led and the cloistered, moneyed lifestyle of the young players at Chelsea and elsewhere in the Premier League today. They have money and plenty of it, we didn't; they have luxurious accommodation laid on, while we either stayed with our parents or found the best digs we could. And I have yet to hear one of today's young stars being ordered to clean the terraces or the seniors' boots. Despite all these changes, one thing we definitely had in common was our determination to succeed as pros. I started that way and finished that way.

Within the youth team, I enjoyed being the fulcrum of the side, the main supplier. I knew I was good at it and I practised like hell to make myself better. I would demand the ball and dictate play, short or long. I enjoyed the responsibility, but it is the men in front of you or on either side who must then exploit the openings. With young guys like Barry Bridges and Bobby Tambling, we always had a chance and it was clear that we were ready for the step up to first-team action.

Indeed, by the time I won my first FA Youth Cup medal, I had already made my senior debut, the moment coming on 6 February 1960 against West Ham. Of all the teams, fate decreed I should face my local club. My nerves before the big occasion were not helped by newspapers describing me as 'the new Duncan Edwards', just a couple of years after the incomparable Duncan had been killed.

I think it is fair to say I could have had a better start to my career, with nothing I tried seeming to work for me. I made it to the dressing room at half time looking for some word of encouragement to see me through the next 45 minutes. It would surely come from one of my all-time heroes, Johnny Brooks. Johnny was a player of distinction, with a magnificent physique, two good feet and an incredible body swerve. His style influenced me, as he was one of the players I studied and copied, trying to emulate what I thought was worth doing. He wandered across to me as I sat hunched, hoping for a consoling word. I normally cope on my own, but after all the build-up and excitement of the occasion, I was feeling very down. I was grateful when Johnny put his arm round my shoulder and drew me in close, but then he said: 'Terry, how do you think I am doing?' I had discovered that Johnny, despite his exceptional ability, was short on confidence.

We lost the game 4-2, and went on to finish the season in 18th place, three points off relegation. Jimmy Greaves was still with us, and his 29 goals that campaign probably ensured we stayed up. His disastrous transfer to AC Milan was still a year away. He was a near neighbour of mine and, as he had a car and I didn't, he would often give me a lift. It would be some time before I was able to fund a car on my own, and when I did I chose a yellow Ford Anglia. He drove a pale blue Ford Popular, as good a model as it got for young footballers at the time.

On one memorable occasion Jim offered to run me to the ground for a game we were both due to play in. I was still 17 and Jimmy was three years older than me and, as always, scoring goals for fun.

He was doing in senior football what I had seen him do with ridiculous ease for the boys' team at the Dagenham Arena. After one of those matches, I had even followed him to the bus stop, hoping I'd get a clue how to score goals like he did. But few could ever manage that – and certainly not me. On this occasion, the first thing he asked me after he'd picked me up was: 'Fancy something to eat?' He looked at me with sharp, darting, bright eyes. I liked my food but I drew the line at eating before a match and said that to him.

'Don't be stupid,' he replied. 'I do it at every home game.'

'But we haven't time,' I argued. 'It is only three hours to kick off.'

He got his way and we ended up in the Dinner Gong restaurant at Gants Hill. The waitress asked what we wanted. Not wanting to overdo things, I asked for boiled chicken and toast, but Jimmy ordered roast beef, Yorkshire pudding, roast potatoes, vegetables and gravy. I can't remember him ordering a pudding, though he probably did. I told him he was having a laugh. His reply was he always had the same roast beef lunch. We made the match against West Brom on time and won 7-1. Jimmy was sensational and scored five. Having seen how he performed on his diet, I said to one of the lads: 'I think I'm eating the wrong food!'

He left for Italy at the end of the 1960-61 season as the top striker in Europe, after scoring 41 goals in the league for Chelsea. I always felt his best period as a goalscorer was at Chelsea, but wherever he went he scored goals. With Jim in your team you always felt you would win. We knew he would score, so it was up to the rest of us to make sure we didn't let in any at the other end.

That season was significant for another reason. Up until January 1961, all players had been restricted to a maximum wage of just £20 per week. It didn't matter if you were one of the game's biggest stars, like Stanley Matthews, able to draw in thousands through the turnstiles, you were still kept to a wage of £20. When the maximum wage was abolished, I anticipated negotiating a fabulous new deal with Ted Drake, even though I was only just 18 at the time. Now, thanks to the Professional Footballers' Association (PFA), there would be no ceiling to my earnings.

I went in to see him, perhaps hoping I would receive something close to the £100 a week Johnny Haynes famously secured from Fulham. At the time, I was still on £18 a week, the sum agreed when I'd turned professional. We talked things over, and after our chat I emerged with a pay rise after all – to £20 a week!

That change, coupled with the ending of the retain and transfer system in 1963, which effectively tied a player to the club that held his registration, meant players could move freely between clubs and could negotiate better and better pay deals for themselves. In the space of 50 years, footballers would go from £20 to £300,000 a week for the top men, because of the determination of players of my generation to no longer be 'slaves' to the system. But there was a more immediate change about to take place in my career.

# 6

# DOCHERTY'S DIAMONDS
# ON SONG

IF THE 1960-61 season was momentous for all of professional football because of the abolition of the maximum wage, then the following season was just as significant at Chelsea for a change much closer to home: Tommy Docherty arrived as player-coach in September 1961 to give manager Ted Drake some support. When Drake was sacked as manager early in the 1961-62 season, with us already involved in a battle against relegation, Docherty replaced him, initially as caretaker-manager before getting the job on a permanent basis in January. The Doc soon brought in Dave Sexton, one of the smartest of the young coaches at that time. That does not mean the other coaches didn't give a damn and were happy to remain entrenched in the old ways, but Dave was one who studied the coaching business in many sports, drew his conclusions and put his ideas into practice. He offered a fresh new perspective to coaching.

The English game was changing from an age of not such splendid isolation to awareness about the coaching developments already established and used in Europe and parts of South America. We had been slow to react properly to the lessons that should have been learned from England's defeats against Hungary in 1953 and 1954. We were in the process of emerging from the tactical dark ages; men such as Dave, Malcolm Allison, Ron Greenwood, Noel Cantwell, Phil Woosnam, John Bond and John Cartwright (one of our best youth team coaches) were making an impact with their ideas. Further north, there was Alan Brown, who managed at Burnley, Sheffield Wednesday and Sunderland and was an outstanding teacher to his players and an inspiration to young, aspiring coaches.

We talked about the game as players among ourselves and with players we knew from other clubs. There was a desire to learn from each other and from the new coaches, such as Dave, about how we could evolve our approach. We would talk endlessly at Chelsea. I was fascinated by the impact good coaching could have on players and teams – and still am. Even in these very early days of my playing career, I knew I had discovered what I wanted to do with the rest of my life.

It was not just the coaching side that interested us, but how the great managers of the day ran their clubs. We had a heaven-sent opportunity to do that when a small group of us met Leeds United manager Don Revie, and I asked him question after question. Don spoke about every aspect of administration, about how they ran their training HQ and how they maintained their pitches, even about the grass. There were some good-natured murmurs that I was asking too many questions, but Don said: 'No, no, that is why I am here, but I think we have had enough for now.' The group began to break up, when I chipped in to say: 'Can I have one more?' Don looked surprised, until he realised I was joking. I believe these meetings were vital, as they gave the men with experience the opportunity to pass that on to players who hoped one day to follow them.

We had read plenty about the Busby Babes and Drake's Ducklings, a description that always seemed corny to me, but once the Doc took over we quickly found ourselves dubbed Docherty's Diamonds. As a unit, the young players were exceptional, though it would take a year of working together as seniors before we began to play as an excellent winning football team. There was real affection between us as a group. Sadly, there was nothing the Doc could do to save us that season. We were relegated, five points from safety, with the Doc increasingly looking to the future and trying out the younger players, as he realised that relegation was unlikely to be avoided.

The players quickly adjusted to Docherty and Sexton's new approach, but I was always being inquisitive, keen to find out more. So when the Doc put a point across, I would normally ask why and what the benefits would be. It wasn't always meant as a put-down, certainly not initially, but he was clearly irritated by my constant questions, not realising that I just wanted to understand the thinking behind the tactics. I was a young footballer (not even 20 years old), a bit saucy and he was a young manager of 33, with his strategy of how things should and would be done. Nothing, I suspect, could have averted a collision between a hard, ambitious Scot and an ambitious, young cockney who liked to question everything.

Despite that, I recall that these were uncomplicated days. I was young, happy and doing what I loved: playing football. But that was never my only passion: singing interested me more and more, as I came from a singing family. After my mum and dad came home from the pub on a Saturday evening, we'd often have a singsong. We would all gather round the piano and sing whether or not we were any good at it. It was the way we entertained ourselves and our neighbours. My parents were very good singers –

they would harmonise – and that is where I must have got the urge to do the same. To see if I had a real talent for it, they even took me to a social club. There, I tried to mimic Spike Jones and his City Slickers, a well-known act in the post-war era who would parody famous songs. It gave me a taste for performing in front of a crowd. So when I got the chance to enter a singing competition at Butlins in Clacton, I couldn't resist.

In those days, the Butlins holiday camps were extremely popular. You would stay in a chalet and all meals were taken together in massive dining halls as part of the package. Each camp would organise a variety of competitions, including singing ones, and the papers gave them a lot of publicity. It was almost like a small-time version of *Britain's Got Talent*, and there were several acts who got their first break this way.

There was a group of us who would trek to the camp on the Essex coast during the summer: Terry Moore who was a team-mate of mine with England Schoolboys; Dennis Butler, who played right back for Chelsea, Ron Harris, and Ronnie Hanley, who has remained a close friend over the years but who never quite made it at Chelsea. Ronnie was devastated not to be offered a pro contract. He came round to our house afterwards and my dad spotted that all was not well. He asked Ronnie what was wrong. 'I don't know what to do about a job,' Ronnie replied. Dad immediately came up with the answer. He told him he had friends at the docks who might be able to help, but if they did find him a job then he should not let Dad down. Ronnie got his job and he worked on the docks until he retired. We have remained friends ever since, and talk regularly, and he will even put his little grandson on the phone to talk to me.

We got up to the usual tricks of youngsters on the loose, but it was all pretty harmless stuff. We had so much more freedom than the modern player who can often not do anything for fear of the press or people recording it all on their phones. Anyway, at the age of 17, I won that particular competition and was due to go through to the final, which was scheduled for September. Sadly, it was the wrong time of year and Chelsea wouldn't allow it. It was a fair decision. Despite missing my shot at the big time then (I heard that it was the Bachelors who eventually won), I kept it up and subsequently had the opportunity to sing with the Joe Loss Orchestra at the Hammersmith Palais, which is not far from where I live now. People said I was hyperactive, always wanting to be involved in things. That was true, as I couldn't envisage a situation where football took up every minute of my adult life. It meant everything to me, but I found I could be successful at that and still become involved with other things.

The papers latched on to the fact I was singing with Joe Loss, and that was the start of me making headlines for matters outside football. I got some mixed reviews, and when I ran on to the field the crowds would often shout: 'Stick to singing!' I just saw it as a bit of fun, a healthy distraction from my football career, though I'm not sure Tommy Docherty saw it in quite the same terms. In those days, footballers very rarely made it into the newspapers for anything other than football. I enjoyed the celebrity that came with being a Chelsea footballer and quite often made the headlines for the right reasons.

I have to admit, I was attracted to the glamorous lifestyle. There were a few from the Dagenham area who went into showbusiness: Victor Sylvester was one of the biggest dance band leaders in the post-war era; then there was Harry Fowler, a fine character actor; the singer Kenny Lynch and comedian and actor Dudley Moore were also from the neighbourhood.

Being a footballer allowed me to meet people who were themselves in the news. I got to know singer and actor Adam Faith (his real name was Terry Nelhams) and Terry O'Neill, who was the finest of showbiz photographers. I used to meet them in the Carlton Tower Hotel in Knightsbridge (now the Jumeirah Carlton Tower), where they would come in for breakfast. Their lifestyles interested me, as did learning more about them. Even as a 17-year-old, I would save up to eat in the very classy and expensive Rib Room.

I also met singer and entertainer Tommy Steele there. He was six years older than me, mad on football and, having been brought up in Bermondsey, a Millwall supporter. I would take him to our training sessions at Chelsea where he worked as hard as us to maintain the fitness he needed for his stage and film work. Despite his success, what he really loved was football and so he was delighted to be able to spend time with us, just as we were with him. There were plenty of other showbusiness figures who trained with us at Chelsea, including Richard Attenborough, who became club Life President.

With Chelsea in the Second Division for 1962-63, you could say it was out with the old and in with the young as far as Docherty was concerned. As players, Johnny, Barry, Eddie, Alan and Ron plus the rest felt we were good enough for promotion, and the Doc made his contribution. He was happy enough to continue with the new, young brigade, and with no money to spend he had very little alternative. Doc had his own ideas on how the team should perform. He had not only been a successful player as a Scotland international and had lined up alongside a superlative player like Tom Finney, he also had all the coaching badges, so you cannot argue that he did not know the game.

For a long time, and with good reason, my thoughts on him have been coloured by our abrasive relationship. To say we begged to differ on many occasions would be a gentleman's way of describing it. And of course he lost me and many others in the awful wake of what happened in Blackpool, more of which later. I was never convinced by Tom as a tactician, but one admirable decision I will credit him with is his appointment of Dave Sexton as his coach. Dave's quiet, unassuming style as a man hid an unbendable backbone of steel, as you would expect from the son of Archie Sexton, a professional boxer of high standing. There came a point, as some players have discovered, when you realised you should never, ever cross the line with Dave. He was a fabulous coach, one of the renaissance men of the modern game.

For Dave coaching was, as it should be, a lifetime's study. He would talk about coaching in various sports; basketball was a particular interest of his. He taught me many lessons that have stayed with me ever since, such as: do not go to floor, stay on your feet and get close in. He would say to players that if your opponent can lift his head to make a pass, you are not close enough. If he had a flaw, it was his refusal to accept that anything that did not happen on the field was important. He hated personal publicity – he did not want that side of the job so he was perfect for us and for Tom.

We had the enthusiasm and energy of youth, and the ambition collectively and individually to drive us on. We were also very good and would prove that by bouncing out of the second tier and back to the top league in 1963. There were some remarkable clashes that promotion season, a couple of which highlight to me the different attitude of fans to the game in those days, especially when it came to big-name opponents. Fans would applaud stars from the away team as they ran on to the pitch, and in that sense none was more widely respected than Stanley Matthews, who was still playing for Stoke City, our main rivals for promotion, despite the fact that he would be 48 at the end of the campaign.

Stan was a godlike figure, at one time the most famous footballer on earth. Franz Beckenbauer told my journalist friend Ken Jones that when he was a youngster the only foreign player he knew anything about was Stanley Matthews. When I was relatively new at

Chelsea, I remember Ian MacFarlane, a very tall, powerful Scottish defender, giving Stanley (then still playing for Blackpool) a rough time with his tackling, and our crowd responded by booing Ian. Stanley played up to it and came out after the interval with the biggest bandage possible wrapped round his leg. That finished Ian on the day. Whenever he went near Stanley the crowd booed and jeered him. Stanley, who had been named European Footballer of the Year as recently as 1956, ran rings round him.

I'll always remember what happened when we played Stoke at the Bridge during that season in the Second Division. There was a full house and a tense atmosphere, as it was a crucial match for both sides, but that did not stop the crowd welcoming Stanley. They went silent when first Eddie McCreadie then Ron Harris went for him with full-blooded tackles. I forget whether it was Ron or Eddie who sent Stanley stumbling over the hoardings, but they were both booed from then on, and at least one newspaper reported how our fans were not happy at us going for promotion by kicking an old man. Fortunately, even though we lost the game 1-0, we still earned promotion as runners-up to Stoke.

Once we returned to the top flight, we became a force in the league, finishing a highly respectable fifth. In the summer of 1964, the Doc signed George Graham from Aston Villa for £5,000. Although still a teenager at the time, he was virtually a giveaway, costing a few thousand pounds, and the two of us quickly began a friendship that has remained strong through the years.

George had arrived in England from Bargeddie, a working-class village outside Glasgow, and his first tasks when he moved to London were to unravel the mysteries of the tube system and find suitable digs. The Doc made sure he felt grateful by telling him that he had saved him from being 'doomed' at Villa. It didn't quite have the desired effect, as for a time George was known to the rest of us as 'Doomed'. He hated it and subsequently earned the nickname 'Stroller'. He had great ability but was initially very quiet until one day, while the rest of us were playing cards or reading as we travelled to a match, he began singing loudly as he looked out of the window. He was one of the boys from then on.

With London being so new to him, he decided the most sensible thing was to find digs not too far away from either the Bridge or our training ground at Hendon. Understandably, he didn't fancy my tortuous travelling routine from Dagenham. But Ron Harris explained he was staying at Stamford Hill, which sounded perfect, as George assumed it would be close to Stamford Bridge, though in fact it was a long way out of the West End of London and the travel involved was considerable.

By now the London music scene was very lively indeed. The main attraction for me was Denmark Street, or Tin Pan Alley as it is better known, close to Oxford Street. I would often go there with George and Ron Harris, and we got to know Tony Hiller and Pat Sherlock, the guys from Mills Music who had an office with a recording studio.

The level of our sophistication at the time was watching George order his favourite meal: lasagne and chips. There was so much going on in the music scene at the time and we loved being around it. Mills Music was *the* place then. At the time, there were two youngsters working as general dogsbodies in the basement of the offices, Reg and Eric. They would distribute the post, make cups of tea and coffee and carry out all sorts of jobs to teach them about the music industry. Reg was a fat little fellow, who had a superb gift as a mimic, and could do a brilliant impersonation of Carry On star Kenneth Williams, while Eric was an extremely extroverted character. But they would not stay hidden away for long. Eric Hall went on to become one of the most famous showbiz and sports agents, but for a while I lost track of Reg, who wanted to make his way as a musician.

It was there that I also got to know Bill Martin, who like Tony

My dad, Fred, was a petty officer in the Royal Navy when I was born during the war, so I didn't see much of him at the time. But he and my mum, Myrtle, did all they could for me.

Celebrating with my dad after I was selected for my first England Schoolboy cap, aged 15.

Sitting at home with Mum and our poodle, Shandy. My upbringing in 'Corned Beef City' gave me a set of values that I have taken through my life.

Valence Park in Dagenham was one of my first football training grounds.

Practising in the garden. It was here that scout Jimmy Thompson tested out an injury I was trying to overcome – to both our cost.

Jimmy led me to Chelsea, and soon after we were winning the FA Youth Cup, my first significant trophy.

Training on a mudbath of a pitch was something we all had to get used to in the 1960s – nothing like the manicured surfaces they play on today.

George Graham and I pack for another trip. He and I have been lifelong friends.

Turning tables on the press at Chelsea. John Hollins is behind the camera, while manager Tommy Docherty also tries his hand as a photographer. I'm taking the whole thing very seriously.

In the directors' box at Stamford Bridge with the Doc. My relationship with him was never an easy one.

All dressed up at the Norbreck Hydro in Blackpool, but it was a trip there that ended up in the most ridiculous fallout with the manager, and soon I would be on my way.

I wanted to extend myself beyond football
and followed up numerous other interests:

I've always been keen
on singing, and here I am
rehearsing with Joe Loss
ahead of a performance at
the Hammersmith Palais at
Christmas 1960.

In order to help my writing
career – novels I wrote
with Gordon Williams
were turned into the *Hazell*
television series – I learned
how to type. As you can see,
not many men did in those
days!

Norman Wisdom, who
became one of the big
supporters of a tailoring
business I helped set up.

My senior England career was sadly brief, but at least it meant I got to play at every level for my country. Here I am in conversation with manager Alf Ramsey.

Following Bobby Moore out on to the field for my debut as we faced Belgium. Bobby was one of the true greats of English football, and it was a tragic waste that he was not used more after he retired.

On the coach to make my Tottenham debut against Blackburn Rovers. Left to right are: 'Nice One' Cyril Knowles, me, Phil Beal and Dave Mackay, one of the greatest footballers I ever played with.

Celebrating winning the FA Cup after beating Chelsea 2-1 at Wembley at the end of my first season with Spurs, but despite this my spell there as a player wasn't entirely happy.

I really enjoyed my time as a player at Queens Park Rangers: there were some great characters in the squad, and it was just what I needed after Spurs.

When I joined Crystal Palace, my career was drawing to a close as injury problems got the better of me. It was time to make the next steps in my career and move into coaching.

was a song writer, and both have been my friends since. They are both Eurovision Song Contest winners: Bill was the first British winner with Sandie Shaw's 'Puppet on a String'; Tony won it with 'Save Your Kisses for Me', performed by Brotherhood of Man, and also wrote the famous song 'United We Stand', while Bill wrote major hits such as Cliff Richard's 'Congratulations' with one of the best-known lyrics ever written. He wrote for Elvis Presley and had number ones worldwide. His footballing connections continued when he wrote the words of 'Back Home' for the 1970 England World Cup squad. We still regularly meet at Philip Lawless's Motcombs restaurant in Belgravia.

A few years later, those days at Mills Music came back to haunt me, when I went to a function at Harrison and Gibson, a major retailer in the centre of Ilford organised by Watford FC in honour of the Morgan twins Roger and Ian, whom I'd got to know after I'd joined Queens Park Rangers in 1969. As the event went on, Elton John made a guest appearance and came up to us, which wasn't immediately surprising, as we knew he was a keen football fan.

He greeted me by saying: 'Hey, Tel, how are you doing?'

'I am doing fine, Elton. Nice to meet you.'

'We've met before. Don't you remember me at Mills Music?'

I couldn't remember him at all, but as soon as Elton did his Kenneth Williams voice I realised that he was Reg Dwight, the lad who had been working with Eric Hall years earlier. We stood and talked for ten minutes or so, mainly about football, not music. I remembered how he had always been keen to talk football in Mills Music, and of course in later years he spent a lot of the wealth he created from his music to finance Watford, with Graham Taylor doing so well for him as manager at the club.

Another big name our group would regularly meet was Norman Wisdom. He was always immaculately dressed off screen, but on it in character he wore those bloody awful suits that didn't fit him and that silly little cap, but he was one of the funniest men I've ever met. His films were for all the family and would have people queuing up to watch them with the kids night after night.

In truth, it wasn't just those who were involved in showbusiness that I was keen to meet, I also enjoyed the company of journalists such as Ken Jones, then of the *Daily Mirror*, and Brian James, who worked on the *Daily Mail*. Most of my team-mates would probably have been slightly wary around the press, though not to the degree you find nowadays, but that didn't worry me. I saw them as more knowledgeable and more successful than me in their field. I wanted to know why they were successful, and I was keen to hear their stories, and to understand their perspective on things.

I learned from Ken and Brian how difficult Alf Ramsey could be in his pomp as England manager. He would be embarrassingly rude to some if not all the people he had to work with, particularly journalists: offhand, brusque, dismissive – and that was on a good day. We discussed things like my moving into coaching and how I had to have a personality to go with the job. It was a useful insight into the role, because being a manager is about so much more than just getting your coaching badges, which isn't to say you can overlook them.

I knew I wanted to go into coaching when my playing career was over, so when I was 24 I took my FA coaching badges, supervised by Mike Smith. I couldn't believe it when I passed with distinction – a 95 per cent pass mark. Before that I had never been sure that I could make it as a coach, yet there were those, my mother included, who believed I would be a manager and a better one than I was a player because I was always telling others where to play and who to pass to. At the time, I didn't realise that was coaching – it just came naturally to me. Once I had that certificate, it gave me a huge amount of confidence. I was so keen to coach I would stay on once a week to work with the new lads coming through, such as the young and supremely talented Alan Hudson and his brother Johnny, who did not make it at Chelsea. It was so enjoyable for me. Eddie McCreadie was another who would learn how to coach at these sessions.

After doing so well in our first campaign back at the top, we all believed the 1964-65 season could be special for us. But before it had fully got under way, it produced a game that highlighted the attacking genius of one young player and the collapsing career of another. The genius was George Best, and the event was when he played against us for Manchester United at the Bridge on 30 September 1964. The Northern Irishman was just 18 years of age and had already shown himself to be a player with unique ability. He had yet to confirm that potential consistently at the highest level, though there were few doubts he would succeed. His ability with the ball, his pace and his trickery mesmerised the fans and bewildered his direct opponents.

On this day he was up against our full-back Ken Shellito, who was a defender of quality and, at 24, seemingly entering the prime of his career as one of the best of his generation. As players we knew what he was worth to the team and the Doc thought extra highly of him: in fact, he loved Ken as a class footballer who had been playing well enough to be selected by Alf Ramsey for England in 1963. Ken had been seriously injured when it was his misfortune to shatter his knee in a tackle involving Sheffield Wednesday's Edwin Holliday. Ken's studs caught in the turf, his knee twisted and that was that. It was a sickening injury, particularly so when medical knowledge struggled to cope with such a potentially catastrophic injury. It had meant a prolonged period of rehabilitation before Tommy Docherty had to decide if Ken was ready for a return.

I remember well enough the trouble the club went to to ensure

Ken was fit to play against United, despite having begun his come-back the previous season. The Doc certainly would not have okayed a return that in any way would have hampered Ken or Ken's ambitions, with the World Cup very much on the horizon. Ken was confident all was well, though having been out for such a protracted period meant there would have to be doubts about him lasting the full game. And it was taken into consideration that Ken would be facing George Best, who was emerging as a special talent.

Ken ended the day having been taken apart by George. He was run ragged, turned inside out, beaten every way possible, call it what you like. It was a drubbing. As Ken's team-mates and friends, we could only watch in dismay. There was nothing any of us could do to stop what was the most one-sided contest I had witnessed on a football field. It was the performance that confirmed to the foot-ball fraternity that George was every bit as extraordinarily talented as had been claimed; a young man surely destined to conquer the world.

George scored one of United's two goals and made the other for United's established legend and players' player, Denis Law. United that day were not short of other great footballers, among them Bobby Charlton, Pat Crerand, Nobby Stiles and Bill Foulkes, who died in 2013 having been (like Bobby) a survivor of the Munich air disaster. There may be film of George's performance somewhere on the internet, but the reason I recall that day is also to highlight the circumstances of it all, which were a major contributor to George's success at Stamford Bridge. George was in strident, killer form and Ken was not as he and the rest of us thought he would have been. It was an embarrassing, unequal duel. Ken was ready to gamble on the day and lost, despite the best intentions. His injury eventually curtailed what could have been a far more glittering career for club and country.

It is possible George would have been equally impressive against a fully fit Ken, but I suspect he would have had a much more difficult time. I believe Ken was good enough to have made Alf's World Cup 1966 squad and challenge for the place won by George Cohen. Instead, he never fully recovered from the injury, retired prematurely, was appointed a coach at Chelsea and elsewhere before making a successful coaching career for himself in Asia.

Despite that setback, we had developed as a team of high quality. We had toughened up as a group. Even a youngster like John Hollins, who made his debut as a 17-year-old, had quickly learned how to protect himself. He learned the hard way. In one of his first games, he was the victim of a terrible tackle from Everton's Alex Young, a marvellously talented forward who had come to England from Hearts. Alex was known as 'the Golden Vision' and had a great reputation for scoring. I can remember looking across as John went down and lay on the turf. I had a go at Alex: 'Why did you do that? What was the point of that? He is just a kid and you did that to him.'

He looked at me and replied: 'I know he is new in the game because if he hadn't been, I would have gone in harder.' I can hear those who remember Alex as a player least likely to do such a thing saying 'no way'. There were many more such full-blooded challenges that would today result in red cards and lengthy bans; then it was almost seen as a part of the game. I have no doubt that the modern game has got it right on this issue.

The raw material that had been secured by scout Jimmy Thompson had all by now matured, and with additions such as George Graham we felt we were a team capable of competing for the First Division title. For starters, we lifted the League Cup in April 1965, when we beat Leicester City in the final over two legs. We played the first leg at home on 15 March, and Bobby Tambling scored our first in what turned out to be a full-blooded confrontation. Leicester equalised through their skipper Colin Appleton, then I scored with a penalty. Again they came back at us, this time with a Jimmy Goodfellow strike. Eddie McCreadie clinched the first leg when he went on what seemed like a never-ending 60-yard run to score the decisive goal with less than ten minutes remaining.

With a narrow 3-2 advantage, when the return at Filbert Street ended goalless, the cup was ours. The team that day was: Peter Bonetti, Marvin Hinton, Eddie McCreadie, Ron Harris, John Mortimore, Frank Upton, Bert Murray, John Boyle, Barry Bridges, me, Bobby Tambling. John Hollins, Allan Young and George Graham had all played in the first leg. It was Chelsea's first silverware since winning the league in 1955, and we felt it was the beginning of something special.

We were a terrific team, praised for the style of football we produced; exciting and fluid with an elegance that represented the image of the club and its surroundings. I felt we were a year or two off winning the title, but could maybe even emulate Spurs and win the Double and go on to be a force in European competition. I believed everybody, including the Doc, would be happy about that. The players certainly were up for it. As the campaign reached its climax, there was still an outside chance we could win the title, while a cup double opportunity ended only when we were knocked out of the FA Cup by Liverpool in the semi-final.

Sadly, for all the bright prospects ahead, there was a cloud on the horizon, as my relationship with the Doc had become increasingly remote, despite the fact that I was the captain of the team. You could argue it had been building up to an unexpected and unwanted confrontation. It came when we went into our last three matches of the season, against Liverpool on Monday 19 April 1965, Burnley on the following Saturday and then the final match two days later at Blackpool. It was a tough call: three away matches to end our campaign and the Doc had reasonably decided to base us in the North West in Blackpool's Norbeck Hydro.

We had dropped a bit of form and were in third place behind Manchester United and Leeds United, which did not please us but could not be described as disastrous. And we would give it all we had left, knowing our high position was an achievement. We had come a long way and were so near to title success, even if we knew that other results would have to go in our favour for us to stand any chance of taking the league crown. Our target was three wins from our remaining matches, and certainly no one was looking to cruise through such important matches.

When we got up to Blackpool, the Doc had agreed to give us a night off after we'd played Liverpool. This wasn't a time to rampage round the bars of Blackpool, but a chance to go out in our groups and have a couple of beers if we wanted to. However, we lost 2-0 at Anfield, which was hardly a disgrace, but the result must have upset the Doc to such a degree that he told us our night out was cancelled.

It was our turn to be furious. Why had he done it? Was he looking for a confrontation? We were not going to run amok, but surely we were entitled to a night off? So eight of us – George Graham, Barry Bridges, John Hollins, Marvin Hinton, Eddie McCreadie, Joe Fascione, Bert Murray and me – decided to take it. We had a couple of drinks but no more. We returned to the hotel in good order only to be confronted by the Doc. I do not know if it was the pressure on him or his way of trying to impose discipline on us. People react to stress in different ways, but it turned into a major scandal when the Doc decided, in what could only have been a moment of madness, to send us home, supposedly because we broke curfew, had downed a couple of pints and sneaked back to our hotel. The Doc has since said that he did not cancel the night out, but merely cut it short and his anger was provoked when we had gone out again. I don't remember it happening like that.

I still find it hard to believe. I still do not understand how a manager would take such a decision against players who were working hard on behalf of him and Chelsea. Our success would be his success. It was his team, yet he chose to humiliate us and embarrass our families. It was *the* big football scandal of the year. I thought the punishment was severe and outrageous: all eight of us were told to pack our bags and go. He chose to turn a small storm that could easily have been dealt with in-house into a full-blown tornado.

He must have known the significance of what he had done and the serious repercussion of his action. Sending so many players home was bound to reflect on team performance and long-term morale. He had to send out a scratch team made up of what was left of the first team plus reserves and lost 6-2 at Burnley on the Saturday, before we were reinstated and lost 3-2 at Blackpool on the Monday. If we had all deserved it, I would concede the Doc was right. But he had initially given us permission to go out and then, when we lost a tough match after a season of considerable success, he changed his mind and then punished us severely.

It was hugely costly to Chelsea. He had made us appear to have been drunken yobs. When we arrived back in London, the world's press were waiting for us. Years later, people still ask me about it. What infuriated me and the others was the betrayal in deciding to leak the incident to the press or rather to one reporter. Bernard Joy, now dead, a former footballer and a friend of the Doc's who then worked for the *Evening Standard*, was not at Blackpool but he broke the story in London. I don't blame him for that, as he had a job to do, but I can't forget what the Doc did to us or work out why he did it. In my opinion, it was crass, stupid and self-defeating.

I have wondered if there was another reason behind it all, and that maybe he felt my influence as captain was growing too strong. I had angered him in an earlier incident when he caught me singing in the ballroom of a hotel the team were staying at in West London.

He had ordered an early curfew on the eve of a match at Stamford Bridge and had himself gone out. Knowing he was away, the players had taken the opportunity to have a couple of drinks in the hotel. However, when he returned they all scattered, leaving me up on the stage singing my heart out. He was not best pleased.

It wasn't just a question of discipline off the pitch, either. There had been all sorts of talk about the players not obeying his tactics during the game on occasions. And it was true: we did change things on the field if we thought that was necessary. I never considered it open defiance, but a sensible response to the situation we were faced with. After all, isn't that what good players are supposed to do: adapt to the circumstances?

The Doc had never been opposed to us going out as a group, or in small groups, because he understood it was important to stop us from becoming bored on our travels to matches. He was hardly a wilting flower himself, and he always met life face on, so he knew all about the importance of players being able to enjoy themselves.

I remember an occasion when we had to play Blackpool – there must be something about the place – this time over a Christmas holiday period. They had a number of outstanding players, including a young and highly impressive 17-year-old Alan Ball, England full-back Jimmy Armfield and Tony Waiters in goal. We had been booked into one of Blackpool's best hotels where we had to wear black tie when we sat down to dinner. We had to hire the suits, which the club paid for. It was a fine place, if a bit too grand, but nonetheless we enjoyed our stay there. After dinner, there was a dance in the ballroom, and the Doc said to us we could go out but we had to be back by ten. We returned bang on time to find the Doc asking, as if all surprised: 'What are you back for?'

'You had told us to be,' we said.

'You don't need to bother about that,' he replied.

I would have laughed if I hadn't been so angry with him at his inconsistency. There had been previous occasions when he had been furious if we were a couple of minutes late. So we sat down at the dance and ordered fruit juices, but hid a glass of sherry behind each pint of orange. With our match only two days away, none of us really wanted to drink too much, so we ordered the sherries because we knew it would annoy him if he spotted them.

As we watched, the Doc was approached by a lady who said: 'I recognise you – you are a football manager.'

Doc could have left it at that but spotted a way of giving us a laugh.

'Would you care to dance?' she asked him.

They took the floor. She did not know it, but she was going to be the butt of Doc's sense of humour. The dancefloor was choc-a-bloc as they ambled round, with the Doc playing up to us by pretending she had bad breath. He tied a hanky round his face at one stage. When he rejoined us, we were all preparing to go to our rooms for the night.

'Where are you going?' he asked.

'We have a match to play.'

'Don't be silly! You are young boys, enjoy yourselves.'

Doc did and kept us amused. He went up to a man who was the double of the comedian Freddie Frinton, and very drunk. When the man fell over, Doc grabbed his legs and pulled him up a long corridor in the hotel. I think the man finished the night propped up in a telephone booth. It was a silly prank, perhaps, but it was a lot of fun at the time. It was moments like this that made those of us who were sent home feel angry: all that players look for in their managers is consistency.

These pre-match getaways were sometimes extended to three or four days as a bonding exercise. We would go to places like Lancing College, just outside Brighton, where we could relax and prepare ourselves as a squad. It worked for us. You didn't have to go abroad,

Lancing was fine. In later years, Brian Clough used breaks to relax his teams, taking them away to Majorca as often as was possible. The good thing about it was if you did have a few beers, you felt dutybound to play well.

The Doc's idea of a joke could have unintended consequences on the club and the players. When we played AS Roma at Stamford Bridge in September 1965, having qualified for the Fairs Cup with our performances the season before, everything was going well until Eddie McCreadie was sent off. I was captain and Eddie just didn't want to go, so I had to usher him off. Their trainer came on and started abusing Eddie, with the Doc giving him a full and robust response, as he felt the Italian tactics had been provocative. That was in the first half and we were a goal in front. We went on to win 4-1 and I scored a hat-trick for the first time in a major competition. However, the Italians completely lost the plot.

The problem was we then had to visit Roma for the return and they decided to host the game in a small stadium where the crowd would be extremely hostile, rather than in the Olympic Stadium, where the atmosphere might have been more diluted. Even when we trained in the little ground, it was full of ranting Romans and the target was the Doc. They were giving him hell and he in return was giving them it back. The police rushed in to protect him. They tried to persuade him to go back to the dressing room, but he decided on another technique: he dropped his shorts to the crowd. Chaos! The crowd went even crazier and Doc did not give a damn. He was doing exactly what the Roma coach wanted him to do, working the Italians into a frenzy.

On the day of the match, it took us what seemed like forever to make it to the stadium by coach. The crowd lined the approach and were incredibly hostile. We eventually reached the main entrance, but even then it took a long time for us to make it to the relative sanctuary of the dressing rooms. Roma put back the kick-off time, another way of stretching our nerves. I looked on to the pitch to see that seats had been ripped up and thrown on to the playing area, but most extraordinarily there was a huge block of ice on the field. I have never found out how they managed to push or carry it on to the pitch, but it was going to take some shifting to get it off.

Bernard Joy, who had access to our dressing room, said to the Doc: 'Tom, go for them. You have to.' We thought the opposite and believed we should play with a sweeper, keeping things really tight – after all, we had a three-goal lead. We also had Marvin Hinton, who was superb in that role, but the Doc decided we would a play a normal game because of our lead. We knew that if the Roma players were caught up in the hostile atmosphere created by the crowd, we could find ourselves in trouble, so we agreed among ourselves that Marvin should play a little deeper, like a sweeper, when the pressure was on.

Eventually we drew 0-0, which in the circumstances was a great result. I cannot remember a game where so many missiles were thrown onto the pitch. Joy came into the dressing room after the tie and shouted over at Tommy Doc: 'I told you we didn't need to play a sweeper, didn't I!' He hadn't even noticed what we'd done, though I'm sure the Doc must have seen what we were doing, but because it had worked he decided to say nothing about it. Despite the success of the strategy, I am sure he must have felt this was another challenge to his authority, and so realised that something would have to be done about it sooner or later.

The hostility on the way out of the stadium was even greater as we drove very cautiously away from the ground. It was made worse by the fact we had knocked Roma out of the Fairs Cup. Brian Mears, who would eventually succeed his dad Joe as club chairman, was sitting in front of me in the coach beside his wife June. A brick came through their window and glanced June on the face, leaving blood streaming from the wound, but it could have been so much worse. I shouted at the players to lie down in the aisle of the coach, which would offer some safety from the maddened Italian supporters, and we escaped with June our only casualty.

For my own part, despite the dispute with the Doc, I was continuing to enjoy life, and also looking for other excitements away from football. I was never one for leaving training and going home to watch horse racing on the television, although I am not criticising those who do. It might have been different had I joined West Ham, but having decided to go to Chelsea I had to travel through the centre of London, making it easy for me to stop off in the West End and enjoy some lovely Italian food, often accompanied by chips. It was there that I agreed to set up a partnership in a tailor's business.

My fellow directors were George Graham, Ron Harris, Ken Jones and Tom Barclay; Tom was the tailor, a tall Scotsman and a lovely fellow. Men's fashions were changing and we thought we had enough bright ideas to produce a viable business. We had a lot of support from our contacts in Denmark Street, while Norman Wisdom said he would give us his business, and even allowed us to use his name to say we were his tailor. In the end, we thought better of it when we realised he was not known to the public for his elegant clothes, but for the ones he wore in his films, which wasn't quite the impression we wanted to create. In fact, he sent round a van with about 40 jackets for alterations, and as anyone in the tailoring business will tell you, there isn't any profit in alterations – at least not enough. In the end, the business went bust. As one of our cynical friends put it, we were the best dressed bankrupts in the West End.

Despite this off-the-field setback, I was playing full of confidence, in control of my game and contributing to those players around me. We were still incredibly young as a squad and we were like a family. I would have been quite happy to stay at Chelsea for my whole career, but that was never going to be the case unless the Doc decided to quit or was asked to leave. If it was going to be a case of him or me, then the odds were always stacked against me. From the Blackpool scandal onwards, I felt I was on borrowed time. Near the end of the 1965-66 season, when we didn't do quite as well and finished fifth in the league, Docherty decided to make his move.

He has written that he felt I had become too central to the team's style of play, and that opponents had worked out that if they could stop me, they could stop Chelsea. In order to make his side less predictable, Doc discussed the matter with Joe Mears, and it was agreed that I should be put on the transfer list; I felt as though he had made it into a case of him or me.

He signed Charlie Cooke from Dundee to replace me and he went on to do brilliantly for Chelsea. Charlie was a classy footballer and, although I wasn't often able to watch him, I knew he came as the latest in a long and distinguished line of highly talented players reared north of the border to head south, guys such as Dave Mackay, Alan Gilzean, Eddie McCreadie, Ian St John, Jim Baxter and the wonderful Denis Law. Charlie came in to the side and did a different job from the one I had done but it was perfect for the new Chelsea.

I was on my way to Tottenham, the club I had admired as a boy, and made my debut on 9 May 1966. George Graham was also sold, moving on to Arsenal. I remember one day after we had both moved on that I was best man at his wedding. The ceremony took place in the morning and we played against each other in the afternoon, George for Arsenal and me for Spurs. Arsenal won.

Moving to Spurs was hardly a downward step, and I was very nearly not the only major summer signing for the club, as they also tried to sign my pal Bobby Moore. By the time my transfer to Spurs was being negotiated, I was living at Beechwood Gardens, Gants Hill, where I had bought our home for £7500, paying for it outright from the proceeds of a signing-on fee. Bobby was in Glenwood Gardens, just round the corner. Our friendship flourished when we became neighbours and it was there that we learned Spurs wanted to sign us both. We were the two players manager Bill Nicholson had agreed to buy for the new season. I signed for the club for an £80,000 fee just before the World Cup, and waited on Bobby to join later in the summer.

I had hoped I might be busy myself during the summer as I was part of Alf Ramsey's list of 33 possibles for the finals. He had selected me for two matches in late 1964, and I played reasonably against Belgium in a 2-2 draw and then against Holland in Amsterdam when we again drew, 1-1. There should have been a third cap, but I was injured and not available. As it was, I did not make it to the final 22. Alf did not see me as an essential in his squad, but I was delighted he had given me a chance and my two caps. We were both Dagenham lads, but I am not sure he liked to be reminded of that. I remember one occasion when I had met a former neighbour of his and when I saw Alf at training I mentioned that Sid passed on his good wishes. Alf didn't say a thing but turned and walked away.

However, the World Cup was about to change everything for Bobby. Once he became England's World Cup-winning captain, and a national hero, that made it impossible for West Ham to let him go. He was choked, as I was. It meant Bill Nicholson was left to find another defender and the man he chose was Mike England. Mike had a fulfilling career at Tottenham, but although he was an excellent replacement he was second choice to Bobby.

As for Docherty, I have never tried to analyse our relationship. There was no need to. I knew why we battled each other, principally over the Blackpool business. What I do not want to do is find myself in a position where my anger with him ignores his achievements at Chelsea. I asked a journalist I knew was a lifelong Chelsea fan, to assess the Doc through his eyes. He said that for him the Doc was impetuous and that a major mistake was made when he sent his own players home from Blackpool. However, during his reign he was not scared to blood the young players available to him, he won immediate promotion after relegation, and his team challenged for a title and even a potential treble, after winning the League Cup.

I have met the Doc over the years and when we did I would feel uncomfortable about it. More recently, we agreed we were both too old not to say hello. That makes sense. In the autumn of 2013, Bobby Tambling organised a gathering of the Chelsea lads that won the Youth Cup in successive years and I went along, and so did the Doc. He may have been 85 but he had not changed a bit: the one-liners keep coming at you and he never stops.

Back then in 1966 it was goodbye to the Doc, but my sadness at leaving Chelsea and my mates was mixed with the excitement of having a new focus in my life. It was time to see if I could help Spurs get back to the top of the table.

# 7

# DON'T TANGLE
# WITH YOUR HERO

MY WELCOME TO Spurs was not an extended hand but a two-footed lunge which connected with my groin. I can still feel the pain of that collision, as I tried to take the ball past my opponent. It was the second hit I had taken from him in quick succession, and was the moment I realised that the first, which I am told also involved a short sharp punch, could not have been an accident. My reaction was to retaliate with a swinging fist that connected with the face of my tackler. I felt another shot of severe pain as the rather large ring on my finger twisted and ripped the soft flesh on the face of Dave Mackay.

If ever there was a moment of panic that was it. Those of you who know Dave will understand how I felt. To those who have only seen old film of him in his pomp, I should explain that he was a lion of a man. He was the guvnor, a powerful figure who happened to possess skill on the ball almost beyond compare. He was not a tall man, but had the build of a Sonny Liston. When he tackled, legs apart, if you were on the receiving end, as many opponents have told me, you just prayed you came out breathing. The nearest modern-day comparison would be Paul Gascoigne. They both had a unique confidence, astonishing skill and great physical strength. They also possessed a similar swashbuckling attitude to the way they lived their life. Bryan Robson too was an equally excellent footballer, but less flamboyant, though like Dave he had a reputation for not hanging about when it came to defending his territory.

Dave was a towering figure in British football in 1966 – for me the greatest, a man who has been too easily dismissed as a thumper and a destroyer, although this was another of his skills, as I can testify. It is impossible to overstate the importance of his contribution to any team he played in: at Hearts, Tottenham (where I ran into him, or rather he ran in to me) and latterly at Derby, not to mention his 22 caps for Scotland, his influence was pervasive.

That morning he 'welcomed' me to a practice match, during a highly competitive five- or six-a-side game in the Tottenham gym we called the Ball Court, a cramped area with a tarmac floor and only one door. When you were in, it felt there was no way out. Dave's tackle could not have been more forceful had a bull charged me and connected. It was fearsome. My retaliation was instinctive. I was not going to take that from anyone, though my response was a reflex action, and in no way did I intend either to cut him or hit him hard. I am told he laid a playful return right-hander on my chin. I remember nothing of that, probably because I was stunned, though I am prepared to accept he did – and it was just as well he didn't turn it into something more serious. The confrontation could not have lasted more than a few seconds before we were separated and Dave could do me any real damage. I do remember I walked around with a very painful hand for some time afterwards and my finger was so swollen I could not slide off the ring for weeks.

I had run up against him before in a cup tie when I had just started at Chelsea. As I got close to him early on in the match, he shouted: 'Take a good look at the ball, son, because you are not going to see it again.' He was right – I didn't. He was that good, he could shut you out of a game.

If my introduction to life at White Hart Lane was brutal, I soon realised that the atmosphere at Tottenham was so different from anything I had previously experienced at Chelsea. It had the air of a much bigger club, and certainly the expectations seemed higher. It was obvious to me that either I focused on my game and got on with it, or else I would wilt.

There was no question how I would respond – I was up for it. I had arrived with a considerable reputation as the central player in a fine Chelsea team. It was a position I revelled in. I knew I was an influential part of the Spurs side, but I would no longer be quite as dominant. I was now lining up among some of the finest and most experienced players seen in the British game. There were Scots like Dave, Alan Gilzean and Jimmy Robertson, Welshmen such as the brilliant Cliff Jones and fellow new signing Mike England, and Irish lads like keeper Pat Jennings. From England there was Alan Mullery, who was a strident, forceful player for club and country, and Jimmy Greaves, the most naturally talented English goalscorer around and a former team-mate from my Chelsea days.

I was not going to talk my way through these men, some of whom were Double winners from 1961. They were not going to be overly impressed by the words of a confident 23-year-old with just one League Cup medal and two England caps to his name. They had achieved far more than I had as a player.

They had done all of this under the leadership of manager Bill

Nicholson and his assistant Eddie Baily. There was a lot more to Billy Nich and Eddie than on first meeting. Nicholson had a dour exterior but was a man of great passion and emotion; he loved his football, and coached his teams to play great, passing football, putting together teams that entertained and were often awesome to watch. His teams were a blend of talent, skill and power and had a distinctive attitude. You didn't play for Bill and expect to lose. That I would learn.

Baily, meanwhile, was a little Londoner we nicknamed 'Alf Garnett', which summed him up perfectly as he always seemed to be moaning about something. He would watch Mackay and his fellow Scots standing together and then murmur something grouchy before saying in admiration: 'Aah! My Scottish soldiers.' That was the closest you would ever get to receiving praise from Eddie, who had spent the Second World War as a member of the Royal Scots Fusiliers. Being part of a Scottish regiment can be a scarring experience for any Englishman and I suspect especially so for an argumentative cockney, though you can be certain Eddie would have given as good as he got.

Eddie had been an extremely skilful footballer, a fact lost in the passing of time, helping Spurs to the title in 1951 and winning nine England caps. He was up there with the best and when I started training under him I realised what a brilliant, innovative coach he was. In those days even the best teams were often still chasing round tracks and then off home. The time when a coach could have his day clothes on under a high-zipped tracksuit was on the wane. He was big on exploiting skill in his sessions that would test you to the limit – unless you were Dave Mackay.

There was one unforgettable occasion when we all stood on a line. On the wall behind us were three lines, each a different colour. Eddie told us he wanted us to hit the ball in sequence to each colour area, control its return and volley it on to the next colour and so on, starting with our backs to the targets. The ball must never touch the ground. A voice was heard asking for more explanation. At that Dave picked up a ball: boom, return, boom return, boom return. 'Is that what you mean, Eddie?' Stunning!

I cannot disguise the fact that joining Spurs was a decision I took with a mixture of stomach-churning excitement and wonder. I did not know what to expect. I have never, as stated earlier, been lacking in self-confidence and that remained with me when I made my entry to White Hart Lane. But there were a number of challenges ahead. I did not know how the others would take to me, which can always be a problem for a new signing, especially one who had played all of his career for one club. Just as importantly, how would the supporters accept me? As a childhood fan of Spurs, I knew they could be a fickle lot. If they saw you as an imposter in their great team, life would be difficult; survivable, but very uncomfortable.

It was only a couple of years since the great John White had died in a tragic accident, when he was struck by lightning, and some fans saw me as having been brought in to replace the irreplaceable. I did not want that additional burden, so I decided to get on with it, play on, and do my best. I felt there was no point in me going into Tottenham and making a big fuss, giving it the big 'I am'. But in taking that conscious decision to go about my business quietly, I let myself down. I didn't want to cause ripples when in fact that is what I should have done. The result was I lost a bit of my game. I knew what Spurs wanted and would give it to them: I would be neat and tidy in midfield, pass the ball, give them 100 per cent involvement, but really I should have been more forceful. I should have been my real self.

The compensation was that I was working alongside some true greats of the game, all the way from Pat Jennings in goal to Alan Gilzean and Jimmy Greaves up front. But Dave Mackay was the centre of the team, a man with a lust for life. He was loath to let anything or anybody stand in his way. He was multi-talented and, for those who have never seen him perform, I can only say they have missed the greatest player of his generation. I remember sitting round a table with old players who knew Dave, having played against him and with him. When the subject was brought up to name a World XI, a normal part of these get-togethers, the votes would often go for Dave, not just as a player but the first name on the team sheet. The man could do anything with a ball – any ball, leather, full size, plastic, golf ball or tennis ball, you name it.

I would sometimes play golf with the three Scots: Dave, Gilly and Jimmy. We would line the balls up on the tee ready to drive off, all of us except Dave. When we had driven, he would throw the ball high in the air and wait on it dropping. He would play his shot from wherever it landed. It could be on a perfect lie or in a divot or more uneven ground. It didn't matter to Dave. As we watched, he would bring his club round and swoosh, he would hit it 250 or 275 yards straight down the fairway. He would do anything not to lose, except cheat, but he would employ every advantage available to him and against his opponent. He called all the shots and always had an opinion.

Dave could do tricks with the old half-crowns that would make you say 'Jeezus' and then promise to spend hours trying it yourself when no one was looking. For example, he would drop the coin on to his foot, flick it on to his shoulder then on to his forehead where he would drop it on to his eye, his top pocket or into a glass. It was a show stopper. His preference would be to let the coin slide into a glass of champagne. He did this at a British Embassy residence in the USA when we were on tour. A few drinks had been consumed and Dave was the centre of attention. Down went the coin, on to his shoulder, no problem. We all wondered where it was going to end up: on his eye, in his pocket or in the long, slender glass he was drinking from? Dave chose the latter, just as the Ambassador returned from an appointment. The coin fell and shattered the glass. Total silence, all eyes on Dave, but he just smiled.

As I've said, there was so much more to him than skill, there was real presence. If you nutmegged him in training, the look you would get told you what would happen if you actually managed to do it again. He didn't need to say anything. Everything about Dave was big, with a set chin and a barrel chest that always seemed to be inflated and legs like oaks. The rest of his body – neck, shoulders, arms – were all immensely strong. He ate big and he drank big. He'd been given the nickname 'Marquis' by a pal in Edinburgh, though I never found out why, but although it somehow suited him, I never felt I could call him that.

Dave may have been as hard as they come, a real warrior but there was another side to his nature that was rarely revealed. I learned from a friend that after Scotland had been beaten 9-3 at Wembley in 1961, a result that was a total humiliation for his side, Dave left the dressing room and walked up the tunnel in the old stadium. It was empty apart from a few Wembley staff. He looked around at the scene of a quite shocking defeat and began to cry. It would not have been for himself, but for the thousands of his fellow countrymen who had trekked south hoping to celebrate victory never thinking they would have to swallow defeat on such a scale. I must admit I found it hard to imagine a result that would make him shed a tear.

I have to say that I enjoyed playing in a great team alongside some of the strongest characters in the business – who could fail to? It was a privilege to be in that side. The crowd were, as I feared, not openly hostile but certainly undecided about my value. I felt I did not immediately do myself justice, though if I had to award a category to my first-season performances it would be 'reasonable'.

But the team itself did really well. We finished the league season in third place, four points behind champions Manchester United and we went on a successful run in the FA Cup that took us all the way to Wembley, where we would meet my old club Chelsea in the first all-cockney Cup final. We began that campaign by beating Millwall (1-0, after a 0-0 draw), Portsmouth (3-1) and Bristol City (2-0), all of whom were in the Second Division and all of whom had to come to White Hart Lane. Our first away tie was at Birmingham, another Second Division side, in the quarter-finals. That ended goalless, so it was back to North London for the return. Birmingham had had their chance and they were not going to have another. We beat them 6-0, and I remember with satisfaction that I scored two of goals, as did Jimmy Greaves, with Alan Gilzean and Frank Saul scoring the others.

The semi-final was at Hillsborough against a very fine Nottingham Forest team, who finished just above us in the league, but a goal from Jimmy and one from Frank earned us a 2-1 victory and our trip to Wembley, where we would meet Chelsea, who overcame Leeds to get to the final.

Because I had only recently left them to join Spurs, I was given more attention than might otherwise have been the case. Tommy Docherty caused much smirking behind hands at a reception before the game when he gave a speech in which he made the point he could not lose. If Chelsea won they would of course celebrate, and if it was Spurs then he would be happy for me as one of his former players.

On the morning of the final, Dave Mackay asked if I fancied going for a walk. As we strolled down towards Piccadilly, I asked how he thought it would go. With not a second's hesitation, he fired back: 'We'll win.' And he added, in case I was wondering why he was so confident: 'We'll win because we're too good for them.' So simple, but you cannot buy that sort of positive thinking.

I do not believe he felt the pressure the rest of us were feeling. It was all so normal to him. He knew he was better than anything Chelsea could offer up, despite the talent they had, which I knew better than anyone else in the Tottenham camp. They were a good enough side to cause any opposition damage, but he would not concede that, insisting we were the better team, we had the better players and we would win.

He was proved right: we won 2-1. The Spurs side represented every section of the British Isles, such was its diversity. There was one Northern Irishman (Pat Jennings), full-back Joe Kinnear was from the Republic of Ireland, Mike England of Wales was in central defence (while Cliff Jones was on the bench), then there were the three Scots – Dave, Alan Gilzean and Jim Robertson – and the other five were all Englishmen: Cyril Knowles, Alan Mullery, Jimmy Greaves, Frank Saul and myself.

Jimmy Robertson gave us the lead before half time and Frank Saul added our second goal midway through the second half. My old mate Bobby Tambling earned Chelsea a consolation goal minutes from the end, but in truth it was nothing more than that, because they had been outplayed, just as Dave said they would be. I looked it up recently and of the 24 players on show that day in the biggest game of the season, including the two unused subs, 14 were eligible for England. Compare that with what Roy Hodgson, the current England manager, has available. Roy would be lucky to have two or three in any major Premier League match or cup tie. As a former national coach, I understand and sympathise with the pressure that comes from having a relatively small number of players to choose between, although Alf would disagree, as we'll see in a later chapter.

I must also admit that earlier in the season I had had a bet on the outcome of the FA Cup, which I shouldn't have done. It happened quite by chance. I had arranged to meet the Scottish trio for a game of golf and went into the bookies with them. I am not keen on gambling, but as I waited on them placing their bets – I think it was just Dave and Gilly who were betting – I noticed they were offering

25/1 on Chelsea winning the FA Cup. That interested me, since they were my old club, so I placed £20 on them to do so, meaning that if Chelsea won I would have collected £500 tax free. My cup bonus at Spurs was £500 before tax, so in theory I would have been better off had we lost, but such thoughts never entered my head as I had the opportunity to add the medal to my collections, and I had never imagined that we would meet in an all-London FA Cup final when I placed the bet.

Dave began his celebrations the moment we were back in the dressing room. By the time we had arrived at the official reception, he was flying and in magnificent, if rowdy, form. One of the directors, Arthur Richardson, came over to our table with a tray carrying the commemorative medals which Dave flicked out of Arthur's hands spilling the medals over the floor and under the table. Arthur was mortified, but Dave just sat there laughing as the rest of us scrambled to pick them up.

Unfortunately, Bill Nicholson was in one of his dour moods and made a graceless speech, complaining about it being a disappointing final and so on, which provoked Dave to begin heckling him. Even he couldn't keep going all night and was eventually carried off to bed. I know it was Bill's way, but I found the manager's pessimism and downbeat approach galling, frustrating and downright misery-making. He couldn't help it. When I spoke to him much later in the evening, all he could talk about was the new season some three months away and the need to bring in new players. It didn't fill me with enthusiasm.

Some of the players decided to attend an alternative celebration organised by Morris Keston, one of Tottenham's biggest fans and a long-time friend of mine. Morris is a giver not a taker, an enormously generous man who lived and breathed Tottenham Hotspur when he was not making his money in a successful clothing business. The directors of the club tended to dismiss him as a hanger-on, and so were not keen for us to go. However, Morris had arranged a lavish celebration, and several of us were more than happy to share this moment with him.

To my mind, there was no real secret to Tottenham's success; Bill Nicholson simply bought the best he could: Dave, Gilly, Jimmy, John White, Bill Brown. I was lucky enough to join a classy squad. However, within the Spurs set-up I have to say that Cliff Jones was the most underrated of them all. Bobby Moore explained to me why he was such a tricky opponent, even for a great defender such as him: 'I knew what would happen. I would wait for the cross and prepare for it. It would be that much from my forehead and just as I was ready to meet it, Cliff's head would pop up and head the ball, take the ball away from me and probably score. He was sharper than a new pin.' He was a devastating forward and Bobby rated him as one of the very best. I will go further and say that to me the little Welshman was the best. If he did have a flaw it was that he always seemed to cut himself. In my mind's eye, I would always see him sitting or standing with blood coming from a cut in his head or somewhere else.

Cliff was also one of the really fun-loving members of the team – a lot of us were like that, which meant the atmosphere was always great. He was full of laughs on tour, wonderful company. He would keep things going, the type of person you are always glad to see. I remember one occasion when we were on an outing to Switzerland, and found ourselves on the opposite side of a lake from our sumptuous and very expensive hotel. A certain amount of strong beers and liquor had been consumed, and so we were ready for whatever life would throw at us. We were relaxed as we waited for transport to our hotel, but when it took an age to turn up, three of the players decided to commandeer a rowing boat that was tied up to a jetty, and row back. With some difficulty and to ironic cheers from the bank, they sorted out the oars, dipped them into the water and proceeded to row. There was a problem: the boat was anchored. In trying to pull it out of the water, they all fell in. The look on the faces of the staff in our hotel when we eventually returned, with the three of them led by Cliff dripping puddles onto the two-inch pile carpet, was priceless.

These tales are trivial in themselves but highlight the strength of the camaraderie in the squad. That is vital. You can pack your team with five-star players, but if the atmosphere is wrong, if there is no bonding, you will not achieve your full potential. I also learned from my time how important it was to have a mixture of youth and experience in a squad, and never to ignore the value of having older heads in a team. I also recognised how valuable it could be to let the tension out at the end of a long, hard season.

Sadly, all of that didn't help us during the next campaign, when we slipped down the table and were soon knocked out of the European Cup-Winners' Cup. Although I was being picked by the manager, I was still finding that the fans had not yet warmed to me, and even if you are getting the manager's backing most players will agree that having support from the terraces also helps a great deal and builds your confidence.

At the end of the season, I had a chat with Dave Mackay. He was in serious mood, and told me he was leaving. He was heading off to Derby County, which astonished me, and I asked why it was happening: 'Oh, it's about time. People keep saying I'm finished and all that.'

We were having a few beers at the time, and I told him it was nonsense and he could not be finished at his age (he was 33 at the time), with so much invaluable experience to offer the game. I understood how that sort of belief can set in when a senior player has had a few poor games and has reached the age where everybody expects him to be over the hill. If you were ten years younger, and people began to criticise your performances, you'd just say to yourself, 'I've had a few bad games,' and forget about it, but it's not so easy to do that when you're getting towards the end of your career.

He added: 'I do think I've a lot to offer going to a good team like Derby.' And so it proved. The move was a huge success. He joined up with Brian Clough and Peter Taylor and helped steer Derby to promotion into the top league. They worked out how best to exploit Dave's assets, and the end result was that he was voted FWA Footballer of the Year that season, along with Tony Book. It is what I always believed was possible if you have the right manager in the right club. A few years later, we did something similar with Frank McLintock at QPR when he joined from Arsenal in 1973. Admittedly, he had slowed down but he could use his wealth of experience to help the team, he could drive people on and he could pass the ball like few others. We also organised the tactics of the side so that he wouldn't have to run too far, utilising the younger legs of those around him. Sometimes junior players object to this, but experience can be as valuable as youthful speed and energy. And often, as Bobby Moore showed, the most important element of pace is in the mind, and how quickly you see things, not your raw speed across the ground.

Things did not improve much for me or the team during the next season, 1968-69. The fans continued to ask questions about me, as they had done since I arrived. I have to admit it, they were probably right to do so. I had lost that spark from my game which had made me the controller of the tempo at Chelsea. I was not overawed by the great players around me, but maybe I paid them too much respect. Perhaps I should have ruffled a few feathers, made a fuss, demanded the ball as I used to. Don't get me wrong: I have no complaints about how my team-mates responded to me; I was treated impeccably as one of their own. They realised how tough it was for me to be accepted in the team, especially when so many fans saw me as the replacement for the truly great John White.

What made the whole situation particularly painful was that Tottenham were my team and the thought of leaving under a cloud did not appeal to me in the slightest, but that was the way it was heading. I do not think it was just me. The squad was in a period of transition at that time, as Bill tried to build another side that would be capable of winning the league again. During 1968, he sold Dave, Cliff Jones, Jimmy Robertson and Frank Saul, while Jimmy Greaves would leave the following year. All had been massive contributors not just to winning, but winning with style. How do you replace that unique group? You can't.

Bill Nicholson tried to recruit the best players available, such as Martin Chivers and then Martin Peters, but it was always going to be a tough challenge. For me, it was clear my time was up, too. Did I feel a failure at the club I had supported? No. I was disappointed that I had not pleased everyone, but I wasn't left moping around like a lost soul. I was delighted to be a part of an FA Cup-winning side, but I had to accept that after three years at one of the great British clubs a section of the support were not on my side. Bill always backed me, although we didn't ever talk about it until near the end and I thanked him for that. However, in the summer of 1969, Queens Park Rangers made an approach for me, and the deal was settled at a fee of £70,000, just £10,000 less than Spurs had paid for me. I was heading west to Loftus Road and a new learning experience.

# 8

# GREGORY'S BOY

I CANNOT THINK of a transfer blessed with so much good fortune as the one that took me from Spurs to Queens Park Rangers in the summer of 1969. It changed my career; hell, it changed my life, although I didn't know it at the time. I had heard rumours that Rangers owner Jim Gregory was keen to sign me, but only if the price was right.

What finally swung the deal, however, was down to a little thing called luck involving a very nasty tackle between me and my pal Bobby Keetch, the Rangers defender. Our clubs had met during the 1968-69 season and Bobby, with a nice line in gallows humour, had told me to expect no mercy. He said it in a way that suggested I hadn't thought of the possibility. I was ready for what I presumed would be a very physical match, after which I knew we would be friends again and enjoy a beer and maybe a late meal together. It would have been just what I needed, because I was still feeling down about not being able to win over the Spurs fans.

As a defender, Bobby was the toughest of tacklers, a player who could have been taught by Dave Mackay how to do it as humanely as possible. Apart from being a top pro, he was also a clever businessman and the very best, most generous and wittiest of men. There was no holding him. He lived his life in a way that was bewildering to those who trailed in his wake. And, like his tackling, he gave it 100 per cent effort. Bobby's personality also placed him at the very top of London's social scene. His contacts were impeccable, but I knew our friendship and all the rest of it would count for nothing out on the field. If I had any doubts, he made his position clear when he said to me: 'I'm going to get you tonight. Just because we are friends doesn't mean I'll be taking it easy, just don't expect anything.'

As the game progressed, I found myself on the edge of the 18-yard box with Bobby flying at me, feet first. I held my foot up and pushed it down, knowing I had to protect myself from what he was going to do. If he had been sideways on, I might not have had the strength to combat him. Thump! It was brutal. On came the stretcher and off he went, shouting at me: 'What were you doing, you bastard?'

I told him I was simply looking after myself – I genuinely believed if I hadn't done this, he would have badly injured me. He was telling me that I was out of order, and I followed him off saying: 'Come on, Bob, you are tougher than that.'

He was having none of it. As he disappeared towards the tunnel, all I could see was him mouthing swear words at me. I knew I had to make the effort of meeting him immediately after the end of the game even though he was clearly unhappy, to put it mildly. To be fair, it was a nasty injury. I was a bit dubious about going into the Rangers dressing room, because I knew what the players would be saying, but I had to. He was my friend. When I went in, Bob was trying to sit up and Jim Gregory was to one side talking to him, and

I could tell that he was giving vent to his thoughts about what I had done.

I chipped in. 'Bob,' I said. 'Sorry about that. I'll see you later.'

'No you effin won't,' he replied, so I sidled out. I decided to wait for him in the car park, and eventually he came out, leaning heavily and painfully on crutches.

'Seriously,' I said. 'Are you all right?'

'Yes, it's not so bad, no thanks to you.'

We made up. Then he continued: 'When you came into the dressing room, I was telling Jim what a rotten little sod you were and Jim said: "He's got some front, though. We've got to buy him. If he can walk in after what he did on the pitch, then we've got to have him."'

I joined Rangers in June 1969 after Bobby had quit for South Africa and Durban City and it was to be an enlightening experience at a club with exactly the ambience I needed at that stage of my career (I was now 26). It immediately felt right. Even our dressing room – surely the smallest in the Football League – was welcoming. Football became a joy again, something I looked forward to with confidence, not mild apprehension.

In Jim Gregory I had found an owner I could work for and learn from. We would talk football for hours. He knew his players and he loved them, though he didn't fawn over them. He would invite them in to the boardroom after matches, something no other club owner/chairman would have allowed. He liked to be involved in it all and was certainly the fittest chairman in the business, even if he didn't look it on first appearance. After a match against Sunderland, he challenged a player to a sprint – and won. Admittedly, it was 1.30 in the morning when the player may not have been at his quickest. Jim was not to everyone's taste, but we hit it off and our relationship developed over the years.

My first concern, however, was to rediscover my game, the one

I seemed to have left behind at Chelsea and lost at Spurs as my confidence on the field ebbed away. Rangers had nothing like Tottenham's prestige; they were a seesaw club trying to establish a place for themselves at the same table as the big boys Arsenal, Manchester United, Liverpool and the club I had just left. They had gained promotion to the top league for the first time in 1968, having been promoted from the Third Division just a season before, and perhaps unsurprisingly, having risen so far so fast, were knocked straight back down again. Jim wanted nothing less than their quick return, and my former Dagenham neighbour Les Allen was the manager charged with fulfilling that task, having taken over at the club the year before after Tommy Docherty's 28-day reign had come to a swift end.

Jim and Les wanted to get there playing good football with good players. We had a mix of experience and eager, talented young bucks, most notably Gerry Francis, who was not yet 18 but already looked a midfield player of genuine potential, a prodigious talent. He went on to captain England and was to be another of those quality players who for some reason never received the recognition their ability deserved. Gerry would have been even more successful but for a succession of injury problems.

Rangers just seemed to be made for me, and I was proud to be made captain of the team. In that first season we finished ninth, some way short of putting in a proper challenge for promotion, but bit by bit we improved until we eventually won promotion, though it was to take longer than we had perhaps expected. We got there in the end with a blend of concentrated coaching and quality players. As well as Gerry, the dominant figure in the side was Rodney Marsh, who was in prolific goalscoring form that season. Despite beating Blackpool 6-1 at home (they would eventually be promoted) and going on a good run in the FA Cup, where we would lose out to eventual winners Chelsea in the quarter-finals, we were not consistent enough.

Sadly, we didn't progress as much as we had hoped in 1970-71, when we ended up in 11th place. If there is such a thing as a false position, that was it for us. We learned from our mistakes, which were simple enough: we were losing too many matches we should have won. Rodney was top scorer (23) and I finished next, a long way behind him (with 11), thanks to a number of penalties we were awarded. Jim Gregory was depressed enough about the overall situation as to consider selling his club, but fortunately there were no buyers. He also decided that a change of manager was needed, and midway through the campaign brought in Gordon Jago to take charge.

Gordon was looked on by some, Rodney Marsh for one, as a soft touch, a boss who could be bullied. He did have to live with a lot of banter from yours truly also, but I believe he shrugged it off. Although a quiet man, he made some ground-breaking decisions, one of the most important being the introduction of Ron Jones, who had captained the British Olympic team in 1960, to improve our fitness. What I learned from him was a fitness regime that would be used to the benefit of every team I have since worked with. It demands an awful lot of the individual, but it works and in time makes players very much fitter than normal track work. It consisted of doing a series of flat-out 220-yard sprints against the clock, designed to build power and stamina. At first, some could manage only one sprint and we rarely did more than three.

It appears simple enough but was hell when I first was introduced to it by Ron. I very quickly realised the huge benefit of vastly increased fitness and greater stamina. Every time I have used it, the players have revolted. They wanted to know what I was trying to do to them, telling me that they didn't need it. But after going through the agonies of being forced to do it, they were astonished to realise how much fitter and stronger they were – just as I was when I worked under Ron's instructions.

Frank McLintock, who joined Rangers in 1973 after we had moved back to the top division, tells me now that he believes it lengthened his career, just as Arsène Wenger's training expertise would later prolong the top-level careers of players such as Tony Adams and Lee Dixon. It was a hellish discipline, and the effort expended could make you vomit. Rodney would even have a bacon and egg breakfast if he knew we would be sprinting that morning, just so he had something to bring up.

In later years, and after I had returned to Rangers as manager, the naturally fast Kenny Sansom found it worse than he would running up the side of a mountain, but he became faster and fitter. It gave him, and therefore us, an edge. I continued to use the idea at Crystal Palace and Barcelona and would pin up a sheet with the players' names and their times. When I later managed at Rangers, Barry Silkman and Rachid Harkouk became fanatical about it and developed super fitness. They even bought spikes to improve their times, so competitive had it made them.

You would expect to run the first 220 yards in around 22-23 seconds; the next sprint would be timed at around 26-27 seconds and by the third you would be at 34 seconds. It is crucial the players are made aware of what they had achieved, so I would write down the results and pin them on the noticeboard. We thought we were working hard until Olympic javelin thrower Fatima Whitbread came to watch us one day and asked why we did only two or three runs and why did we restrict ourselves to just 220 yards. I told her that was all they could manage, and was astonished when she told me the top athletes would do the same exercise over 440 yards, and they might do as many as a dozen separate sprints. For all that different sports require different kinds of fitness, it certainly made the players respect the work of Olympic athletes.

Whether it was Gordon's new fitness regime or not, 1971-72 saw us make a breakthrough and we finished in fourth place, just two points off promotion, which was far more encouraging. He was often caught up in administrative work and so he allowed me even more opportunities to supervise the training, especially after coach Bobby Campbell left to go to Arsenal. He would say: 'You take it, Terry.' It developed my interest in that side of the game. After a time I was taking full sessions, exploring different methods. I was allowed free rein to express my ideas and try them out, and soon began to realise that the players were enjoying the way I was doing it, which was very encouraging.

I believe I played as well as I ever did during my period at Rangers, and there's no doubt that being given this freedom to coach helped my game. Along with a few other players, I worked with the coaches to find the best system and to develop the little tricks that would give us an edge. One of our cheeky numbers was at free kicks awarded within shooting range of the goal. The opposition wall would form, while the player taking the free kick would wait and, just as he was about to take the kick, one of us would run along the wall and grab the last man's outside arm, spinning him round and leaving a space for the free kick to curl towards goal. It worked.

Just as we seemed on the brink of returning to the top flight, we lost Rodney Marsh, who was sold to Manchester City in March 1972 when they paid a club record £200,000 to sign him up. He had already scored 20 goals that season for us, so it was a big loss, not just as player for I also lost a good friend. Rodney was a star at Rangers before the arrival of Stan Bowles and the emergence of Gerry Francis. It was Rodney who scored when Rangers, then a Third Division side, won the League Cup at Wembley in 1967 against West Brom.

Rodney was a fantastic individual: he was funny and a mickey-taker, as well as being big and tall, and striking with his blond hair, but it was on the pitch he did such exceptional things. He earned only nine caps with England but should have had many more. He did things others could not do. His control of the ball was astonishing, and he worked hard to improve what came naturally to him. The perception of players such as Rodney is that they have god-given talent and that their success is just down to the luck of the draw. There is a degree of truth in that, but they still had to work and Rodney put in the time to improve his skill. To watch him in training was an experience. If he was working in an indoor hall, with a basketball hoop fixed on the wall some 30 yards away, he would hit a half volley time and again onto the net. He didn't always 'score' but he rarely missed. It set him apart among his team-mates.

For a time in his last season, Rodney played alongside a striker who had been signed from Coventry but had played for various teams before, and since, including Chelsea. John O'Rourke was a goal-hanger who could score goals, which he often did very well indeed, but didn't always offer a lot else, and like every striker he had his off days. In one particular friendly, he tried a straightforward shot that went badly wide, then Rodney tried to go round two defenders, overdid it and also missed the target. At that, John shouted at me: 'Bloody hell, he keeps fluffing easy goals.' It's all in how you see it, I suppose. John scored goals because he never gave up. He was not one of those strikers who would disappear when they hit the ball over the bar. John would do it again and again. The chance would eventually come that he'd score from.

Initially, Rodney didn't want to know about coaching or the tactical side of the game. He thought what he did he did better than everybody else and he was just about right with his self-belief. Coaching and tactics were for others, he did not see the need and did not want to know. In those days, a group of us would go to Lilleshall for two weeks in the summer, even if it meant missing our annual holiday. Malcolm Allison, Don Howe, Bobby Robson and

Dave Sexton would be there, because they didn't want to miss anything. I eventually got Rodney to turn up and he enjoyed it. He took it all in because he was smart and realised the benefits. Sadly for him, he never quite reproduced his best form at Maine Road, despite the help of Malcolm Allison's motivational skills. His arrival is blamed by some for costing City the title that season, because the way the team was set up had to be altered to fit in Rodney. In his search for individual brilliance Malcolm had gambled and lost.

Gordon used some of the money received from that deal to sign Republic of Ireland international Don Givens from Luton. As the new 1972-73 season began, he then recruited Stan Bowles from Carlisle and Dave Thomas, who joined us from Burnley for a hefty fee of £165,000. They were three great signings, testimony to Gordon's skill in the transfer market. So good were they in prospect, I felt sure they would give us the extra impetus we needed finally to win promotion back to the First Division.

Stan was the best, as entertaining a footballer as this country has produced. There is nothing he could not do with the ball, including the most important thing of all: scoring. The fact he was playing for Carlisle, and Rangers could buy him for the equivalent of a song, is an indictment of football's inability or unwillingness to take on players labelled as different if not difficult. And Stan was certainly different. I never saw him as anything other than a playing asset to have in the team. Famously, he was an obsessive gambler, but I can think of a few of those without a quarter of his talent. I remember he had a bet with Tony Hazell about who could hit Sunderland's recently won FA Cup trophy, which was paraded on a table at the club's old Roker Park ground before a Division Two match. Stan shot, and spun the trophy off the table with a shot that ended up damaging it.

He and Don formed a seemingly unstoppable partnership up front. Between them they scored 44 goals, with Don the league's

top scorer (with 23), happily served by Dave Thomas. We won promotion to Division One as runners-up and had been assured of
promotion a handful of matches before the end of the season, finishing 11 points clear of Aston Villa, the team below us, thanks to
an even more magical playing relationship between Stan and Gerry
Francis.

Gordon brought in Arsenal's Double-winning captain Frank
McLintock that summer, and the addition of another superb new
face, steeped in the game with all the experience we needed,
ensured that we did very well in our first season back in the top
flight, finishing in eighth place. By then I was 31 years old, and I
was beginning to struggle for fitness, as I was suffering from a bit
of arthritis in my ankle. I thought that coaching would be the future
for me, but I also began to open my mind to matters outside football, or at least not directly related to playing or coaching.

I was a strong supporter of the Professional Footballers'
Association (PFA) and became vice-chairman for a spell. I attended
meetings wherever I had to, in the Midlands or the North. Even
back then, Gordon Taylor was on the committee, before he went on
to run the association and become a force for good in the English
game. We would link up in Manchester, say, attend a meeting on a
Sunday afternoon, and when that had finished go for a pint and a
meal before I headed for the railway station at Piccadilly to catch
the last train south.

During that period, I remember having to represent Dave
Thomas against his old club Burnley at a tribunal. Dave asked me
to put his case and, although I was no barrister, I agreed. We were
up against Bob Lord, that monument to fearsome club chairman-
ship. In those days, they always seemed to be local butchers, and
with his massive frame, a ruddy face not remotely handsome, and
a self-assurance that came from getting his own way for decades, it
was going to be difficult to win. Thomas had been due a season's

bonus of £1,200, which Lord said he was not going to pay now that Dave had signed for Queens Park Rangers. When we won our case, Lord gave me a look on the way out which said: 'Just wait, you cockney bastard, I will get you back for this.'

Dave was so thrilled at winning, he and his wife insisted I should be their guest for dinner. He didn't drink or gamble, and appeared to take a slightly dim view of those who did. His idea of fun was his garden, which he was obsessed with. So I'll never understand why he chose the Sportsman Club in central London, with its strong link to gambling, for our celebration dinner. The club stood against just about everything he believed in.

Despite that, we had a pleasant evening and his wife was enjoying herself when he decided they should leave. As we were going out, he let out a cry. He had spotted the man he most admired; not a sportsman or a politician or a celebrity from TV or film, but Percy Thrower, the gardening icon. He had all his books and idolised the man. I didn't know Percy of course, but I recognised him, so I said: 'Hang on, and I will go over and say you are keen to meet him.' But Dave didn't want to meet him and walked out, as he had spotted Percy was smoking, drinking and gambling. That was too many 'vices' for Dave.

The other area I had started to get involved in came when I met the writer Gordon Williams in my mid-20s. He was to become another of the important and extraordinary characters who have been a big part of my life. He was a QPR supporter, and I am sure he would be offended if I called him a mentor, but without doubt he fired in me an enthusiasm to do what I had never done or thought of doing before then – read, read and read. It was not only that, he cajoled me into writing pieces first with him and then on my own for newspapers.

When we first met, he was ghosting articles and books for a living and would write these with the likes of Bobby Moore and

Bobby Charlton and me, and he would then sell the articles to the newspapers. He was also an acclaimed novelist, too, which is why he saw himself very much as a 'proper' writer. He was a larger than life character, a Scot who loved a drink and lively company and we grew to be close friends. That suited me, though as a sportsman I couldn't always be quite as boisterous as he was. He was great fun, though he could occasionally go too far if he went over the top on drink. He was very well read, very intelligent and that appealed to me.

Gordon, like Jim Gregory, was prepared to share so much of what he knew. Usually, we would write articles together for the newspapers, and we'd share the proceeds, which tended to be no more than £50 per piece. He eventually suggested I try writing my own stuff, so I did. I bought a typewriter and I joined a class to learn how to type. I was the only male in a room full of flirting females. I remember that my first piece was called: 'Jokes the Fans Don't Hear.' It may not have been Hemingway, but it was a start and I loved it. I was a proper working partner, and I reckon typed out one third of what we produced.

Then I started to compose stories, taking Gordon's advice to write about what I knew, so I began with a tale about two footballers who got themselves into trouble. It was full of dialect and local characters, and that was the basis of our first novel together, called *They Used to Play on Grass*, which was published as a joint venture in 1970. Gordon thought it was very Runyonesque. I didn't have a clue what he was talking about, but I read up on Damon Runyon, who was most famous for *Guys and Dolls*, which became both a stage play and a film, based on two of his stories. Learning about the man through his biography and his writing was a revelation, but it was Gordon who coaxed me into it. He pointed me in the right direction and I set off to increase my knowledge of literature, which admittedly had started off at zero. He and Jim taught me so much, expanding my horizons, and it helped that by now I was a willing pupil, which probably had not been the case when I was at school.

When our novel was published, we sent a copy to all the managers in the First Division. One went to Bill Shankly, and Gordon persuaded me to speak to Bill after we had played at Liverpool. I was reluctant to approach the great man on such a self-promoting matter, but when I saw him in the corridor after the match, I called out: 'Mr Shankly! Mr Shankly, please.'

'Aye?' he said, turning round to face me.

'Do you know who I am?' I asked.

'Yes,' he replied. 'You're Venables.'

'I just wanted to know if you received a copy of my book.'

'Book?' he said. 'Book?' Then he leaned forward: 'Aye, son, you are the H.G.Wells of football.' He made it sound so good I actually believed him.

Gordon convinced me I had an ear for dialogue and I worked harder on developing that aspect of my writing. After we'd done our first book, there was a lull for a spell when he moved down to the West Country to write his bestseller, *The Siege of Trencher's Farm*, which was developed into the highly controversial film *Straw Dogs*, with its notorious scenes of violence and rape. Gordon was not happy with the way it had been dramatised, but the book and film made him a lot of money. When he moved back to London, he got in touch again.

'Let's write a novel,' he said. 'We'll create a character.'

The result was to be the Hazell books. They were conceived and produced as a partnership. Gordon was not keen to use his name, and I realised if people saw my name they would think I was involved only to attract readers from football supporters who knew of me, rather than being a genuine partner in the project. We'd both been irritated that our earlier book had not been taken seriously, but tended to be reviewed by sports reporters and dismissed as a gimmick. Therefore, we decided to write Hazell under the name P.B. Yuill.

We named the main character, a cockney detective, after Jimmy my friend from Dagenham and not my Rangers team-mate Tony Hazell, who was a big enough personality to inspire the character. Tony was another of the Rangers squad who did not hang back when he wanted to say or do something, even if it was undiplomatic. He would often team up with Stan in a series of pranks like the FA Cup stunt, and if he was involved you could guarantee it would include some side bet.

Working with Gordon Williams almost on a daily basis was so stimulating for me because it forced me to concentrate on a project other than football. We put in a lot of effort to get our book the way Gordon wanted it. We would rewrite sections time after time. Although we worked hard on them, it could not have been more enjoyable or worthwhile to me. I knew the London scene, so I would report back to Gordon. We would discuss things and then we would get down to writing. Because I was always looking for ideas to translate into fiction, I became more aware of what was going on around me. I always had been, but now I was putting these observations to good use. For example, when I went to hospital to see my second daughter, Tracey, after she was born, I noticed a bangle or band on the floor of the maternity unit. It was what looked like a tiny bracelet and I asked the nurse what it was. She said it was a baby name tag. It sparked a story idea about how easy it would be to mix up babies after they are born. That idea eventually became the basis for the book *Hazell Plays Solomon*. We wrote three of them in total, and they were successful enough to surprise a lot of people who had not given them a chance.

The books had strong storylines and our central character was appealing enough to attract television interest. We were thrilled to be contacted about the idea of producing a series based on the books. For me it meant when I had finished my training and coaching at Rangers, I would then work on my other career as a TV series collaborator with Gordon Williams. I would head for the studios in the afternoon and make my contribution and learn from what was going on around me. It was so exciting and new for me. We were involved in the decision to choose who would play Hazell. Basically, what happened was a group of women employees at the studio studied tapes of the actors on the shortlist for the role, eventually coming up with Nicholas Ball, who turned out to be ideal for the part. The first episode to go out was 'Hazell Plays Solomon' in 1978, but the show ran for two series and a total of 20 episodes in all. I was really proud of that.

By developing my writing career and doing the work with the PFA, I was trying to prepare for the day when I wouldn't earn any income from playing. I had my coaching badges, but who can forecast what life holds for you? There was certainly no guarantee that I would be able to find a job in that area. There was never any chance of me going to university or of me proving my worth with a degree, so I had to find the right options to secure my future.

At Rangers my coaching duties had become more all-consuming. I adored working with the players. It was our university, and nobody was barred, everybody could have input. The more that was said, the better we would understand each other. We had lost Rodney, but I was now working with Stan and Gerry. Stan had that intuitive ability always to make the right decision on the pitch, which I found exhilarating. Only Steve Archibald of the players I ever worked with had that same intuition. If I could see the centre-half was close, Stan knew to knock it off before the defender had a chance to dig him. And then, when I would call for him to hold it up, he would sometimes set off on a dribble, shoot and score. He was always right with his decision; it was uncanny. Stan always played for the team, not just for himself. If he was playing today, I have no doubt he would be a sensation.

Stan had an understanding with Gerry from the first time they trained together and played together. It was a one-off. Gerry told me it was one of the great disappointments he had as an England player and captain that he never once played alongside the one player whose game he knew best. I was the captain who also coached, so they came to me and from that first time you could see they were on fire as a partnership.

I had them working on what we called double one-twos, where an extra pass often left the final receiver free to burst through on goal. It can be a highly productive ploy, and one you see more often now than then. I'd first watched it between Brazil's Pelé and Tostão. Pelé knocked the ball to Tostão and then started to run, but before he got into his stride Tostão had passed it back at him and Pelé then returned it to him again and Tostão was through on the defence with a lot of space. We were the first to use this ploy in English football. I was fortunate enough to play behind them, and to see them in action from that position made you realise how exceedingly good they were.

I knew I was coming to the end of my playing career during a match against Chelsea when I had to face a young player I used to work with when he was a kid: Alan Hudson. The boy was now a young man, and he left me standing. It was a moment of some soul searching, with my mind turning over and asking: 'Is it time, Terry, is it time?'

What I didn't know was that Jim Gregory had the same thought. He also supplied the answer: transfer me. My only regret was that neither he nor Gordon Jago got in touch beforehand. The deal was this: Crystal Palace, managed by Malcolm Allison, would sell Don Rogers to QPR while Ian Evans and I would move to Palace. The man who eventually took my place at Loftus Road was Don Masson, a Scotland international, who joined the club from Notts County in December 1974, one of new manager Dave Sexton's first signings after he joined Rangers in October. Don made QPR a better side, just as Charlie Cooke had been the ideal fit for Chelsea after my exit.

Ironically, Sexton (who had replaced the Doc at Stamford Bridge) had wanted me to return to Stamford Bridge, but I knew I could not possibly justify a return to Chelsea and as it was, he was gone from the club within a couple of months in any case. I was aware that my career was winding down and I didn't want to stumble through and be below par for a manager, coach and club I had so much respect for. Rangers, with Masson, would have been a truly exceptional side to play in, and indeed they went on to finish as runner-up in the 1975-76 season, but I had to change direction and work for Malcolm at Palace.

Rangers were aware of the problem I had with arthritis in my ankle, but what they did not realise, ironically enough, was that Don was struggling with arthritis in a knee. They were replacing a dodgy ankle with a dodgy knee, even though Don rarely missed a game for them before he was eventually sold on to Derby in October 1977.

I began this chapter talking about my great friendship with Bobby Keetch and will end it in the same way, though I have to move forward to 1996. Bobby's fertile mind was always searching for business opportunities. He was behind the Football, Football theme bar and restaurant in London's Haymarket, which is a great success. To me he was a friend, the man who would keep me sane in times of stress. He was always telling or rather retelling jokes. When he asked if he'd told you a certain joke, you'd always say no, even if he had, as you wanted to hear it again and he always found a new way of telling it or would introduce something different into an old joke.

His loyal support helped sustain me when the hounds were trying to drive me to distraction, following the fall-out at Spurs. He would phone every day to say: 'Come on, keep going. Don't let the bastards get you down.' During Euro 96, he enjoyed my success with England, partly because he knew it embarrassed my enemies in the media, who had now become his enemies, too.

A few days after we had been beaten by the Germans, Bobby and I and our respective wives Jan and Yvette went out for dinner. It was a beautiful evening: great food, great wines, all in company you want to be with. I had a commitment on the Saturday to present Alan Shearer with his official award for being the leading goalscorer at Euro 96. It was to take place at the Hilton on Park Lane. I arrived in good time and was waiting to be told what was planned when a call came through for me. It was Yvette. She was sobbing and so distressed I knew something bad had happened. She eventually blurted it out: 'Bobby's dead.'

'What?'

'Bobby's dead.'

'Oh, my God.'

I thought back to the night of our dinner. When we parted, I had said: 'See you at the club, and don't let me down.' Bobby had then wandered off with Jan, and that was the last I saw of him. It was the suddenness of it all. I was in shock. I informed the organisers my friend had died unexpectedly and that there was no way I could deal with a presentation. They understood.

I wandered down to the front of the Hilton. I couldn't face a taxi for the moment, and I needed a drink. I went to the bar near the entrance, expecting it to be busy, but I knew the barman and was sure he would find me a quiet spot. However, when I entered the bar it was empty, not a soul was in it. I found a stool at the end of the bar and ordered a drink. I sat there for how long I don't know and still on my own. I thought of poor Jan and

Bobby's children, Nicolette, Christian and Karl. What must they be going through?

I was looking into my glass when a voice I recognised said: 'Are you all right?' It was Bobby Robson, who was a guest at the presentation to Alan. 'No,' I replied, and told him about Bobby. He knew Bobby, but it didn't seem to register with him which shouldn't have surprised me. My pal's sudden death at 54 from a stroke made a considerable impact on me. Suddenly, all the problems I had to solve, the people I had to take on, regrets about previous events in my life, all became, like Jim Gregory's opponents, an irrelevance, insignificant.

# 9

# LEARNING TO FLY
# WITH THE EAGLES

M ALCOLM ALLISON WAS there to meet me when I arrived at Crystal Palace. His presence made it easier to accept my transfer from a club with real prospects in the First Division to a side recently relegated to the Third Division. That was to be the bonus I would receive from the switch from West to South London. We had known each other since the late 1950s, when he had tried to convince me I should join my local side West Ham United and had been so disappointed that I chose Chelsea instead. Despite that, we had stayed in touch, and like everyone else in the business I had been hugely impressed by his impact at Manchester City, where he and Joe Mercer had built such a magnificent team.

Working with Malcolm was highly instructive, inspiring and never less than entertaining. After he signed me for Palace in the summer of 1974, he very quickly realised that my playing days were all but over. I made just 14 league appearances for him, each very painful due to my arthritis. On New Year's Eve he asked me how things were going, as if he didn't know. He offered me a range of options: first, I could play on but for what? Second, I could just quit. But it was the third option he gave me that was most enticing: I could quit playing and accept his offer to work on the coaching side with him, which is what I did. Even though he had Frank Lord on the staff at the time, he decided to promote me instead, which could have made things difficult with Frank, but we were able to work together.

It was the beginning of a six-year love-in between me and Palace, during which I would work with impressive young players and eventually build a great young team that the media would tag 'The Team of the Eighties'. I hate that sort of presumption, but truthfully we were very good. We went from the Third Division to the top of the First Division, if only for a week, all inside three seasons. That was after Malcolm's team, still in the Third Division, made it to an FA Cup semi-final in 1976. The ending, when it came for me in October 1980, may have been an unhappy one, but unless you are Manchester United, Liverpool, Arsenal or Chelsea, that is par for the course. During that time we had some great days, often played in front of huge crowds. And it wasn't just the seniors: we won the FA Youth Cup twice and developed many outstanding talents such as Kenny Sansom.

Most of our players came from the youths and worked their way through the ranks. There were a few we brought in from outside, some on free transfers, and we blended them together to make a marvellous, entertaining unit. I remember them with pride: Sansom, Jim Cannon, Vince Hilaire, Peter Nicholas, Terry Fenwick, Jerry Murphy, Dave Swindlehurst, Barry Silkman, Rachid Harkouk, Ian Walsh, Billy Gilbert, Steve Lovell, Mike Elwiss, Nicky Chatterton, plus Welshman Ian Evans with a 'mad' but highly effective elder in goalkeeper John Burridge. They were not all as superbly gifted as

Kenny, nor did they enjoy his illustrious career at the very top of the English game, but they worked, they listened, gelled and flourished as a team for a short but glorious time.

My first season as player then coach was respectable, as we finished in fifth place. The second campaign, 1975-76, was far more exhilarating for the players and our fans. We were challenging for promotion all the way until the build-up to our historic FA Cup semi-final tie against Southampton at Stamford Bridge, only to stumble again. We lost that game 2-0 and ended the season once more in fifth place. That in no way rewarded the players for the effort and commitment they had given. The cup was a disappointment, but that did not compare to losing out on promotion.

The game that did for us was against Millwall, prior to the FA Cup semi-final, and we had the chance to win it when we were awarded a penalty. A fired-up crowd of 34,893 at Selhurst Park was willing the ball into the net, as Peter Taylor stepped up to take it. Millwall were one of our main rivals for promotion and the match was then goalless. Sadly, he missed and the two points that would have come our way became one – it was the story of our season, as too many home draws (12 in all) cost us dearly. I would never blame any player for missing a penalty, but I was less than enthralled by his decision to demand a transfer after we missed out on promotion.

I could understand his ambition, but I felt it would be better for him, and ourselves, if he stayed for another year. I explained to him that he could not do better than stay with us. He had made all sorts of breakthroughs during that campaign, including being selected for England and making his debut on 24 March against Wales. To do that from the third tier is an exceptional achievement, and one that confirmed Peter had a great future. Understandably, numerous clubs wanted to sign him, with Leeds United offering £180,000 while Spurs were ready to pay £200,000.

I wanted him to stay, but there was a selfish aspect to that as I was certain he was one player who would win us promotion. However, it was not all self-interest, and I hid nothing from him, saying that I was sure he would lead us to promotion the next season, adding: 'If you had scored with that penalty we'd have had it, wouldn't we?' He laughed, but nothing I could say would sway him. He eventually signed for Tottenham, though ironically, for someone who felt he needed to play in the First Division to further his England career, he never again played for his country after winning four caps with us.

Peter wasn't the only one who decided it was time to leave Palace. Malcolm also found the disappointment of missing out on both Wembley and promotion too much, and chose to move on. Maybe it was having to live with just one lung, after suffering from tuberculosis when he was a young man (I remember visiting him in hospital as he was recovering from the operation), that determined the cavalier way Malcolm conducted his life, both privately and professionally. He and his partner for many years, Serena Williams, were a special couple. Because they were both very charismatic people, they attracted lots of publicity, though I'm sure many of the stories about them were exaggerated.

But more importantly from my perspective, Malcolm was a football innovator who taught me so much. I developed as a coach under him and enjoyed working with him. For all his flamboyance, there was also a quiet side to him and you could tell when something was getting to him.

We talked about coaching to the point of exhaustion. He knew the business like few others, so I was able to pick up so much from him. He was engrossed on what went on in the game, not just in this country but wherever it was played. He was determined to get me started properly on the coaching side as soon as the decision had been made to retire, so he encouraged me by saying: 'What I want you to do is get in there, you're the first team coach.' Gordon Jago at Rangers had said the same, leaving me to take charge.

Sometimes there were mornings when Malcolm didn't even come in, perhaps because he'd been out late the night before, and so he would ring and say: 'Take over. I'll see you back for lunch in town.'

If things weren't going well with the team, he would suggest that we met up to talk through the tactics we were using. I'd always find what he had to say illuminating, and he was often funny, sometimes when he was not even trying to be. However, when things were going smoothly, I would barely see him at all, and had to plead with him to come in and take a session, but he'd just tell me we could meet up afterwards for lunch. It got to the stage where I said to him: 'I realise what you are now. You're not a coach, Malcolm, you're a professional luncher!'

There is no doubt that he had a brilliant coach's mind, but Malcolm's behaviour exposed a weakness in his character, and the lack of responsibility that he showed even then would eventually cause him even more problems. A few days after I had gently remonstrated with him in the hope he would see the light, he made the headlines in a big way. He had been discovered outside his house, parked on a yellow line and slumped over the wheel after suffering from an asthma attack, or so he told the policeman who woke him up. His condition had absolutely nothing to do with champagne. Of course not!

After he failed to show up for training, the phones at the club were ringing non-stop and reporters were arriving in droves, and they weren't just the football scribes we knew and mainly trusted but also the news men. In the midst of trying to divert all the criticism, Malcolm contacted me to say I had to meet him at the restaurant we used. When I arrived at his table, he looked up at me like a naughty little boy, as if I was the older one and he was the kid. The first thing he said was: 'Do you want a drink?'

'Not much! All the bloody press I've had to deal with this morning makes that necessary.'

'That's okay,' he said. 'What would you like?'

My reply was to the point: 'I'll have a glass of that asthma you've been drinking!' He grinned.

Malcolm could be irresponsible and never more so than when he turned up in a Rolls Royce with the model and actress Fiona Richmond, who was not known for her shy, retiring disposition. She was associated with Raymond's Revue Bar, as owner Paul Raymond's girlfriend. Unbeknown to me and the players, who had just finished training, she sashayed into the changing area, whipped off her coat and jumped naked into the communal bath with Malcolm. As soon as the players saw the photographer who had arrived with them both, they grabbed their towels and headed for the exit door. At the very moment she slipped into the bath, Peter Taylor, who had just been picked for England, jumped in, not realising there was a naked women already there. I warned him what had happened, and he was off before the photographer could take any pictures of him. It would have looked bad for Peter at the FA if he had been involved, even innocently. It was a stunt we could have done without.

There were one or two others who, when the photographs started appearing, had a lot of explaining to do to their families. It was just typical of Malcolm, who dismissed it by saying: 'Oh it's all right, isn't it? There's no harm in that.' While I was asking him what the hell was going on, he replied: 'No, it's okay, it's good for Peter. A bit of publicity is good for you.' I've often wondered if that was the incident that did for Malcolm at Palace. It could have been, but I imagine it would have been overlooked if we hadn't missed out on promotion.

Malcolm was a nice man, clever and aware. He just had a streak of madness, something that told him to go ahead and do what he wanted to do. We would call it chronic misjudgement or misbehaving, but he wouldn't recognise it as in any way wrong. As a consequence, it was very hard to be angry with him. People say he was over the top, but he was just enjoying himself. He would blow his money on champagne if that is what he felt like and often did.

The FA Cup run had been glorious. It was made for Big Mal in his fedora (which he said was a lucky charm that would see us through to Wembley) and a greatcoat with a huge fur collar. He would get the opposition fans worked up before the start when he would walk round the pitch and use his hands to forecast the score by which he believed Palace would win. We couldn't stop him and why should we? He was entertaining and we were producing results. The run, which went on a lot longer than any bookie would have predicted, started in low-key fashion, as we took on non-League Walton and Hersham at Selhurst Park. A 1-0 victory didn't suggest we were about to start something truly special. We had to overcome Millwall in the second round, needing a replay to do so, before continuing at non-League Scarborough, who we beat 2-1.

The draw for the fourth round was going to be made when we were journeying home from Scarborough by train. It was time for a little psychology. Malcolm said to me: 'It doesn't matter who we get. We are going to show the players we are happy with it. When we find out, we should start congratulating ourselves. If the team think we are confident then that will boost them, lift morale, whoever we have to face.'

When the news came through that we were drawn against Leeds United at Elland Road, it was hard to respond as he had suggested, but we both leapt up excitedly, saying how this was the perfect draw for us and how it had always been a lucky ground. The truth of the matter was that Leeds were as close to their peak as was possible. They had an excellent home record, and had been European Cup finalists the season before, so it was fair to say the odds were against us. Malcolm sent me to watch them, and after doing so I said we had to go with a sweeper, which we did and it worked, as we won 1-0, playing good football too.

Chelsea, my old club, were next. By now they had slipped into the Second Division, but we still had to take our young team away to Stamford Bridge, and again the odds were stacked against us, despite which we won 3-2. We then travelled to Sunderland, themselves winners of the trophy just three years earlier, for our quarter-final. Our team was on such a high that we saw no reason why we could not go all the way, especially as only two First Division sides would remain in the draw if we won, which we did by 1-0.

We now faced Second Division Southampton at Stamford Bridge for a place in the final. We knew we had a good chance of winning and had quite a high-profile build-up, with Malcolm an obvious magnet for the media. Southampton were shaded by comparison. They seemed to disappear as we took the brunt of the media interest, which in those days was very demanding as the FA Cup had much greater prominence then. We were somewhat disadvantaged, because we also had a league game that week, while Southampton were able to relax and have a clear run.

When we arrived at the ground, Malcolm went straight on to the pitch in his fedora and fur coat in front of the Saints fans and again used his fingers to predict the score in our favour. I think he got the scoreline right, but unfortunately it ended up the wrong way round. Peter Taylor, who was our best player, was injured in the first ten minutes and that took quite a bit of our threat away. Lawrie McMenemy's team ended up beating us 2-0 after they scored a couple of goals in the last quarter of an hour.

After that, the fedora and coat went into retirement. In fact, there was a rather sad end to Malcolm's hat. He had enjoyed the publicity of the FA Cup run, milking it for all he could. When it was over, he decided to put it up for auction. Unfortunately, someone had placed it under a counter and when they went to collect it there was a great big hole right in the front where a receptionist had stubbed out a cigarette. Despite that, they still managed to sell it and received quite a lot of money for charity.

There were other crazy incidents from that run, created purely for publicity by a hypnotist called Romark. He was on television a lot and had contacted Malcolm because he believed his 'powers' on behalf of Crystal Palace were the real reason behind our success. Big Mal and Romark had a fall-out prior to the semi-final and I recollect him causing us all sorts of embarrassment in public when he started denouncing Malcolm and placing a curse on Palace before the Southampton game.

Despite the severe disappointment of missing out on a Wembley place, the satisfaction came from the way we had maintained a high performance level against major clubs such as Leeds United, who were packed with international footballers. It's possible that the exertions of playing in such high-profile matches affected our league form just enough to deny us promotion, though the FA Cup can also stimulate a team, too.

By this time, Malcolm was more or less giving me complete charge of the coaching. He had joined Crystal Palace from Manchester City, where he had worked with talent such as Franny Lee, Mike Summerbee, Colin Bell and a squad of players, most of whom were international footballers, and who had won several trophies. When he suggested that I should do most of the coaching, I now realise that he was perhaps struggling to impart his knowledge and demands to a group of Third Division players. He had noticed that I took a different tack in dealing with them. I kept it simple, starting from the basics and working my way up.

He told me: 'I see in you a lot of me when I was young. You are doing simple things thoroughly, which is what I used to do. I've come here from City and began coaching from that high level.' He couldn't get going with this squad because he was doing top things and too many of the Palace players couldn't handle some of the ideas he had. For example, you often hear people say after their team has had a good result: 'We should start where we finished.' But that is the wrong way to look at it: if you win 5-0, you actually need to start where you began the last time – that is when you put in the work that enabled you to dominate the other side and score all those goals. If you start as you finished, then actually the last quarter is when you were beginning to run down.

For whatever reason, Palace now seemed to want Malcolm out, but he was prepared to quit without any prompting from them, partly because he was having family problems. He also felt he was at the end of what he wanted to do at the club. He had joined Palace as a very big coaching star. Malcolm did a lot, put a lot of work in and it took a lot out of him. He was not sacked or forced to resign. Malcolm was under intense pressure due to circumstances it is none of my business to talk about. When you combine that with losing an FA Cup semi and missing promotion and the feeling that he had done his bit in finding and developing young players, then he saw it as his time to say goodbye.

I was ready to walk with him. I told him in a very emotional meeting that I would quit too, as I felt that was the least expected of me, but he wanted me to stay, explaining: 'Why leave some other coach to benefit from our hard work and planning?' He had no problem with me taking over. 'Just do it right,' was his final piece of advice.

Having agreed with Malcolm that I would carry on regardless, I then made a verbal agreement with the club chairman, Ray Bloye, that I would take over as manager. Before agreeing terms and signing the contract, I said I wanted to go on holiday with my two daughters, Nancy and Tracey, who were still in infant school, before I decided anything. It was my first proper holiday in years and the first time I had been able to have a three-week break with my girls, because usually there was an end-of-season tour, or I would go off on a coaching course.

However, while I was in Mallorca in June 1976, I took a call from Jimmy Quill, an old friend. With his brother Patsy, Jimmy ran the Blind Beggar, one of the East End's most famous pubs, which had been used, if I can put it that way, from time to time by the Krays and was where Ronnie notoriously shot George Cornell in 1966. Jimmy was well known in the London football scene and was in business for a time with Bobby Moore and Frank McLintock.

Jimmy was also a major Arsenal fan and a friend of Ken Friar, who was then the Arsenal secretary. He apologised for disturbing me when I was on holiday, but what he said next shocked me: 'Ken Friar's been in touch and he is trying to contact you. He wants you to have an interview for the Arsenal manager's job.' This had come completely out of the blue. I had no inkling of any Arsenal interest, there had been no prior contact, not even a gentle nudge or a newspaper rumour after the departure of Bertie Mee, the man who had won the Double for them in 1971. I said I found Arsenal's interest hard to believe when I hadn't yet even started as the Crystal Palace manager, so how could I take the job to manage one of the great English clubs? Jimmy reminded me that all Ken wanted to know was would I be prepared to consider the job as Arsenal manager.

When I put the phone down, I sat for a minute or two wondering what the hell was going on. It was a huge compliment that a club like Arsenal were interested, but why me? More importantly, there was the complication that I had given my word to Ray that I would take the Palace job and finalise everything when I returned from holiday. Whichever role I took would be my first managerial job and it was vital I considered every possibility, as a wrong move at this stage could derail my career before it had even got started.

Ken has a great reputation within the game as an administrator and was soon on the line to me. He asked me if I would be prepared to have an interview with the relevant directors and I told him about my situation at Crystal Palace. Ken was reasonable and he suggested I call him back when I'd had the time to think about it a bit more. He did also add: 'Can you just come back for one day and explain your position to our directors?' There was no question: I had to accept the invite to be interviewed. What I could not resolve in my own mind was why they wanted me? My head was spinning – and not just from the call.

Earlier that day I had quite literally fallen out of the sky. I had been watching the parasailing from our beach in Mallorca and thought, as it was a brilliantly sunny day, that it might be a good idea to have a go. I was strapped into a harness and, with my girls Nancy and Tracey watching, I took off into what there was of a wind. It was exhilarating for however long it took me to reach 60 feet above the blue sea below, when suddenly the harness snapped and I fell like a stone.

Water does not provide a soft landing from that height. It could have been concrete. I hit the water with a force that numbed me down one side, but luckily I remained conscious and even more luckily I had not landed in a way which could have broken my neck. People came rushing up to pull me out of the water, and it was only then that I began to recognise the extent of my injuries. The broken harness had badly ripped an ear and there was a gaping hole between my thumb and index finger where you could see straight into the white bone below. I needed 40 stitches in the wounds and was badly bruised. It was the first time I'd had three weeks' holiday, and now I was bandaged up and painfully sore with a week remaining. Just to make matters worse, I eventually took most of the stitches out myself, but fortunately no lasting harm was done.

That scary incident, coupled with the Arsenal contact, meant my mind was on overdrive. I have often been surprised by what life has given me, but I was dumbfounded by the turn of events. My dilemma was twofold: how could I be good enough to run Arsenal when I had never managed a club, and could I break my word to Ray? I called him to let him know what had happened, and he was panicking. He had not anticipated anything like this. Although I had said yes to Palace, we hadn't discussed anything about my salary or what I would be able to spend on new players. I knew that, with Palace struggling financially, the salary wouldn't be very much and certainly nowhere near what Arsenal could offer.

I thought back to how my dad was an Arsenal supporter and how he was always saying to me when I was a lad: 'Train with Arsenal. Go to Arsenal, son.' I never did then, but now I might have the opportunity to do so. I tried to work out why they wanted me. They must have studied the list of managerial contenders and come to the conclusion that I was good enough. I had to do a lot of talking to myself to convince myself that they might be right, before telling myself that if I was offered the job I must accept it, as I might never again have the chance to manage such a great club.

Then the doubts set in. Yes, I had coached with Malcolm, and the club thought I was good enough to succeed him as manager of Crystal Palace, but as of that moment I had no actual experience of working as a manager. Because I had been working with the Palace players for two years as a coach, and had been given a chance to try it at QPR when I was still a player, I was comfortable with the coaching side of the role. But I knew management was about so much more than coaching. How can anyone go into one of the top jobs in any sphere on the whim of some people who believe they know that person's potential? They were going to gamble, and being top men in banking and the City they were used to taking big risks. If it went wrong, they could easily bring in someone else, but I might never get another chance and would be dismissed as not being up to the job. In fact, I would be the one taking the biggest gamble.

I flew back to London and Ken picked me up at Heathrow and took me to meet the board, headed by the old chairman Dennis Hill-Wood, who were waiting to speak to me and keen to hear what I had to say. They asked me all sorts of questions about the job, and the atmosphere was very pleasant, official but laid back. They quizzed me about men I knew and had played against, such as Peter Storey and the skipper Eddie Kelly. They basically went through every player asking me my opinion on each, and what I would plan to do to help improve them.

At the end of a very long interview, Dennis Hill-Wood asked Ken to take me for a walk round the garden so we could have a chat. I confided in him my concern that it would be such a leap for me to move into Arsenal when I was just preparing for my first managerial role at Palace. His answer was that I seemed to be doing well and why shouldn't I do the job? He believed I had a very good chance of being successful.

When we returned to face the board, Dennis Hill-Wood said: 'We've made our decision and we would like you to take the job.' I thanked him and told him I then had to advise Ray Bloye. So I rang Ray and told him I was going to join Arsenal. Understandably, he was upset at my change of direction and kept saying: 'You gave me your word.' I agreed not to do anything until I had spoken to him face to face, and we arranged to meet that night. I was becoming overwhelmed by it all. Arsenal's offer was the greatest compliment I had received, but my head told me it had come too soon.

I have always advised anyone taking their first steps in a managerial or coaching role that they should either start low down in a big club or higher up in a middling club. Instinct told me that was the right way to go about it, and if that was what I would advise others to do, then I felt I should stick to my own advice. So I told Ken Friar that, even if I might have been making the worst professional decision of my life, I was going to remain with Crystal Palace. I just knew I wasn't ready for a club of Arsenal's size. I might have learned a lot of the tricks of coaching working with Malcolm, but now I had to learn about management under my own steam away from the glare of attention that comes from a big club such as Arsenal.

I can't remember exactly what pay package was on offer from Arsenal, but it was a helluva lot. By contrast, Ray Bloye offered me a much lower salary, but there was to be a generous £100,000 bonus if my team were promoted to the First Division within two or three years. Now that was big money for me, never having made more than £100 a week as a player. Those who consider me a money-grabber may be interested to know that I didn't have this written into my contract. At the time, I didn't think it would be important, but when we did reach the First Division, Ray seemed to have forgotten his offer.

That first season when I took charge, we had lots of bright young players coming through, who we hoped would be the stars of the future. The press quickly began to lavish plenty of attention on them, and perhaps they received too much praise too soon. The players I worked with were strong characters, physically capable of taking care of themselves, but I had no intention that we would kick ourselves out of the Third Division, as one cynic had suggested.

Despite the club's difficult financial position at the time (the phones were cut off a few days after I started), I had been promised that I could spend a good proportion of the £200,000 we had received for the sale of Peter Taylor, but my first deal was to sign

Barry Silkman on a free transfer from Hereford. I then tried to recruit Rachid Harkouk, a freakishly talented player we had spotted at Feltham. They wanted £1500 for him, which was a bargain. I first saw him after I had gone to watch some games in South London, ending with Rachid's match. As I walked towards the action on a sunny evening, I saw this player collect a ball from his keeper and run through the opposition like they were not there before driving a shot at goal. I was transfixed by the skill of the player, and knew he must be our next transfer target. When I told the chairman what fee Feltham wanted, I was astonished when he replied: 'The bad news, Terry, is we can get no more money from the bank.'

I could not believe the club hadn't the financial resources to fund such a small amount. 'You don't understand,' Ray explained. 'There is no money from the bank, nothing, no extra funding. I am really sorry, but there is nothing I can do.' I argued with him, saying that the pressure he was putting on the team was intolerable, like taping their legs together. I wondered how the club could do this after we had had such a good pre-season and with a promising season ahead.

So I called his bluff. I told him I would pay the £1500 to ensure we signed Harkouk, but I'd do this on the basis that I'd take 50 per cent of his transfer value when he was sold on. In all honesty, I had no intention of using what money I had, but I was interested in Ray's next move. His reaction came first thing in the morning: 'Terry, I have spoken to the other directors. You can have the money for the player. Fifteen hundred will be available to you.' He made it sound as if he had produced a miracle scraping together all of £1500.

It was very much a warning about the precarious position of working for a club with no money. Our lack of cash would affect me and continue to do so for the length of time I was manager there, but they had entrusted me with giving them a chance of survival and progressing as a team despite that. If I could develop those who were there into an even more credible unit and exploit their talent, then maybe the future could be bright. It was the beginning of a highly pressured, exhausting and fulfilling time.

I accepted the title of manager, because a coach worked the players while a manager would also select and administer things, so the title was important. Furthermore, a manager earned much more than a coach. I brought in Allan Harris as my assistant. Titles are not necessarily important when there is a friendship involved, but I needed his support, not only to coach but also to look after my back, as I knew I could trust him and I valued his opinion. Allan had great antennae that made him sensitive enough to suss out a potential problem.

In those days a manager would probably have a team of four or five men working alongside him, whereas nowadays that number might be 20 or more, each with a special area of expertise. My youth team coach was John Cartwright, whom I considered to be the very best in the business. Malcolm had devoted a lot of effort into finding and signing talented youngsters like Kenny Sansom. He also signed Peter Taylor, who quickly matured into a very fine young player as well as a valuable asset when the club needed money. John had worked with and helped develop a great number of players, and was so good at his job I could not lose him. Keeping him in the same role may have meant he missed out on a promotion in our structure, but it was no reflection on his status. I wanted him to be with the young players for as long as I could keep him at the club. I believe he should have been placed in charge of England's youth development and left to get on with it. He was employed by the FA, but yet again a man of independent opinion was never going to feel comfortable there for long.

The workload for us all meant we had little time for anything other than total devotion to the club. I had six to seven weeks to prepare the squad during the close season. We would train the players, and then I would deal with the numerous problems that had to be resolved to sort out whatever administration was on my desk from the club secretary and his staff. I also had to talk to the press non-stop, a task that became more frenetic the more successful we were. During the season we would go to watch two or three evening matches. These were the days when managers and coaches did not have the advantage of satellite television. If we wanted to look at a player or our future opponents, we had to travel to see them; we could not sit in front of a computer and download detailed information on just about every player involved in the game worldwide. It may have been hard work, but it did allow us to meet up with other managers and the media in more relaxed conditions than on our own match days.

We were very industrious, often only returning home in the small hours after driving from somewhere like Crewe or Sheffield. I would then grab a few hours' sleep and then be ready for an early arrival at the training ground. It would only have been tough had I been forced to live that sort of lifestyle, but to me it was normal.

I had to squeeze a lot in to that first close season. We had a crop of young players who had to be prepared for a campaign I was determined would end in promotion. I started by speaking to each of the players individually. It is a procedure I have used at every club I have managed since. I found these one-on-ones very revealing. I wanted to know the commitment of each player, whether he was confident or lacking in self-belief. I wanted to know which players would give the club 100 per cent and those that would be happy to pick up the money and do little for it. I had to present my case to them. I would always expect them to speak out, to have an opinion and express it publicly. If they questioned what I was doing, then I wanted to hear it from them direct, not from a second-hand whisper. They might be embarrassed if they were proved wrong, but they would not forget what I'd said. I always felt it was better to hear what their concerns were, as sometimes they would make a good point.

At the beginning, I kept my message to the players simple and straightforward, so it was unlikely to be misunderstood. Malcolm had perhaps been guilty of cluttering them up with too much information. I would not make that mistake. He wanted to do different things, but you have to go back to basics – keeping the shape of the team, for example – to learn where you are. It is a phrase you hear often enough from coaches: back to basics covers a multitude of options, and these would be different from one coach to other, but essentially what the coach is saying is that his players have lost what had taken them to where they were. To rediscover that quality, they would have to go back to the start and work from there. I felt I had to do the dirty work at the beginning, cleaning everything out that was not good and keeping the things that would help us go forward. When they took in what I was teaching them, we could then move forward to where I wanted them to be, but that would take time.

I was confident at the start of my first season because I knew the strength of the players I was working with and I knew how hard they had worked in pre-season. We had a crop of young talent I listed at the start of this chapter, plus an older group to go with the younger legs, so it was a fair mix. Initially we didn't hit top form but we improved as the season went on. As the campaign reached its climax we found the cash, around £30,000, to sign Jeff Bourne in March 1977 from Derby County, who had loaned him out to play in America. I was convinced Jeff would produce the goals that could win us promotion. He hit the ground running and scored nine goals in 15 matches to see us through.

We had survived the loss of Peter Taylor and won promotion

from a battle that was incredibly tight. What made it even more intense was the rivalry we had with Brighton, who became our local derby opposition. It developed into some formidable confrontations that continue to this day. As my former Tottenham colleague Alan Mullery was in charge of Brighton, that added an extra dimension to the encounters. Harkouk rose to the challenge with his very own *Roy of the Rovers* show at the old Goldstone, when he went up the right wing and along the byline, cut inside, gave himself a bad angle and with his left foot smashed the ball into the net. He fizzled out as often as he freaked us out, but there were moments when he was sensationally, awesomely special.

The promotion race went right to the end of the season, and it was Harkouk who clinched it. Three teams were to be promoted from Mansfield, who were sufficiently in front, the enemy Brighton, Wrexham, ourselves and Rotherham. Wrexham manager John Neal, who managed at Chelsea for a spell, had brought in Bill Shankly as an adviser after Shanks had quit Liverpool, which was a smart move and we wondered if it might tip the balance their way.

Our late run meant we had to win our final match against Wrexham by two clear goals to stand a good chance of going up. If we won by one goal that would have left Wrexham needing just a point from their final game, also at home, against champions Mansfield. However, a two-goal margin meant they would need to beat Mansfield to leapfrog us. It was an evening match in May and we soon moved into a 2-0 lead. Silkman was struggling badly with a 'flu bug, so I took him off and replaced him with Harkouk. Before long they had pulled it back to 2-2, and time began to ebb away.

It was then that Harkouk produced his moment of brilliance. All the Wrexham lads wanted to do was play for time and John Roberts, their central defender who had been part of Arsenal's Double-winning side of 1971, took a kick on the back of his leg and went down, trying to waste some time. While he was on the floor, we shouted at Kenny Sansom to run across from left-back to take the throw-in on the right-hand side, just inside their half. He had a long throw, and we knew he could easily reach the penalty area from there, setting up a vital chance for us.

Everyone was putting pressure on the goalkeeper, so Harkouk moved further back so he was not too close to Kenny, who launched the ball. It came to Harkouk at face height, but he tried a scissors kick and hit a wicked volley into the top left-hand corner. We were in front again at the vital time, the last minute of the 90, but we still needed another goal as the game moved into injury time.

Always expect the unexpected. Suddenly, there was Jeff Bourne to hit number four with no time left for Wrexham to recover. We won 4-2. Wrexham then lost their last match 1-0, and we were up. When people ask me which are the most satisfying moments of my managerial career, then that match and that particular moment from Harkouk is up there with the very best I can remember from England and Spurs, QPR and Barcelona.

After the game, Ray Bloye came into the dressing room to speak to the players. He was misty-eyed as he began to read his end-of-season address. He knew we had won, but he had prepared his speech when it looked as though we would have missed out on promotion: 'Well done boys, we are really proud of you ...'

I shouted over to him: 'What are you reading that for? We have won. You can tear that up.'

As someone who had been encouraged from an early age to get involved in coaching, I was always keen to bring in others, not least George Graham. He had come to the end of his playing career after a season with Palace and then a brief spell in the States, and was thinking of getting out of the game altogether. I happened to have a vacancy in my coaching staff, so persuaded George to come in and run the youth team when John Cartwright eventually left. The Palace junior sides, who won the FA Youth Cup in 1977 and again in 1978, were lucky to have coaches like John and then George.

Initially George was reluctant to become a coach, but he soon developed into a great one. I was both flattered and surprised at a recent awards dinner when he went out of his way to thank me in his speech, saying if it had not been for me, he has no idea where his professional life would have taken him.

So much was happening and so quickly. We had been known for as long as anyone could remember as the Glaziers but now we became the Eagles, which I felt suited us. Having won promotion and the Youth Cup in 1977, we discovered how that sort of success built confidence and improved morale. It also attracted the media, who wanted to know what was going on. I was delighted to have the young players available in the first team. It was a combination of their youth and quality that intrigued the media, who dubbed them 'The Team of the Eighties'. That was fine and dandy, but now they had to prove they were worth the billing.

George wasn't the only distinguished former player I brought in to work as a coach, Frank McLintock and Bobby Moore both came to coach as well. Bobby had this amazing presence that lifted all of us. I can still see the look on the faces of the young players when Bobby stood in front of them, ready to take them for a coaching session. He was surely destined to be a manager/coach and it looked as though he was going to take charge at Watford, until owner Elton John mysteriously changed his mind and gave the job to a very young Graham Taylor. Although it was a huge disappointment to Bobby, you cannot say Elton picked the wrong man, as Graham led Watford to the top league and preceded me as England manager. For Bobby there was subsequently a managerial role at Southend, but he was soon to be lost to the game, which struck me and all those of us who knew his qualities as a tragic waste.

My friendship with Jim Gregory had continued after I had joined Palace from Rangers. He would often phone me and we still met up on a fairly regular basis. When we met, he was often trying to do a deal, to sign one of my players or he would want to sell one to me. Sometimes we'd reach an agreement there and then, but the next morning he would be on the phone, having realised he had had too much to drink over lunch, to clarify what we'd agreed. In fact, what would have happened is that when he told a colleague who he'd arranged to buy or sell, they would tell him he was mad and the whole thing would fall through.

One of those deals that did go through was for Rachid Harkouk, who I'd decided to sell. As I've said, he was capable of brilliance, but increasingly often he did not play well. He played football the way he chose to live his life, with no middle ground. When George Best, then playing for Fulham, broke Ian Evans's leg in a bad tackle, Harkouk grabbed George by the throat.

If that was bad, there was worse to follow. The first I knew about it was a phone call I received in the middle of the night saying that he and his friend Barry Silkman were in custody at a police station. They had been discovered in possession of $250,000 of counterfeit bills, which they had been trying to sell, having received them after playing a friendly match against a Prison XI. If the police had mentioned any other names but theirs, I wouldn't have believed it, but with Barry and Rachid anything was possible. Their case went to court and they both received a nine-month suspended sentence.

Despite his inconsistent reputation, which I warned him about, Jim decided to sign Harkouk for £90,000. The first chance he had to watch Rachid after buying him was at Loftus Road when my Palace reserves were playing a Rangers reserve side. He was hopeless. I turned round to look for Jim and he was glaring at me as if to say: 'What are you trying to do here?' At the end of the game, Jim came over to me fuming. 'Hoy, you!' he shouted. 'If I wanted a fucking clown I'd have gone to Bertram Mills Circus for one. Thanks a lot.' And then he walked out.

During our first season in the Second Division, 1977-78, we were essentially a mid-table side, but nothing could restrain my enthusiasm or confidence in the wonderful young players I was in charge of. Having taken a gamble in turning down Arsenal, this went some way to proving to myself that I had not made a wrong career decision. We were clearly on the up; often we would take the field with a side whose average age was about 20, so to do this well was a remarkable achievement, and I knew they would only get better. Indeed, one of the advantages of a young team is that they are all keen to learn and progress, which is what I hoped we would do the following campaign.

The climax to the 1978-79 season proved to be extraordinary. Our final match was a rearranged fixture with Burnley and this meant we played after our rivals had finished their campaign. All season we had been battling it out again with Brighton. We knew exactly what we had to do: if we beat Burnley we would leapfrog the Seagulls and lift the title, if we drew we would be promoted along with Brighton and Stoke City, but if we lost we would miss out on promotion altogether, with Sunderland going up in third place.

With so much at stake, a club record crowd (51,482) turned up to see the match, with thousands more locked out. It took us until 14 minutes from the end for Ian Walsh to head us into the lead. Dave Swindlehurst then scored the second to make absolutely certain of the title. Meanwhile, Brighton had flown to the United States to go on tour without knowing the result. They discovered en route that they were runners-up, which further intensified the rivalry between the two clubs.

The Eagles were soaring, and the work I had been doing was getting noticed further afield. I received various offers to go elsewhere, the most lucrative of which came from New York Cosmos. I always felt I should see out my contract, but the money on offer was so much that I spoke to Ray about it, and he agreed to improve my salary. In the end, I didn't want to leave as I was excited to see just how far my team could go. In fact, we even got to the very top of the First Division, albeit for just one week, and it was October before we lost our first match back in the top flight.

I was delighted with how well we had taken to the top league. I had brought in two experienced figures in Gerry Francis and Mike Flanagan to help our young squad cope with it. We drew our first three matches, then won four of our next five. Before the end of that first pathfinding season, we managed to claim the scalps of Arsenal, Leeds United, Manchester City and even European champions Nottingham Forest. We finished a comfortable 13th place, but unfortunately that was to be as good as it got.

I did not know it, but I was only months away from leaving the club. That summer we signed striker Clive Allen from Arsenal, swapping him for Kenny Sansom. If I hoped the arrival of a top goalscorer like Clive would be the next step on our rise, I was to be hugely disappointed, not that Clive was in any way to blame. Everything went wrong as we lost nine of our first ten matches, and I could not find any solutions as to why things were no longer working. Furthermore, the club was in increasing financial difficulty – they were all over the place – which meant there was no scope to bring in new players. Indeed, on one occasion we even had to have a whip-round to pay our travel costs, after the club had failed to pay its bills.

During this period, I found out the directors had gone behind my back in their search for a replacement. There was no need for that. I was prepared to see it through, because I knew we would get better if we could add to the playing staff. If they wanted me out, all they had to do was talk to me about it. In view of what had been achieved with me in charge, and how I had turned down various offers when we were on the rise, I found their behaviour disturbing and disloyal.

I would have had mixed feelings about leaving, despite the

board's actions, because of my contractual responsibility. Furthermore, I would miss the players: they were a quality group who were growing up together, much as I had experienced in my early years at Chelsea, and they had achieved so much: a great FA Cup run to the semis followed by two promotions – how bad is that? I felt I could have achieved more with them over the next season or two, if only there had been more money for signings, but that was never on the horizon.

Palace's attitude towards me was a surprise, but not one that should have come as a great shock. It was simply a reminder of what can be expected from the often ruthless men who run clubs. When I heard the stories about the club looking for a replacement, I sought out Ray Bloye to ascertain exactly what plans he and his board had for me. Would they come out and tell me they were talking to other managers? I made it clear that they would have to push me out, as I wouldn't walk away as I wanted to see out my contract. That threw them.

Subsequently, Ray told me that Jim Gregory had been in touch, as he wanted me as the Rangers manager. He'd even offered them compensation of £100,000 to take me, the first transfer fee between clubs for a manager. I explained that if he wanted to take the money, he should do so and I would go, on the understanding that no one should think that I was forcing my departure. That gave Palace a way out. If they wanted me to stay, they only had to turn down the money, but I knew there was no chance of that from a club whose board may have had personal wealth but were slow to spend it on behalf of Crystal Palace. Ray was a thoroughly decent man, but a man under pressure to keep the club afloat. So I closed the boardroom door behind me and left the club. As I was going, I was spotted by a member of staff who asked me what was wrong. 'Nothing,' I told him. 'Absolutely nothing.'

# 10

# DON'T STOP ME NOW

WE WERE GOING to change the world, Jim Gregory and I. An exaggeration? Perhaps. But we certainly thought we could change things for the better at Queens Park Rangers. In the process, we felt we might make a broader impact on the game. We achieved that and ruffled some feathers along the way, with our plastic pitch and our success as a team.

We came together as owner and manager in 1980 when you could sense the mood for change, with a few of us progressives, mostly inside Jim's office, aware that the way football was administered would have to move on and, more pertinently, be prepared to do something about it. The pace of change would quicken after Hillsborough, the setting up of the Premier League and the arrival of Rupert Murdoch and Sky Sports, but that was some years away. It was still desperately slow for small clubs like ours, and that is why we set about creating our own new way of doing things.

We had no shortage of plans – they were all but bursting out of my head as I returned for duty at Loftus Road, this time as manager.

We would install an artificial pitch at the ground; we planned a covered stadium for added comfort and to make it multi-purpose for other events, such as pop concerts and the like.

I even suggested changing the club's name, but I have to admit that Jim was uneasy about the idea. His love affair with QPR was genuine. When I put it to him that London FC would be a name for the future, he could see what I was trying to achieve but never sounded convinced.

I find it astonishing that London is the capital city, yet there is not one club with London as part of its name. Compare that with Paris, Madrid, Rome, let alone the other big cities in England: Birmingham, Leeds, Liverpool, Manchester, Newcastle and so on. In London, Arsenal, Tottenham and Chelsea are big clubs who represent areas of the city, but Rangers is not even in Queens Park. That was why I wanted to see us adopt a new name. London FC would have been simple, straightforward and instantly recognisable but it didn't happen, as it went against the grain for traditionalists such as Jim.

All these ideas came about because we knew it was essential that we increased our revenue so that we could have the financial wherewithal to compete with the big clubs, even though we would still be at a significant disadvantage to the likes of Man U, Liverpool and Arsenal. We were compelled by necessity if we wanted to be able to challenge them.

When I arrived, however, I was simply relishing being back with Jim Gregory, plugged into his business brain. Jim was so different from other highly successful businessmen who take over football clubs and pretend they run them. Jim never forgot that you can have all the ideas in the world, but the first thing to lavish your money and energy on is the team. Without a good group of players, you don't have a decent team and without that you don't have a business worth the entrance money for the fans. Too many forget that.

Although Jim's family had started out running a fish stall, he now had various business interests in car sales, with Kings Motors and Blue Star, which had made him his fortune. He introduced the All Star Card for petrol sales that was way ahead of its time. He had considerable assets, all of which had generated the money that allowed him to run Rangers.

He was also a moneylender, and may the gods help you if you did not repay on the agreed date. I was in his office when one very tall and rather self-confident man had turned up with some excuse about how he could not pay as agreed. Jim was incandescent. He ordered him out and, as he left, picked up a large glass ashtray and to the utter surprise of the man flung it at him. By the time the now terrified man had arrived in reception, Jim had phoned down ordering him to return to his office suite. The man had made a serious error in showing that he considered Jim to be a person he could dominate with his superior intellect, or toy with. Now he knew what he was really up against. If Jim loaned you money, he wanted it back. He would always pay on time and he expected those who owed him to pay on the dot as agreed.

I can recall numerous occasions when he would demand of his staff that such and such a bill had to be paid. 'It must be paid when requested,' he would warn them and add: 'Not a second late. I do not want trouble over this.' He was all for free enterprise, too. When Ken Friar, Arsenal's general manager, visited Jim's office to negotiate a transfer, he admired Jim's desk. Jim's reply was classic: 'Everything is for sale here, Ken.'

I have heard the story repeated about Jim selling his car or almost anything else he possessed that was complimented in front of him. Jim was powerful financially but he wouldn't try to overwhelm you. He was quietly spoken, even when angry, and would never be on top of you, shouting or remonstrating. He had his enemies, some of them loud and nasty. He dismissed them as irrelevant, but he enjoyed the rough and tumble. Perhaps unsur-prisingly, all sorts of stories did the rounds about his involvement in this or that. I have heard it said, though not to his face, that Jim was even the brains behind the Great Train Robbery. I ask you? Total rubbish!

He was as hard – I mean physically hard – as any man I have known and he loathed unjustified criticism of him and his club. One of Fleet Street's finest wrote a column in a way that offended Jim and then made the mistake of going into the gents toilets in the Café Royal at the annual Football Writers' Association Footballer of the Year dinner at the same time as Jim. There were just the two of them, and Jim, smaller but more robust, landed the columnist with a right-hander. It came as a surprise and flattened the press-man, who was down and out. It was then that George Kirby, a footballer noted for his physical attributes, entered the toilet looked down at the body, and then across at our chairman. Jim said: 'George, did you see that?'

'I certainly did, Jim, I certainly did. He slipped on the soap. It was an unfortunate accident.'

It is hard for a businessman who deals with figures on a balance sheet to spend money on flesh and blood or to stand in the back-ground and let the manager manage. It was explained to me by a man called Brian Jupp when I was at Palace that you can have the power or the glory, but not both. That is if you have any sense. Jim had the power, but he recognised how the game worked. He would also say to me that if I was struggling he would be by my side, but if I was winning I had to take the accolades on my own and that he would be there again if I needed him.

Jim had been chairman of Rangers since 1965 and seemed to be a permanent figure at the club. Big-name players would come and go, managers would do the same but he would be there sorting it out in the background. I came in initially as his manager/coach in charge of the players, but he would also make me Rangers' managing director and the club's second largest shareholder. The role of MD meant I had more experience of the inside workings of a football club than many people credited me with when I was at Tottenham. If I can put it this way, I had more direct knowledge of business than most club chairmen do of football.

However, all these exciting ideas and plans we had would have to take their place in the queue behind getting team matters sorted out. Survival was the priority to be addressed when I joined at the end of October 1980. What would have been a catastrophic collapse into the third tier had to be avoided. I had agreed to take over from Tommy Docherty, my former manager and adversary at Chelsea. The fact I was replacing the Doc, of all managers, was a coincidence, but one that gave me a feeling of satisfaction.

His team had been stumbling after missing promotion to the top league by two places. In early 1979-80, Docherty had bought three class signings in England international Tony Currie, future England keeper Chris Woods, and Northern Ireland's David McCreery (who had played for him during his spell in charge of Manchester United). But despite these recruits, decent form had been drifting away from his team, as they suffered a very painful hangover from the serious disappointment of such a close encounter with promotion.

Chairman Jim was fed up with managers not delivering, and I also suspect the Doc was too much of a joker for him. When Jim told him it was time they parted company the Doc's reply was: 'I don't think you should go, Mr Chairman. I think you are doing a great job. I would like you to reconsider.' It was a typically quick and clever Doc retort, but not one that would have impressed Jim.

He felt it was time to invite back someone he liked, and who respected and liked him. If it did not work out then he had tried. The call inviting me to be Rangers' new manager came as dawn broke. Jim was an early riser, a legacy of his days with his father in the fish trade. 'Come back, Terry,' he said. 'Sort this lot out. Come back. Nothing seems to work. I want you to run the club. I want you to be me when I am not around. I want you to run the club. I will spend money.'

It was quite a plea, though not an offer as such, or am I splitting hairs? Some things in my life are irresistible and one of these would always be the opportunity to work with Jim. When you took the trouble to find out how he operated and what he could offer in the way of business experience and as a hands-on entrepreneur, he was unmatchable.

Almost as soon as I took over at Loftus Road, I made a move to go back to Palace for the players I did not want to leave behind for any longer than I had to. Sadly, I could not take them all, but I knew just how much Palace needed the money. I knew those players better than anyone and therefore recognised exactly who would be best for our needs. Until I was able to sign them, we had to show signs of revival, be thoroughly professional and drag ourselves up the league.

Initially, we did it with the squad I had inherited, who were not a bad lot but needed a collective injection of positivity. I have always considered it a most important role as manager to create an ambience second to none. If the dressing room pulses with confidence then you have a chance. It is also important that every player knows what is expected of him. That simple formula was part of my coaching philosophy from the start and the one I would operate wherever I went, including in the England job.

It was my role to make training an interesting experience, not a drudge, and to build a club spirit that all the players would feel part of, whether or not they were in the team every match. That was the way forward but not the end. What you do must be purposeful, always making people feel they are moving on to the next stage, when it becomes more and more interesting. Not everyone will buy in to this at the start, but once they notice that others seem to be enjoying what they are doing, it makes them inquisitive. They start to see the benefits and the possibilities that come from work, from athletic training and super fitness.

Once I had the mood in the camp as I wanted it, and our performances improved, then we could build from that base. I knew that was what Jim would want to see and, once he did, I was sure he would produce the money for the players I wanted. My confidence in my methods was acceptably high after the success they'd brought with Palace, and I had no doubt we would achieve great things in West London.

I cannot overstate how close my relationship was with Jim and its importance to me over the next four years. We would meet at his office for discussions twice a week, maybe more often. These were always centred on football and not just gossip. As I've said before, Jim was an extremely knowledgeable football man. He was obsessed with the game and devoted to Queens Park Rangers, although like any fan happily blinkered by bias. He knew what was important: it was the quality and desire of the players found by and then taught by the manager that would decide the club's future.

Our meetings didn't just take place in the office, as we would often meet up at a West End restaurant, and he would even invite me to the yacht he had bought from Sophia Loren, moored in the South of France. The invite was more of a plea: 'Come down! Come down to the yacht!' I would say I had things to do, but he would insist: 'Tel, don't bother with that, we can talk football here.' I would go and we'd socialise while the crew ran the boat. It was no hardship. He would make a point of walking me round the local fish markets wherever we moored up, but above all we would talk a lot about the future and how we could find ways of generating the extra cash the club would need to be challengers in the top league.

QPR is Jim's story, not mine. I played my part, but so did others like Rodney Marsh, Stan Bowles and Gerry Francis. However, nothing is more certain than without that determined little frame of Jim's directing the traffic, finding the money and having the guts to spend it on players and redevelopment, there would be no club left for the various owners who have succeeded him over the years to control.

He was a bad man to fall out with, but a little gem if you caught his eye and he saw you as someone not dissimilar to himself. I was loyal to him and I saw no reason not to be. It was his drive and ambition that propelled QPR when he took over in the 1960s. He guided a club living in a dump of a ground, hardly a stadium, to respectability. The facilities then were virtually non-existent. When I joined as a player, the dressing room was tiny, with a sloping roof that meant average-sized people had to stoop to change. Jim used his own money, not sponsored money or TV money, to transform the club.

He was often misunderstood, and yes he could be tricky, but that can be an asset. He opened my eyes to situations by thinking about them laterally, which in turn made me think more deeply about them and so together we would solve the problems that arose within the club. He was a whirlwind who would bombard you with his ideas, expect to be swamped by yours, listen to them and, if he didn't agree with what you said, move on to something else.

Moving on was also the fate of his managers at Queens Park Rangers. They had been too numerous to mention, regularly coming in and leaving soon after by the revolving door at his office. I was never to be pointed to the exit because Jim understood me and knew I understood him. Dave Sexton and I are the only two managers Jim employed but did not sack. He understood we were on the same wavelength, working to find out how we could make the club bigger and better.

I had played for him and now I was there to help him find stability for QPR, and to plot a way back to the top league. I have to say that we enjoyed ourselves on the way, which is how it should be. I make no apology for the prominent role he plays in this book, because he had a major influence on my life.

Having begun by working to rebuild the players' confidence and raise their enthusiasm and fitness in training, I was delighted that my arrival seemed to have an instant impact: we had three wins from my first three matches. These wins raised us out of the relegation zone and into relative safety, but often this initial lift can be shortlived, and we hit the skids again with a couple of defeats.

I felt that a new face or two would add to the fresh ideas I'd brought in, and Jim gave me the go-ahead to buy more players. New recruits can often contribute to a surge of recovery from good players who have lost direction. When looking for who to bring in, I used a system I called TTPP for short: Tactical, Technical, Pace, Personality. I would mark the potential signing out of ten in each category. A total of 38-40 would be a world-class player and would probably cost much more than I had available. If a player scored 30 or fewer, he would not meet my requirements. Between 32 and 35 was what I was looking for. I found this system worked for me over the years.

In November I brought in Simon Stainrod from Oldham, and while never as prolific a goalscorer as some, he provided plenty of creativity and proved to be an excellent buy who scored well over 30 in his performances for me. Terry Fenwick was a central defender I had the highest regard for and, having seen what he could do when I was at Palace, I was delighted he could rejoin me. Mike Flanagan and goalkeeper John Burridge also moved across London from Palace. With Simon and Mike to score the goals, and Terry and John to keep them out, I knew I had brought in some key figures, who all passed my TTPP test.

Goalkeepers have a reputation for individualism and bizarre behaviour, but John was even more bizarre than most. Some say he was too weird, but he was a fine keeper in his prime and I knew his experience would be an asset for me. I have known reporters who have interviewed him at his home and been asked to throw oranges at him in his own lounge when he was answering questions to keep him sharp. He was nothing but dedicated.

We kept on improving and, encouraged by that, in February 1981 I signed two more players from Palace in Gerry Francis and Tony Sealy, bringing the total of former Eagles up to five. Tony went on to confirm he would be an important part of our attack for a couple of seasons, making 63 appearances and scoring 18 goals. Gerry's return was not only great for me but for the fans, who had rated him so highly and were distraught at his departure in the first place. He was still a superb midfield player and, as I've said earlier, I always felt his ability was crazily underrated.

What marked out Gerry was not only was he highly talented, but he also used his ability as a team player. Some of the other more maverick talents of that era were less interested in being a part of the team. If you are considered to be slightly unconventional (even if that reputation is harsh), then you are often deemed to be a risk. In my experience, the quirky ones are as prepared as the rest of a squad to give their all. They can also do things with the ball that others only imagine are possible.

I've been lucky that in the years I have managed and coached players, I can think of no more than half a dozen that I did not relate to. They may well have been talented but there was a wall between us, with them either refusing to understand what I wanted from them or perverse enough to say to hell with it. I genuinely liked the rest, was happy to work with them and they with me. There was a line I would not cross, and while I would be happy to have a drink with them, it would be just a brief one before they went on for a night out.

Having finished that first season in eighth place, we continued to improve during the next campaign, which was the plan: consistent improvement. To help with that, I signed Clive Allen from

Palace, creating a new strike partnership of Flanagan and Allen, which meant that Stainrod now tended to play in a slightly deeper role. The 1981-82 season was dominated by three things: we finished fifth in the table, missing out on promotion by two points; we reached the FA Cup final; and we laid the first plastic pitch in British football and, as far as I am aware, the first among equals in Europe.

It was the artificial surface that initially got the most attention, but doing it wasn't even a struggle. There was no law against it; no British or football regulation was broken. Having discussed the idea, I travelled to the Netherlands to inspect a plastic training pitch that was the work of a Canadian company. Impressed by what I saw, we decided to go for it. It cost Jim upwards of £350,000, a massive amount of money for such a project in 1981 – and it was his own money he used, not money from an outside backer or through a sponsorship deal.

No playing surface, whether turf or plastic, is ideal, but the criticism levelled at our enterprise was quite often ludicrous. Of course it was different, of course it would need adapting to and yes we could have an advantage at Loftus Road, but people forgot that when we played away from West London we had the disadvantage of having to perform on crappy grounds covered in ice or snow, or on surfaces where the mud was up past the players' ankles. In those days, grass may have been perfect for a week or two, but it was often a hostage to our weather.

Some felt the bounce of the ball was wrong. Sure, but the surface was always true. Others complained that the synthetic surface gave friction burns to the players, but we were sure that in time the scientists would find a way of producing one that didn't. What our pitch did achieve was to encourage others to improve the understanding of grass husbandry, eventually resulting in the wonderful pitches we have now that remain in excellent condition all season long in all weathers. (Of course that didn't always happen, and sadly some years later it helped cost the England national team I was involved with a victory we expected, of which more in a later chapter.) We were not cheating or trying to gain unfair advantage, and we made Loftus Road available to our opponents to train on the day before we were due to play so that everyone could get used to it.

Our first Division Two match on the plastic was against Luton on 1 September 1981. We lost 2-1. Some advantage! We did come out on top in our next home match, four days later, with a 3-0 win against Newcastle United and lost just one more game at home all season, against local rivals Chelsea. However, I truly believe that our improvement came about not because of our plastic pitch but because we bought well and had assembled a wonderful squad which few other clubs possessed then. They enjoyed working as a unit, and they enjoyed the training. If I wanted to switch things round tactically, as we did in the FA Cup, then they were up for it. It helped that Jim was caught up in the optimistic mood and wanted to support us in any way he could to make progress, even if it was going to cost him.

With the arrival of Burridge, I had a decision to make over our goalkeepers, as I now had three of them fighting over one spot, with Chris Woods and Peter Hucker also in contention. I thought there was very little difference between Woods and Hucker, who were both 21 at the start of the season. However, I knew I could sell Chris for £200,000, while Peter at that stage would have been worth about £12,000 on the market as he had less first-team experience, so I decided to let Chris go. That requires an explanation. How could I sell an international-class player in preference to one who was relatively inexperienced and expect to get away with it? First of all, I needed money to buy and, having studied both Chris and Peter, I felt Peter was vastly underrated. I knew it would be a gamble to sell Chris, but I also saw Peter's style of goalkeeping was in tune with my plans to rearrange our defence. Peter was not so assured dealing with crosses, but our new defensive set-up would cover that for him, and he was an outstanding shot stopper.

With Burridge reluctant to play on plastic, Hucker became our first-choice keeper, maintaining his place throughout our run – and he was even made Man of the Match at Wembley. He stayed with us for the next few seasons, where he proved himself to be a first-class goalkeeper and a man's man. He improved with us, and I always found that was one of the pleasures of my job. In some ways I had the same outlook as Brian Clough, who would improve the status of his players in a way that was double-edged. They would be recognised as better players, which was good for their personal morale, but this meant they soon wanted better pay or would be lured away by other clubs.

The FA Cup campaign was not easy. We could have gone out in our first tie against struggling First Division side Middlesbrough. We drew at home – it must have been the plastic! – but won away on a terrible grass pitch. We then drew at lowly Blackpool before scoring five in the replay. After a straightforward 3-1 victory over Grimsby, we put out my old club Crystal Palace in the quarter-final at Loftus Road.

In the semi-finals, we were drawn against West Brom at Highbury. We had been using a basic system all season, but I tweaked it for the semi, giving different roles for our two strikers, Flanagan and Allen. I wanted Flanagan to operate to the left and Allen to the right, working inside the full-backs, which left wide areas clear. Meanwhile, their central defenders, John Wile and Alistair Brown, were confused about who to pick up, which worked in our favour. Just when everybody was preparing for a replay, a Clive Allen shot was deflected in to give us a 1-0 victory and our place in the final, where we knew we would be taking on holders Spurs.

Wembley was the dream for all of us, a chance to take part in what was one of the great days in English football. Having said that, once you've got there, winning the Cup is what you want. With the final relayed worldwide and its reputation as the greatest domestic cup competition, the occasion has often been greater than the actual match. So it proved in our case, which was a poor final that stretched wearily into extra time. We looked to be heading for defeat, when Glenn Hoddle scored for Spurs with just ten minutes remaining, only for Terry Fenwick to drag us into a replay with the equaliser five minutes later.

I was relieved as I felt it would give us the chance to show we could play so much better than we had in the first miserable offering. For the replay five days later, Tony Currie, such a beautifully balanced player, was our skipper in place of Glenn Roeder, who was suspended. Hoddle scored from the penalty spot early on, but I thought we were the better team after that. Gary Micklewhite, who had been signed by the Doc from Manchester United in 1979, scored a perfectly good goal that referee Clive White decided was illegal, one of the major mistakes in White's career. Then John Gregory, who had joined the club from Brighton at the start of the season, hit the woodwork with a shot that dipped onto the bar. Despite those efforts, we just could not make the breakthrough.

It would have been a bigger disappointment had we not left Wembley having given a team that featured Hoddle, Ray Clemence, Chris Hughton, Steve Perryman, Steve Archibald and Garth Crooks a real scare. They were in their prime while we were still trying to play our way out of the Second Division. I always set out looking for some form of achievement at the end of the season. We didn't win promotion and we didn't win the Cup, but we were improving and I was sure we would continue to do so.

But however well things are going, I came to recognise that as a manager you can never keep everyone happy. At one stage during the next campaign, I had an interesting exchange with a supporter over the form of Tony Currie. I have kept the letter, which read:

*Dear Mr Venables,*
*Why is Tony Currie not playing in the team?*
*You must be one of the biggest idiots I've ever come across. Tony Currie is an international, he can play short passes and never give the ball away, he can hit long passes forty yards on the dot, and he is so strong you can't get the ball off him. Come on you can't be as big a fool as you look. I just want to know one thing. Tell me, tell me, tell me, why isn't he in the team?*

My reply was short:

*Dear Sir,*
*He's broken a bone in his foot.*
*Yours faithfully,*
*Terry Venables*

In quick succession we had gone from being relegation candidates to promotion challengers and FA Cup finalists. I felt we could approach the new season as real promotion contenders. I did not think we needed to buy new players, though we offloaded Ian Gillard, who had been in our Cup final side, Ernie Howe and Burridge.

My main focus was on the team, but I had other duties as MD of the club, which included listening to the moans of the opposition about the plastic turf we were forcing them to play on. Initially, the Football League were surprisingly understanding, mainly, I think, because there was nothing much they could do about our pitch and the ones at Luton, Oldham and Preston North End. The one decision they made was to ask clubs planning to install artificial pitches to advise them first. Eventually, however, they changed their minds and banned them, though Preston used their artificial pitch well into the 1990s. I noted a couple of years ago that one or two smaller clubs were hoping to bring back the synthetic surface to make their little stadiums multi-purpose to generate more cash. What we had instigated still made sense more than 20 years later. The FA have confirmed they will change their legislation to allow the use of synthetic pitches.

Other sports were beginning to use our facilities. It was good for hockey. We had a rugby union mini-tournament and two non-League football sides played matches on the same day when the weather had closed down their own grounds. These were all useful extras, but we believed the real money would come from hosting boxing matches, pop and other music concerts. It would take time for all that to be fully operational, especially as we needed a roof over the ground to maximise the opportunity, and that would cost Jim plenty.

He was up for it, and determined to see it through. His instincts told him a covered stadium with state-of-the-art facilities and with a 20,000 capacity in the west of London had to be successful. The Albert Hall is London's grand concert hall, but it has limited capacity. Our long-term plan allowed us to cater in one night for an audience that would take the Albert Hall three nights or more to accommodate.

But for all these extra opportunities, I knew that my main focus was to produce a team capable of being successful in the top flight. Nothing would improve the outlook more than that. We could have done without having to face Kevin Keegan, making his debut for Newcastle United, in our opening game of the 1982-83 season. St James' Park was heaving with Geordie optimism – which has never seemed to be in short supply – that day and they won. Not the best start to our promotion campaign.

We then went on a run, winning three and drawing one of our

next four matches. We were top of the league well before Christmas and were never lower than second for the rest of the season, with some marvellous winning sequences. It was sheer delight for me in my triple role as manager, coach and managing director. We worked hard, all of us, but it never felt like that.

On 23 April 1983 we beat Leeds at Elland Road to guarantee promotion. The title was the next target, and we had a decent lead. To secure it, we had to win at Loftus Road against Fulham and if rivals Wolves failed to win at Charlton we would be champions. We won 3-1 on 2 May, they battled out a 3-3 draw. The title was ours. It was a team effort inspired by individual performers such as Clive Allen and John Gregory, who had a brilliant season. Perhaps we did not have the virtuosity of a Bowles or a Marsh or a Francis (he had moved on by then), but we had what we needed: regular scorers like Sealy, Gregory (16 each) and Allen (13 goals).

No sooner had we secured promotion to the First Division than Jim came out with the news that he planned to hand over control of the club if he could find a buyer, but that proved more than difficult. In fact, at the time it proved impossible, despite the club being a particularly good going concern, with the team moving into the top level. If Jim was unaware of how respected he was by the Rangers fans, he would quickly learn. Within days of the announcement of his decision, the Loftus Road offices were swamped with thousands of letters asking him to change his mind. He did not take much persuading and was there to see us into the new season.

If he couldn't sell the club to someone else, he came up with an alternative plan involving myself. The deal was for him to lease Loftus Road to me, with Jim retaining the freehold. By this plan, he would allow me the use of the stadium and all facilities for 40 days in a year. That would enable me to complete a full football season, with extra dates to rent out the ground for events. It was a unique, forward-looking arrangement.

Before I could take it any further, however, I had to find the money to buy into Jim's deal. This was going to take a lot of negotiating, and I knew what he was like when it came to making a deal. He was all for it as it was his idea, but then there would be occasions when he appeared less than enthusiastic about the whole thing. I found a wealthy backer, an Arsenal fan who was involved in the music business and saw the possibilities of using the stadium for concerts as well as football.

Now all we had to do was sort it out with Jim. I arranged for the backer to phone Jim in his office when I was present to discuss the details, which would then be confirmed by our lawyers. The call was a disaster. Jim became aggressive, finally shouting down the phone: 'We don't need your sodding money.' I tried to grab the phone, but it was too late. The negotiations were abruptly stopped. Jim was not the slightest bit concerned, but I was fuming and embarrassed. I had no idea where I could possibly find someone else with the same commitment to invest in the club.

I have often wondered why Jim reacted like he did. He could be fiery, but he was never stupid when it came to negotiations if he wanted them to succeed. My only explanation is that he had had second thoughts. His sons wanted him out of a football business they thought was a waste of the family money, but now maybe Jim reasoned that our promotion put us in a strong position where he could enjoy himself without selling out a high proportion of the business to a stranger.

With the Football League now allowing clubs to have their shirts sponsored, Jim saw that would bring in extra cash for the team and mean he would not have to bankroll Rangers to the same degree. We brought in Guinness as our first sponsor in a deal worth to us £450,000. I cannot remember if we chose them or they chose us, but we built up a wonderful relationship with the company. They were committed to the sponsorship and I know, as they looked into the future, it would have suited them if we had been equally committed to renaming ourselves as London FC.

The idea of changing our name never got further than Jim's desk. It has taken 30 years for the question of renaming of a top-league club in England to become a matter of public debate. Assem Allam, the owner of Hull City, is determined to change his club's name to Hull City Tigers, no matter what the fans or the FA (who rejected the idea) think, or how long it takes to get his way. He sees a name change as a marketing asset, possibly not so much in this country but in the massive market in the Far East. Is that a good enough reason for coming up with a name that, to many Hull supporters, lacks a certain dignity?

It is fine for wealthy club owners to want to make changes, even radical ones, but they have to abide by the FA's rules. No league is more successful than our Premiership. It offers excitement and some of the best players in the world. Do you assume, therefore, that no further changes should be made? Do we stand still? The Hull owner wants more, and so does Vincent Tan at Cardiff City, who wants to rename his club Cardiff City Dragons, having already changed the club's colours from traditional blue (they are known as The Bluebirds) to red, as he believes this will make them more popular.

The Americans were the first to test the franchise club system, which was ridiculed elsewhere in the football world, but it has worked for them as the public is used to the concept from American football. They rebranded 'soccer' in the States with jazzy names like New York Cosmos and Tampa Bay Rowdies. They liked fancy titles, cheerleaders dancing round their stadiums, big-screen involvement with their fans when goals were scored or conceded. They also had money to attract the biggest stars, Pelé and Franz Beckenbauer were two, though past their prime. Likewise, more recently, David Beckham helped take the game in the States a few more notches forward. The feeling among their exceedingly wealthy owners was that 'soccer' needed extra spectator appeal. It was not good enough just to have a match.

We haven't done any of that in England because we haven't felt we needed to. That does not mean it will always be like that. It is not a question of agreeing with the clubs who want to change, but recognising that we cannot stand still. That was my argument in the 1980s. You cannot settle with what you have, not for ever. You must consider other ideas. The Hollywood approach has not slowed the progress of football in the States, far from it.

In Australia, another country where they relate to the outdoor life, they have brought in extra elements, too, as the game needs to compete against other, better established sports. They are doing it their way and it has worked and will continue to work. Both nations are in the finals of the 2014 World Cup, and the Americans are now regular finalists, while the Australians are increasingly successful, too. It is essential for them to be at the top table every four years as an incentive for the fans. Their message to the public about their new ideas and their success as a national team is: 'This will excite you.' The Bruce Willis advert, in which he says he wants big things, bigger not smaller, sums up the New World's attitude.

The vision of the owners of Hull City and Cardiff City may not have been the right way forward for the moment, so far as their support is concerned, but I do also understand their argument for change. When I speak to the game's top administrators, they reason that these moves would be too easily misunderstood, but add that if you do not go forward you will end up going backwards. This sort of change is unlikely to come from Barcelona, Manchester United or Bayern Munich, clubs who are making big profits from the way things are currently set up. It will come from lower down the food chain, with a club who wants to try to break into the next level.

Now that Rangers had made that next level, it would be an exaggeration to say we barely checked our stride back at the top, but the team produced high-quality football and played with a confidence that surprised and even shocked a few. We certainly did not tiptoe into the new campaign. We did the double against Arsenal; thrashed Stoke 6-0; had a run of six successive wins; reached third at one stage and finished fifth in the league, having qualified for a UEFA Cup place.

We had come so far in just four years, and our progress could not have been more satisfying. I believe that team could have gone on and won prizes – the players certainly believed it. I was excited about what more we could achieve, and about having the chance to take the club into Europe for only the second time in its history. I had just begun to start discussions over a new contract when I received a call from out of the blue that changed everything.

To my astonishment, Barcelona wanted to know if I was interested in being their new coach. When I told Jim, I was taken aback by his brusque attitude. He more or less brushed off what I was saying in a dismissive way. I imagine he thought I was laying it on as a negotiating ploy to get him to increase my money. I was on £30,000 a year at the time, and he just shouted that £40,000 was all I was going to get, 'and that is it'.

I was so incensed I walked out of his office. By the time I reached reception, he had called down to them. 'Terry,' the receptionist said, 'Mr Gregory wants you back in his office.' I said nothing, walked out, collected my car and decided that if Barcelona wanted me, I would take the job. In hindsight, some 30 years on, I think I probably misjudged Jim's mood. He felt, as I did, that we were on to something big and good at his Rangers, and was disappointed that I was ready to walk out on him. But having turned down the opportunity to work at one big club before, I was not going to turn down a chance like this.

# 11

# THE MAN WHO WALKED
# OFF THE BEACH

'Señor venables, we are pleased for you to become manager of our club.' The offer from Barcelona president Josep Lluis Nuñez was translated by the club's top administrator, Joan Gaspart. It was not quite as precise as I have relayed it. The Spanish never came to terms with pronouncing 'Venables', which became 'Ben-arblez' or some other strangulated version of my name. 'Meester Terry' was the generally accepted compromise as the term 'Mister' had been used in addressing the manager since the days of the club founder Joan Gamper.

To be honest, they could have called me anything they wanted when they offered me the job around noon on 23 May 1984. My outward show of confidence in front of the president and his board of directors disguised the stomach-churning realisation that I was now in charge of one of the world's great clubs, not to mention the world's greatest footballer, Diego Maradona.

What I did not know on my appointment was the state of mind of the Argentine superstar or, more correctly, the state of his bank account. Within a couple of days, it was made clear to me that my first major decision as manager would be to decide his future, with the virtual certainty that he would be on his way. I had been looking forward to working with Diego, but as soon as I heard his extravagant lifestyle had left him with hardly a bean in the bank I realised that – barring some sort of miracle – he would need a big-money transfer to stabilise himself financially. You can imagine how I felt about losing a player for that reason, especially the one rightly lauded as the very best.

There is no such thing as a honeymoon period for the new coach at Barcelona and, despite being unknown in Spain, I was under immediate pressure to deliver success. The club had not won the title since 1974, something of an embarrassment to every Catalan nationalist. Barcelona supporters, however, gave me the surprising impression they had come to terms with losing and crying, rather than winning and celebrating. Either that, or they came up with excuses – there were conspiracy theorists who would recall tales of injustice about how referees and every other official from outside Catalonia had it in for them.

I recognise that my arrival didn't fill the fans with excitement or a belief that the good times were about to return. It wasn't meant as a criticism of me but of the board, and particularly Señor Nuñez, for signing an Englishman who had 'walked off the beach' – the phrase used by the press to announce my unexpected arrival. But the board had their reasons: I happened to fit the profile of the club's ideal candidate. They wanted a young coach with new ideas, someone who was ambitious, rather than a manager who had already achieved everything in the game.

The transformation had been so sudden; I was 41 and had been enjoying life at Queens Park Rangers, planning for the future there.

I was totally unprepared for the approach from Barcelona, and have no recollection of my actual thoughts when I was told of their interest. They asked me if I would consider replacing César Luis Menotti, Argentina's World Cup-winning coach, as manager at the Camp Nou, and I wasn't going to turn them down. Apparently, I was on a list of possibles for the role, along with Helmut Benthaus (who had just won the Bundesliga with Stuttgart) and Michel Hidalgo (who would win the European Championship for France that summer).

I explained to my family what was happening, and that I was on the shortlist to take over at Barcelona. My dad had always supported me and my decisions, whether or not he had agreed with them all. This time, however, he was worried and very emotional. He saw this as the possible parting of our ways, and felt that if I was offered the job he would never see me. On the day I was due to fly out for the interview, I visited his pub, the Royal Oak at Chingford, and tried to console him. 'It is only Spain, Dad. I am not going to Australia,' I said, though that would come later. He could not accept it was only a short hop by plane.

I was worried about him, too, so I tried to help by buying the freehold of the pub, thus securing his long-term ownership of it. That place was his life, and I didn't want the owners turfing him out because they felt he was too old. He was now in sole charge and untouchable. That day, I deliberately left my departure tight, as I was planning to prove to him how little time it would take to get from the pub to Barcelona. After leaving him, I raced to Heathrow and, as I had nothing but an overnight bag with me, I walked straight through and on to the plane. As soon as I arrived at Barcelona's airport I phoned Dad. When he answered, he asked if I had changed my mind – he thought I was still at Heathrow! He immediately felt more comfortable with the idea of my getting the job, knowing that he could join me in Spain in about three hours.

I was driven to the hotel arranged for me by the club and found an army of reporters waiting to ask questions, which did not bother me – other than for the fact that I could not supply any answers. I might have picked up some holiday Spanish over the years, but there was no way I could cope with this. Despite that, they still wanted to quiz me, and I found myself besieged. The best thing to do was find another hotel, so I sneaked out through the back door to find somewhere else to stay.

When I look back to those days leading up to my appointment, I have to pinch myself and ask how did it happen? I must have been somewhat apprehensive, though I cannot remember being overly concerned. I had nothing to lose. I have always been confident of my own ability, probably because I put a lot of work into making the best of what I have. My thinking was positive: I was a successful coach and I was managing a club that was doing well and being praised for its football. I wasn't daunted by my rivals, nor by the fact that Barcelona had employed eight coaches over the previous five years. My sense of humour allowed me initially to consider the possibility it could have been a hoax, part of one of these surprise television programmes like *Game for a Laugh* or something similar. You are set up to take part in a situation that massages your ego but is total nonsense, and then when you do take part they jump out and shout: 'Gotcha! You've been fooled.'

One question in particular went through my mind, however: who was it that recommended me to the club? All these years on, I still don't know for sure, but I salute him or them. Quite a few claim to have mentioned my name in conversation, or have been suggested as likely candidates. There was Doug Ellis of Aston Villa, who was a big friend of the Barcelona board. Bobby Robson had told me during the 1982 World Cup that he had turned down the opportunity to go there, because of his worries about speaking the language. He had remained close to the club and would eventually accept the role there in 1996, so it could have been him. Dennis Roach, who made a success of being an agent after taking over as Johan Cruyff's representative in England, was also known to the club and told me he had recommended me. As did a long-time friend, Jeff Powell of the *Daily Mail*, who knew Menotti. I am happy to credit all of them for any input they may have had.

Having slept soundly in my new hotel, the next morning I was met by Señor Gaspart, who took me to the Camp Nou. His family owned the Husa Hotel group and he had spent time working in their London establishments, where he learned word-perfect English. First of all, he took me on a tour of the stadium and explained everything they were involved in. It was a set-up without compare to my marvelling eyes – a massive complex, catering for many sports, not just football. I had played there some 20 years before, with Chelsea in a Fairs Cup semi-final. Barcelona won the first game 2-0, we won 2-0 at the Bridge (thanks to two own goals) and they won the toss for the play-off, which was held back at the Camp Nou, where we lost 5-0. Fortunately, I was spared the misery of having that result on my mind as I had been transferred to Tottenham Hotspur between the return and the decider.

I was then taken to meet the board, headed by Señor Nuñez, a man of considerable wealth and a Catalan hero since he had taken charge of the club in 1978. Everyone on the board came from the highest ranks of Barcelona society. It would have been easy to be overawed. They asked me many questions in Spanish and I gave my answers in English, which were then translated by Gaspart. As I remember it, they were as much about ethics and discipline as tactics and systems of play, though it was clear they were looking for a young coach who believed in attacking football. They seemed satisfied, but that may have had something to do with my interpreter. Gaspart supported me for the job and knew the answers perfectly, even if I did not.

The next morning, after another interview, the job was mine. The board and I sat down for lunch together to celebrate, before the news was officially announced. At the end of it, I was asked by Nicolau Casaus, one of the directors and a legend in Catalonia for the way he had stood up to the Franco regime in the Spanish Civil War, if I would care for a cigar. I'd never really been a smoker, but Malcolm Allison had persuaded me to try cigars: 'It is what managers do,' he explained. Since that time I had enjoyed the occasional Cuban, finding that they helped me to relax.

Señor Casaus opened the wooden cigar box they kept in the boardroom, but to his acute embarrassment it was empty. He apologised and then picked up a silver cigar box, which he opened with a flourish. To his even greater embarrassment, it too was empty. He was beside himself with apologies. 'May I offer you one of mine?' I said, pulling up my trouser leg and pulling out two cigars that I had tucked into my sock. 'Would you care for a Montecristo? It is Cuban.' With nothing to do the night before, I had decided to buy some cigars and I'd learned that the safest place for them was inside your sock. Small actions like that can win you friends and Señor Casaus was a tremendously powerful ally for me throughout my time there, though I have to say I never once had anything other than first-class relations with the members of the inner board. All of them did everything in their considerable power to help me help Barça.

They said again that they had many experienced men on their list for the job, but wanted to choose a young man full of ideas and energy to follow Menotti. They felt a fresh approach was what was needed. I wasn't nervous about taking on the role, but recognised that to be considered good enough to prepare the future for such an institution carried a responsibility way beyond what you would have to cope with at other clubs, and I felt that pressure.

I decided it was vital I gained as much information as I could about the set-up I had inherited from Menotti before he returned to Argentina. We met on numerous occasions to discuss the team and each individual player. Everything I could squeeze from him I did. I thought he was rather vague on some areas and he certainly had not been as successful as the club believed he would be.

One of Menotti's more self-indulgent decisions was to change training from mid-morning to early evening or later, depending on that week's kick-off time. He claimed it was all down to biorhythms and the latest medical research that said this was the best way to prepare. Fortunately, Spanish players will accept an order from the coach without argument, though they might grumble among themselves.

Of course, he was entitled to his theory and César was a great talker and highly persuasive. If you heard him address the press, you'd believe you were in the company of a Nobel prize winner. His views carried all the authority of a World Cup-winning manager and he presented them in a manner that was as smooth as silk, even if he didn't always stick to the same line. I remember that when news of my arrival came out, he commented: 'I wouldn't have this guy from England; they can't play football.' He also predicted: 'He won't last longer than Christmas.' But when we showed signs of success, he changed his tune, saying it was him who had suggested I should be his replacement.

Because of his achievements, when he lectured about the metabolism of the body you tended to listen. It was all so bloody convincing, the idea that the body needs to be used to making maximum effort at a certain time of the day. He added that bio-rhythmic science would soon be a crucial part of future fitness programmes. I began to wonder if I truly was the lucky coach getting the opportunity to benefit from this revolutionary thinking, but then I wondered if it had anything to do with the fact he was in the Up and Down club until three am? Being there for training at ten am would be a hard start for him, but five pm would be no trouble. By then he was able to get himself ready for evening training and could move straight on to his tangoing at the Up and Down. I quickly decided to return the players to morning training when I took over.

I discovered that neither the players nor Menotti had much good to say about each other, which is what you expect when results have been below expectations. He desperately wanted me to take over immediately, a week or two before the end of season, saying it was at the request of the players, but I told him I would take charge, as agreed with Señor Nuñez, after the final match of the season. I had the feeling that he wanted to get back home early, but more importantly I wanted him around. It suited me to extract as much information as I could about the team, the players, the board – anything that would add to my future plans. Besides, I wanted to take charge when players were fresh and ready for a new season, not at the end of a disappointing one.

Menotti told me there were only two or three players of any worth in the squad: Maradona, the veteran Migueli (who had been with the club since the early 1970s and was revered for his power as a central defender) and Bernd Schuster. The German international was almost added in as an afterthought, which I found strange. Schuster had a towering reputation as a midfield player. I understood that he was an awkward sod, but he could play. I wondered if Menotti was laying it on deliberately to make my task seem even more daunting before I started, so I just told him that I would have to do something about it and left it at that.

Any doubts I had were eased by the fact that I knew I had the support of Gaspart. I also had Allan Harris at my side. He had joined me from England and I could not have had better support than from the man I had known since our days as young apprentices at Chelsea. He had worked with me at Crystal Palace and

Queens Park Rangers. His expertise and his calm, considered counsel were invaluable.

We had been buddies since we were England schoolboys and youth team players at Chelsea and as 15-year-olds we had been invited to join the England team at Wembley when Walter Winterbottom was in charge. We had been around each other and have respected each other ever since. Allan's role never changed with me, nor did his importance as my assistant. We were a coaching/management team, just the two of us; we did not need the massed ranks managers have filling the benches in the modern game. Allan was my confidant, someone I could always rely on.

I was in charge of tactics. The way we played was my responsibility, but it was discussed with Allan, and he would listen to what I said and offer his input. Meanwhile, he was my eyes and ears, in constant touch with the players, training with whatever group needed his attention. A manager cannot be there with the players all of the time, but I knew Allan could and would be. The players liked him because he was easy to like, and as a coach he would never be the one to give them bad news, like telling them they had been dropped.

Moving to this great club was certainly a massive step for both of us, and we helped each other through it. I cannot remember either of us moaning about any aspect of the job we had to do or betraying a lack of confidence of what could be achieved. Not that there was any problem about working with fine players and living in a great city, even though we could initially barely understand a word that was said in our presence. I could happily order a beer in Spanish, but I could not tell Caldere or any of my squad what I wanted from them without help. My lucky stroke was to find an interpreter in Graham Turner who was bloody brilliant, always close to the action, always discreet. He was like a second skin, there whenever I had something to say in the dressing room, on the training field, during matches or when I wanted to talk one-on-one with one of the players.

I hope I was a quick learner and was soon able to make some inroads with the language on my own. It is one thing to learn words like 'shoot' and 'goal', but that is a long way explaining a point in detail. What I couldn't say, I performed with my hands and body movement. That worked; the players accepted it as great professionals would. Graham played his part for me and eventually went on to work for UEFA as a senior media officer.

I also understood that as a manager you are at your strongest when you first join a club, because you represent the illusion of the future. That is the time to ask for what you want. I was pretty certain we were going to lose Maradona, and I knew who I wanted to replace him. The board were none too impressed when I named Steve Archibald from Spurs as the player I wanted as Diego's successor. The president suggested I might be interested in Hugo Sanchez, the Mexican striker then with Atlético Madrid. It was a good shout. I watched him and they were correct in their assessment of a great player. Sanchez eventually signed for Real and was superb for them, but I have never regretted the decision of choosing Steve.

It was a relief not to be involved in the nitty-gritty of players' transfers. I had no part in Steve's transfer or any other signing during my time there. The fine details of transfers in and out were left to Señor Gaspart. I would inform him who I wanted, my target would be confirmed by Señor Nuñez, and Gaspart would then make the necessary moves. In normal circumstances, he would first contact the player's agent, then through him the player, to sound out his desire to play for Barcelona. The official contact with the player's club would then be made.

I do not know if Steve had an agent and, knowing him and his singular approach to life, he probably worked out a deal on his own. It was no concern of mine how they signed him only that they did so, which was confirmed when Spurs agreed a transfer fee of £1,150,000. I had my striker. There was no argument from anyone inside the club about my going for Steve and not Sanchez, though God knows they must have been wondering what they had let themselves in for. They left me in charge of all team matters and that early experience meant I felt as comfortable working with the Nuñez/Gaspart axis as I had been dealing with Jim at Rangers.

Although there was plenty to sort out at Barcelona, I also had a number of matters to deal with at home that I had been forced to ignore as the Barça appointment had happened so quickly. The most important was to explain to my family, especially my daughters Nancy and Tracey, how it would affect them. I could stay for only 24 hours, because I wanted to show everyone at Barcelona that my home was now firmly in Spain. I have seen managers in England taking too long about moving to the heart of their new club, and wanted to avoid that trap. Barcelona would be my life. In future, my family would have to visit me.

Sadly, the move to Spain was to be the end of my marriage to Christine. We had met when we were both 16 and had been married since my days as a Chelsea player, but we had drifted apart. The split was as amicable as possible, and we both wanted to ensure that our two daughters understood they still had loving parents. I had also fallen in love with Yvette, whom I had first met in my dad's pub, and she would visit me regularly before moving out to Barcelona to be with me permanently. We soon moved into an apartment overlooking the Avenida Diagonal, not far from the Camp Nou. It was on the A7 motorway which ran all the way to Malaga in the south. We could also see the Polo Club and occasionally we watched showjumping events from our patio. It was the perfect place for us.

Between them, Nancy and Yvette even persuaded me to have a dog. Nancy brought a pup to the apartment which she named

Bilko. It looked like a big breed to me but she assured me it would not get much bigger than it was, which was big enough. In fact, it was a Pyrenean mountain dog and, lovely though it was, it turned into a monster that caused havoc wherever we went, peeing on our balcony which dripped onto the neighbours below and attacking other dogs. It became so big none of us could control it and eventually we had to find a more suitable home for it on a farm, where it apparently ran the place.

The welcome the Spanish extended to me was generous, open-hearted and genuine. But, for all the support I received from Nuñez and Gaspart, I do not think outside the Barcelona board I was seen as anything other than a temporary figure as I had no reputation in Spain. My big signing, Archibald (or Steve Who, as they called him), didn't appear as extravagant a recruit as they were used to. So at first I was seen as just another coach who would collect the money and run as so many before me had done.

That first summer I had a very interesting discussion while I was sipping a cooling drink and reading an English paper in a café off the Ramblas, the famous thoroughfare packed with bars and restaurants that opens up to the seafront and what is now a marina. It was explained to me that I would be fine if Barcelona beat Real Madrid, as no one expected me to win the championship because it had been such a long time since they did that. I was astonished that that was the limit of their ambition, but this man said that if we beat the Castilians I would be safe in the job for a season or maybe two. That attitude did not appeal to me.

Even now, we English too often think of La Liga as an annual two-horse race between Real and Barcelona. Certainly, they are the two biggest and wealthiest clubs, but it is anything but a league fought out between them, as was shown by the fact that Athletic Bilbao had won the title for the previous two years, while Real Sociedad had won it the two seasons before that. So it wasn't just about doing better than Madrid, but the truth was Barcelona had not won the title for over a decade and that was the challenge I would use as my incentive.

However, before I could start plotting an assault on La Liga, I had to solve the problem of Maradona's future. He was adamant that he needed to leave, but I was desperate for him to stay. I had been drooling over the special skills of the little Argentine from the moment he broke onto the world scene as a teenager in a world youth tournament. He was an enormous talent and I have to say the thought of working with him had occupied my mind when I was first approached about taking on the role.

When I asked why he wanted out I was told: 'He is broke.' The Italian club Napoli were ready to sign him and he apparently was happy to move on. I had to meet him as my priority. I was trying to get it into my head how a player on a huge salary, plus extras through sponsorship, was running out of money. I suspected Maradona would be a touch arrogant, indulged, spoiled rotten, a difficult man. He turned out to be charming, soft spoken and a delight. I asked him why he wanted to leave and told him: 'On behalf of Barcelona, I want to keep our best players – and that means you.'

Unfortunately, the greatest footballer on earth needed to generate cash and that meant moving on. It was not so much about his lifestyle as the lifestyle pursued by his friends. There was a bit more to it: Diego was having problems on the field. His form had dipped after he was diagnosed with hepatitis, which can be debilitating. To add to his apparent misery, he was badly injured (as was Schuster, though not as badly) by the 'Butcher of Bilbao', Andoni Goikoetxea. Maradona's ligaments were shredded by the tackle from a player who was suspended for 16 matches for his on-field brutality. The Basque revelled in his notoriety to the extent of displaying the boots that crippled Diego in a glass case.

Maradona's form was still below expectations, though his team-mates loved him in the same way players loved Paul Gascoigne, as I was to find out years later. They loved him because, like Gazza, he was a giver. Diego had everything, incomparable talent and, before he lost it or gave it away, money that should have been invested to last a lifetime. He would share everything with his fellow pros. Being generous is one thing, being overly so can land you in the sort of trouble he should not have had to worry about.

Diego also had this entourage of friends outside the club, who became his 'buddies'. Despite his wealth and celebrity, he would have gone through lonely periods in Barcelona. However much he was living in luxury, he still needed people around him, so he had his mates living it up on his generosity. I was told he gave them per-mission to have dinner and go clubbing even when he wasn't there. They made him feel comfortable and his largesse made him feel good. Some of them I came across were good guys, but others were poseurs who spent all his money, and even began to run up big debts.

It would have helped had he been on top of his game, but he knew he wasn't and that also reduced his self-confidence, which made him more and more unsettled and vulnerable to new oppor-tunities. He was flying headlong into a wall created by looming bankruptcy with his form floundering. The easiest way out, there-fore, was a transfer bringing in more money and taking him to a new setting for a fresh start.

The problem was now mine: keep him or sell him. I would have been happy to talk him out of a move, and I said that to him. I made it clear I was really keen to work with him, that it would be a thrill for me, though that is not how a coach should talk about working with any player, even Maradona. But how could I deny it would have been a thrill to build a team round him, to exploit his amazing talent? Think of the satisfaction for a coach who managed

to reinvigorate a player of his class and who for the moment had lost
his way.

There was no way he could be dissuaded. He told me: 'I need
to go, it is impossible for me to stay here.' He cited reason after
reason, but in the end it was about money. I sanctioned the transfer, and we sold him for a world record fee of £6,900,000. Diego
thanked me graciously and would go on to inspire Napoli to two
Serie A titles, not to mention leading Argentina to the World Cup
in 1986, with his notorious Hand of God goal against England. I
see him occasionally at football gatherings and he always comes
over and greets me in that flamboyant Latin way. There are those
who rubbish him and would disown him for his addictions and
his strange attitudes, but they should remember his heart is in the
right place.

I did what I could do to ease Maradona's replacement, Steve
Archibald, into the hearts and minds of Barcelona, explaining why
I chose him, and why I knew he would serve the club well. But in
the end Steve was the one who would provide the answer that mattered – goals. I had chosen him because I liked his contribution
when my teams had played against him in England. He always
caused us problems, and I had tried to sign him when I was at
Crystal Palace, but he went to Tottenham instead.

Steve was a singular individual who lived life his way but, and
this is so important, he was not like that as a player. He was terrific
for his team. He was good in the air, quick and brave, he worked
with the others and he scored goals. The Spurs players I talked to
about him said they were surprised I was buying him because he
was a loner, as if that was a minus against his name. Not with me.
He had a reputation for being a bit morose, the type who could
knock the spirit in the dressing room, which might have worried
some, but not me.

I was convinced he would get us goals, as he had scored them for

Spurs and Aberdeen, as well as for the Scotland team. His Scotland manager, the late Jock Stein, saw him as awkward by which he meant single-minded, but would never dismiss his value as a team player. Before the World Cup finals in Spain in 1982, Jock had asked his squad to choose their dinner menu. They were given simple options: soup, steak or chicken or omelette, fresh fruit. When Steve's menu request was returned, he listed courses not on the menu plan. Jock's comment was: 'Trust him to be different.' I liked that aspect of his character.

The more I heard the more the thought of having this Glaswegian as my main striker appealed to me. He may have been too much of an individual at times, but he was the type of player who would take to a new life and lifestyle with ease. If he yearned for the UK, which I doubted, he would never allow it to affect his value to the team. Nor would he be overshadowed by the likes of Schuster. Quite the reverse, he would take him on and did. He would never allow the German to take advantage of him. That is the attitude I wanted from my striker: confident, strident.

Steve knew exactly what he could give Schuster and what Schuster could give him. Shortly after joining us, he held Bernd back after a training session. As the rest of the players headed for the dressing room Steve said to Schuster: 'Let's have a chat. I need you and you need me. If you are on the ball, I'll make a run and if you find me I'll score.' Steve made his runs and did what he said he would: he scored with a welcome consistency.

He did not worry about arguing with me, either. I noticed he had turned up at the club wearing an earring, and I challenged him about it, saying he could wear it on the way to the club and on the way home but not when he was playing. 'Bloody hell,' he replied. 'It cost me a fortune, why shouldn't I be able to wear one? It looks good, it looks smart.'

'I'm telling you not to, that's why,' was my reply, and I added:

'You respect the rules, you respect the club's position and you respect what the manager wants. You don't come to the club wearing a crown, do you?'

The next morning, as I sat at my desk by the window which allowed me to see everyone who entered the dressing-room area, I watched Steve come through the doors, head to the side, and almost walking backwards. My immediate thought was he must be hiding the fact he was wearing his earring. He went out to train, but I said nothing. I returned to my office and waited for him to come in, but when I looked out at the training pitch I saw Steve and two others on all fours. I went out and asked them what they were doing, knowing exactly what had happened. Steve had lost his earring, and I could only laugh. 'Why are you laughing? It cost me a thousand pounds,' he said, which was a lot of money then. 'Tough!' I replied. He never did find it.

It was a totally different life as head coach with Barcelona compared with managing in England. In England, managers do everything – even switching off the lights. At QPR, Palace and Spurs, I would have to prepare coaching right through the teams, supervise training, arrange the buying and selling of players, and deal with players' contracts. I would wear a suit, collar and tie when I was not in training gear. In Barcelona, the role was much simpler: I worked with the players and agreed whom we should buy and who could be sold. I didn't have to be the face of the club at all times, which meant I could turn up for work in smart casual, leather jacket and jeans.

What did surprise me was we had only one pitch to train on at the La Masia training complex next to the main stadium and that was not even full size. One section of the pitch curved in, so if you were running that line you would suddenly have to swerve round to the left. On this one pitch Allan and I had to work with a 30-man squad. There were advantages, one of them being it allowed me to spilt the squad into small groups, each working on what I wanted them to concentrate on.

Despite its limitations, La Masia (which means 'old farmhouse') was an excellent complex for all and I found it a very comfortable place to work from. So too did generations of great players who came through the ranks to emerge in the top team. The squad I inherited included a number of La Masia graduates. Pep Guardiola was a kid on my watch, and already seemed a fine young player, and one we had our eye on from an early age. He showed outstanding ability as did others like Guillermo Amor, who came through the ranks and stayed with the club and had such a successful career at the Camp Nou. Pep was outstanding, though not as prodigiously talented as a young Maradona, but we knew he would have a future in the game, so I recommended he should be retained as a professional and from there on to the next stage in his development.

One of the more surprising visitors to La Masia in my time there was David Beckham. He was a very young and inquisitive visitor to the Camp Nou as his reward for winning a skills competition back home in England. We met, we had our picture taken together, and he also had his picture taken with Steve and the other players. He seemed a pleasant, unassuming lad who we were told was a player of great ability. We never guessed that, like Pep, he would have the world at his feet soon enough.

The beauty of La Masia was the intermingling not just of sports but of the various age groups. We would all lunch together, and I would train and coach them when I could. It allowed me to keep in contact with the players, get to know them not just as footballers but as young men. In England, the dressing rooms were noisy to the point of being rowdy, but the Spanish were serious about their professional life in a way that would bore the average English player. They would neither smoke nor drink, and it had been instilled into them from their earliest days to follow the rules, and that made them the fittest players I have worked with. As the manager, I was always expected to show my interest in the future of the club, but with Allan and me that came naturally. Things have moved on a good deal since then, with much of the training now done elsewhere, but La Masia remains as a symbol of Barcelona's unique approach to developing its players.

I was now ready for the season ahead and, with Allan's assistance, we faced a pre-season schedule that I had not had the opportunity to arrange but fully endorsed. There was a merry-go-round of press interviews and then an open day, which was hugely important to the club as a way of linking with our supporters. Thousands flocked to the Camp Nou to see their men take part in a training session and six-a-side matches. They could watch and assess new players such as Steve, or spot fresher Spanish faces from Barcelona Athletic, our second team that operated as a separate unit in a lower league.

I would not disappoint them on the latter. I had been most impressed by two of the Athletic regulars: Juan Carlos Rojo and Ramón Calderé. Both showed me at a lower level that they had the skill, the commitment and therefore the ambition to be part of the senior squad. They were immediately promoted to the first-team squad. The press were surprisingly critical of the promoted players, asking how I could possibly elevate them. 'They are good enough,' was my deliberately brusque explanation. Rojo was absolutely outstanding and very soon was being acclaimed by the Socios, the Barça members, our wonderful fans who could vote on the future of the club.

Rojo and Calderé would be vital in the style of play I was proposing – the pressing system. I based my decision about our style on what I had seen on the training pitch and in friendly matches, plus many hours of watching videos of the team's performances from the previous season. Scanning the videos was a chore but essential. I would study them in a darkened room for hours and then emerge into dazzling sunlight. It must be what coming out of solitary confinement is like. I would finish with one batch, stretch and thank the gods; then there would be a knock on the door and a messenger would arrive with a large carrier bag containing half a dozen new videos of Barça's matches under Menotti. I would shout out 'Please, please, get me out of here!' long before it became the catchphrase of *I'm A Celebrity* . . .

From these long eye-straining sessions, I knew who would fit the system and who could do what. The forwards we had were not the types who would barge through the middle. The men I had were mobile and that was crucial. The eureka moment came with me shouting out to Yvette: 'I've got it, I've got it.' Menotti had almost made it work. They would attack and press, but their defensive set-up let them down, as there wasn't sufficient cover, and that was what I needed to develop. I would miss Maradona's individualism, and I knew if he had stayed I would have found a way of utilising his strengths for the team. With Diego gone, the key word would be 'conjunto', meaning 'with togetherness'; in other words we would play as a group with a team instinct.

At that time, the Euro 84 finals were taking place in France, so I watched a lot of that tournament, too, as Spain reached the final. Barça had Victor Muñoz, Francisco José Carrasco and Julio Alberto all playing in that game, where they were beaten 2-0 by a talented France team led by Michel Platini and backed by other outstanding players such as Jean Tigana, Alain Giresse and Patrick Battiston.

We began our main pre-season programme in Andorra high in the Pyrenees, then were due to play a series of matches building up to the opening La Liga game, which could not have been more difficult – Real Madrid away! That is when the groundwork was begun on the best way to utilise the players in my squad. My optimism was raised by the success of our pre-season build-up.

Introducing Calderé and Rojo to the squad made a massive

difference, something I cannot stress often enough. They worked incredibly hard for the team, but they were also skilful. Within a couple of months of appearing for me, they were in the Spanish national squad, which was a terrific boost for them. It also showed the players that what Allan and I were suggesting was worth listening to. I played Victor alongside Bernd Schuster in the middle, while Calderé would play on the left. Hard work came naturally to Victor and Calderé, with Victor a tough-as-boots tackler who would confront the opposition. Schuster was a great passer, one of the best in the world, even if he was never an easy player to manage.

You were expected to have the ball winners in the centre, so if Rojo and Schuster were on the attack, Victor and Calderé would slip in to become the central midfield players to offer them cover. If they lost the ball, Rojo and Schuster had to get back to their positions quickly. I also wanted us to press high up the field. For example, if the opposition goalkeeper threw the ball out to his left-back, our right-sided player Francisco Carrasco would immediately close him down and attempt to restrict the damage he could inflict on us. If the left-back moved inside, Victor and Schuster would then close him down. We didn't sit back and allow the opposition an easy way out. That style of play was continued by Johan Cruyff and developed all the way through until the club's golden era under coach Guardiola and on to today. It has served the club well.

We were to be an exceptional team. I wanted them to be confident and to be able to look at the opposition and think: 'If you are going to beat us then you will have to be fantastic.' We had the skill, we would fight, we were super fit and we would not succumb. These are essential qualities and we had them. You could see it in training, in the warm-up matches and during pre-season tournaments. These tournaments made the club money, but for me the main benefit was establishing fitness, camaraderie and raising morale.

Wherever I have been and a team has underperformed, the directors always question the players' fitness. It was as true in England as in Spain. When I asked people at Barça what they thought was wrong with the team, they didn't mention systems, tactics or anything psychological. Instead they said: 'The players aren't fit enough. They haven't the strength to beat the opposition. They weaken before the end. We must work on that.'

But when I saw my players ready for the first session, they made a nonsense of the snide comments from the board about their lack of fitness. Not fit enough? These were the fittest players I had ever worked with. We were going to outrun and outplay any team we met. I have had jobs where the players and the clubs weren't ready for this approach, but this group was, as I found out when I introduced my sprint-training exercise.

Initially, they were horrified and frightened – even supermen like Victor – when they saw what I was asking of them. They hated the long, flat-out, timed sprints over 220 yards – rest and sprint again. They would go to considerable lengths to get out of it and come to me with all sorts of excuses, claiming they were feeling unwell, but when I started pinning the times on a board, that made it competitive and they all wanted to do well. They also recognised that they were stronger for it, and so they soon recognised the benefits.

Barcelona had underachieved under Menotti, and it was my job to find out why and I believe I had because of hours of watching videos of their performances. When you are not winning, you start to drop your head individually and as a group, so you lose more games. It can happen if you don't have the right people to actually improve players' fitness and organisation. To rediscover a great spirit, you have to be prepared to work to become physically stronger and to be aware both tactically and technically. If you get it right, then the players will recover their zest. It's about getting the body right, but also the intangible between your ears.

Any apprehension I had about the job disappeared in the preseason training. My confidence rose when I saw what the squad could do. It could be improved – there is not a squad that cannot be made better – but I was happy and increasingly looking forward to that first clash against Real in Madrid. We beat just about everything that came our way in the way of warm-ups including Watford. We went wild against Boca Juniors, scoring nine goals against the Argentines.

For me, however, the Real clash was going to be the big test. The psychological benefit of winning our opening La Liga match would be enormous, and I could imagine what defeat would do to Real, especially in Madrid. The date was set for 2 September 1984. In the lead-up, I worked with the players, drumming it into them in a way that let them know exactly what I expected from this game: we had to win. A draw – which some may have thought okay – would not be good enough; and defeat would have been a disaster.

The atmosphere at the Bernabeu can be intimidating, but it inspired me. We would play without fear. My players knew exactly what role each had. If we were disciplined then I was certain we would do it. The Bernabeu is a magnificent structure, different from Camp Nou, but striking none the less. To walk out and be greeted by a crowd so shrill it goes through your head and is painful is one of the great experiences. I had been watching, reading about and admiring the great Real teams going back to the Di Stefano, Puskas and Gento sides of the 1950s and early 1960s. I had watched them in wonder. Now, here I was at the centre of the rivalry between the Royalists and the Republicans. I was desperate that the game did not disappoint, and that meant winning. I also wanted to see good performances from Rojo, Calderé and Archibald, on whom I had gambled so much. Steve had been my pick over Sanchez, and so he in particular was under pressure.

Real's early hopes were soon dashed by Angel's own goal, they were despairing when Steve made it two and deflated when Calderé made it three. We had thrashed them 3-0. My team that day was: Urutti, Sanchez, Migueli, Alexanco, Julio Alberto, Schuster, Calderé, Victor, Rojo, Carrasco, Archibald. It was a comprehensive victory against a full-strength side featuring Emilio Butragueno and Uli Stielike. It created a bad reaction in the Bernabeu, which quickly turned violent. The Real Ultras are aggressive and often downright nasty to opposition supporters and teams. There are political connotations involved, too, and let's just say from my experience you would not want to walk into a group of them while waving a Catalan flag.

There were thousands milling about looking for trouble that night. I spotted the potential unrest and realised we had to be careful in the coach where we were most exposed. We were soon surrounded by Real fans shouting: 'Spain! Spain! Spain!' (They were highlighting Catalonia's bid for separation.) Meanwhile, we had to drive from the ground to the airport to fly back to Barcelona. It was a journey that had me concerned and I was on red alert for the possibility of violence. We had to go under bridges, an obvious danger area, and it was from one of them that a brick came straight through our window with the shattered glass cutting the forehead of the driver. Allan was sitting next to me and as I dragged a curtain across our window, a brick or large stone cracked against it but didn't get through. It was all so unfortunate, though perhaps not unexpected. The heavy defeat in such an important game sparked the aggression.

We had achieved a victory few but myself and Allan had thought possible, and even we had never expected it to be so comprehensive. As a start to the new regime, I could not have asked for more. We would have to continue performing like champions and I believed we would. Fortunately, the victory was early enough in the season not to give us delusions about what we could achieve and I did not have to expend effort on keeping the players grounded. We all accepted it was a promising start to what would be a long campaign, but no more than that. Now we had to build on it.

# 12

# CHASING THE CUP
# WITH BIG EARS

Having got off to such a flying start at Barcelona, my target was nothing less than to win the league, ending the title drought, and to move on from there. Steve Archibald would help us achieve that target, and he worked so well up front with Francisco Carrasco. We deployed them working wide of the central defenders. They were both mobile, and Carrasco was great at creating space for Juan Carlos Rojo to come through the middle, just as Lionel Messi does in the modern set-up.

Rojo was fundamental to what we were doing and was a brilliant player for us. He would go at them again and again, which would soften up the opposition defence. We would challenge them in different ways, giving them new things to think about all the time. It was all about variation, just as in cricket, where you can't keep using your fast bowler as the batsmen become used to it, so you introduce a leg spinner and quite often the change brings a wicket.

However, no sooner had we begun to establish ourselves than we were confronted by a major problem, one I had never considered – a players' strike. There were a panicky few hours before I realised this was not so unusual in Spain and there were already regulations in place to cover it. The players were serious about money they considered they should receive, and as coach I sat in on their meetings even though I was powerless to do anything about it. The only person who could solve the problem at our club was President Nuñez.

We were due to face Zaragoza on the Saturday and I was concerned we would be struggling to find a team and play. Graham Turner, my interpreter, explained to me what was going on. I learned that when these situations crop up, the fixtures still go ahead as scheduled, but with players from the Under-19s fulfilling the fixture. Hardly ideal, I figured, but there was no option. Allan and I studied our younger lads and sent them out to represent the club. They performed superbly at the Camp Nou to beat Zaragoza 5-0, and I said afterwards to Señor Nuñez: 'Maybe we should keep it like this.'

As negotiations continued, I received a call from Jim Gregory. He had obviously read about the strike and spotted a weakness, or thought he did. He sounded very sympathetic, but I knew he was up to something, and anyway I was always glad to hear from him, especially as I hadn't had a moment to call him to sort things out after our fall-out.

'Are you going to come back, son?'

'How can I do that?' I replied.

'Listen, son. Come back. They don't take the game seriously at Barcelona ... Why are you laughing, son?'

I had a lot of laughs with Jim over the years, but that was one of the more memorable ones. I had immersed myself in my new life and, while I was touched by Jim's confidence in me, there was no way he would inspire yet another return to West London. Instead, I persuaded him to visit me. He normally used a car and ferry when travelling in Europe and had never flown in his life, but he did it on this occasion, which made it even more worthwhile for me. He stayed for four or five days, visited the stadium, watched a match and ate memorable meals in one of Europe's great restaurant cities. It made him realise why I would not volunteer for a return to English football until there was no alternative.

Although the job was intense, after training I could go home, have a late lunch, read, watch television or meet friends, including Manolo whose restaurant I frequently used. Occasionally friends from England would come over for a few days, such as Malcolm Allison or Jim, and liven things up. Malcolm always rang before he flew out to ask what I would like him to bring, but he knew what my answer would be: pork sausages!

Malcolm was always an entertaining diversion and we had time to enjoy his company. I even managed to fix an ankle problem for him on one visit, when it was obvious he was in agony. I arranged for him to have the op immediately with a top surgeon. I went to see him in his hospital room late one night after I had been at some function or other. He was sitting up looking bored. I asked him if there was anything I could get for him. Somewhat to my surprise, he asked for a couple of bananas, so I found a restaurant who supplied them. He was always different, was Malcolm.

Members of the English press would also arrive on a regular basis and they kept me in touch with the game back home, and provided snippets of news. Life can pass you by when you are as preoccupied as I was at Barcelona. Sure I loved it there, but I tended to think about the job and ignore the peripherals.

There were only a few occasions when we did not do ourselves justice and perform at our best during that long but enjoyable season. We stalled badly against Metz in European competition, going out in the first round of the European Cup-Winners' Cup, despite winning 4-2 in France in the first leg. In La Liga we lost just twice, against an extremely strong and brutal Athletic Bilbao side, who were the current champions, and against Hercules just before we clinched the title in March 1985. Otherwise, it was almost flawless.

The defeat by Metz exposed the petty-minded petulance of Bernd Schuster, when he blamed Archibald for one of the very few failures we had to dissect. Schuster was a player of enviable talent, but at times a very indifferent guy. A footballer with his unique skill is so used to being indulged that he often struggles to consider others. He didn't get on with Archibald at the beginning, but once he saw Steve could play and score goals they warmed to each other a bit more, though they could both be difficult when it suited them.

We had been playing exceptionally well, but that night against the French the wheels came off and we lost a game we should have won. We had a team meeting the following morning to discuss the defeat where we tried to work out why we had been beaten, what we had done wrong and what we could do to ensure it did not happen again. Steve hadn't played well and just could not get the ball. As the discussion continued, Schuster came over all indignant as he tried to offer an explanation for defeat. He said to me: 'How is it possible for us to win the game if we are playing for such a long time with ten men?'

He was having a shot at Steve. I fired back: 'Bernd, don't worry. You weren't that bad!' It could have been either a jokey comment or a dig, but it was definitely a dig.

We were playing football that pleased me to watch. We were organised and we were fit and scoring freely. We hardly glanced back after we had beaten Real in the opener. We did for them again, this time 3-2, in the return at the Camp Nou in December 1984. It was the best possible offering to our support, who were by now deliriously happy. The next morning we awoke to headlines in the football-mad papers of Barcelona that pronounced us 'UNSTOPPABLE' and going for a 'LANDSLIDE'. It was all so positive from the start to its climax.

The Spanish know how to party and none do so with more enthusiasm than the Catalans. You can imagine, therefore, what they are like when their football team comes out on top, with their greatest and most reviled rivals trailing in the distance. It is quite something and I got to experience it, starting on 24 March 1985, when we clinched the title against Valladolid.

The atmosphere in our dressing room pre-match was, I hoped, controlled tension. Valladolid is not what we would recognise as a glamour side, but at Barcelona we knew them as thoroughly professional and very difficult opponents. They would certainly want to beat us or at least stop us winning the title on their patch. The fact that we had four more matches to finish our schedule did not in any way reduce the pressure on the players. Matches have a nasty habit of running out when you need them most. We were in Valladolid to win, and that we did.

We clinched the title with a 2-1 win to complete a comprehensive triumph, and we did it playing quality football. The dressing room afterwards was a joy to be part of. They had had such a long wait and we had succeeded. I thought back to my arrival less than a year before and how, despite my confidence, I wondered what I had taken on. There was the language problem, a different culture to contend with, being away from my family, and the concern about how quickly Allan Harris and I would get our ideas and playing plan through to the players. Training can always be done by demonstration, but you also want to understand what makes your players tick, what motivates them as a group and individually. And for that I needed to be able to talk to them. I picked up the language quickly and made an effort to speak it, though I had Graham

Turner interpreting for me. I learned key phrases to give instructions during training and in matches and worked from there to being proficient but still needing help from Graham.

I thanked the players for their intelligence in adapting to a new style, for their effort and their loyalty. They had given everything they had for a great club. The celebrations had begun in the dressing room between the staff and the players. We returned to our hotel for a dinner. President Nuñez was beside himself, giving kisses, hugs and passionate embraces all round. If it was a gamble to appoint me and go with my plans and my signings – and I would accept that it was – then the outcome was what he had hoped for. The directors were beyond delighted for us all, including for themselves, as success would mean an extension of the usual two-year term of office for them, as they had to rely on the fans to be re-elected.

That night in Valladolid I knew I could work on without any immediate threat to my position. In England, the celebrations by the players would have been wild, but I was about to find out another difference in Spain. The captain Julio Alberto, who contributed brilliantly all season, wandered over to my table with a glass in hand. 'Meester,' he said. 'I tricked you.' Was he going to reveal some amazing incident or conspiracy that I was unaware of? No, Julio was referring to the fact he had not drunk red wine, but some Coca-Cola the night before the game, when it was a tradition for each player to have a glass of wine. I believed there was little harm if they shared a bottle of red between four players. It was hardly mandatory and no one was expected to end up roaring drunk. If they drank with lunch, they would then retire to their rooms for a siesta. The medical staff believed it was better for the players to drink a glass of good wine than a soft drink full of sugar. Julio went on: 'I tricked you, Meester. You think I was drinking wine, but I threw it away and drank cola.'

To break a rule, however trivial, was rebellious to them. They rarely drank, they didn't smoke, and they looked after themselves. I had left behind a drinking culture in English football, where we would often meet as a group after a match because it was the thing to do. The Spanish culture was different. There, professional sportsmen are taught to look after themselves and not take chances with their fitness, so they would avoid doing that. Julio clearly enjoyed telling me about his rebellious streak – and how he had only pretended to drink alcohol – and he wasn't finished.

He wanted to tell me something on behalf of the squad. 'We all thought you were crazy, Meester,' he continued.

'Why is that?' I asked.

'The team always dropped back when we played before you changed the system,' he said.

He was referring to a couple of changes I'd made. As well as the high pressing game, I'd told them I wanted them to 'show inside', encouraging the attacking players to move inside, towards the centre-half, where we were very compact. If an opponent went on the outside, then they could get in a potentially dangerous cross. This tactic had been considered risky by my players, as we were effectively bringing the opponents towards our goal, but they were also going to where we had the most strength to stop them.

He went on: 'You pushed us up right to the halfway line. We started pressing everybody. We had done some of that before, but it was not the same. So we thought: "This guy is mad." But then we won our tournament matches before the season and we thought maybe we have something here. And then when we won our opening match in Madrid, we said together maybe he is not so mad, not as crazy as we thought.'

It was good to hear coming from Julio. Normally the players do not talk like that to the coach and you very rarely know what they are thinking. Julio was a very important player who had just broken into the Spanish international side before I arrived. Within months of my taking over at Barcelona, he became a regular part of the Spain side, while Rojo and Ramón Calderé were also brought in to the national squad for their debuts, which pleased me. There were a lot of hard-working, long-serving players, such as Migueli and Alexanco, in the squad and this was their moment as much as mine.

We flew back to Barcelona in the morning to a welcome that was very emotional for me and everybody else. More than a million Catalans lined the way on the journey from the airport into the city. Almost anyone who could walk was out there. A journey that would normally take 15 to 20 minutes was stretched to nearly six hours. Women pushed their babies up to the coach windows, old ladies prayed, young men, old men, children, they were all thanking us. To generate that degree of worship was humbling. We were the champions, we had put Real Madrid in their place and for these people we could do no wrong.

So much of what happened on that remarkable homecoming is a blur to me. We made it to the mayor's reception, and there were more embraces and handshakes. After it was all done, we returned to my apartment for a private celebration. Nancy had come over to join in, but Tracey and my dad were stuck in England. There had been a lot of interest in England over an Englishman winning the Spanish title, and my dad spent days giving interviews inside his pub. He loved it.

There was a formal dinner at a later date where we were presented with our winner's medals and I received a gold stud from President Nuñez which featured the club crest and had a diamond set in the middle. I still have it in a safe place.

The return of the title meant the Catalans could now surely forget all thoughts of persecution and bias against them from officials. The days of paranoia must be over. Even if their fears had ever been true, we had proved we could beat our perceived enemies. I am not averse to conspiracy theories, but that was one I did not subscribe to.

With our La Liga triumph came increased expectation. There was never any question of us relaxing as a group, but having tasted long-awaited success, everybody had their eyes on more and more, with the European Cup now *the* target. It had to be an incentive to us all. We worked pre-season as we had done 12 months before. I planned for us to start not as we finished, but as we had begun the campaign just won. All was well inside the club and I looked forward to my regular meetings with Señor Nuñez. I was taken by surprise on one occasion when he said that he had bought me a present. 'That's kind,' I said. 'What is it?'

It turned out to be a who not a what. 'I have bought you a striker from Zaragoza,' he said.

The signing was Raúl Amarilla, a Paraguayan, a thoroughly good professional and a first-class striker, but he was not what I wanted for my team set-up. 'Señor Nuñez,' I said, 'in future I will buy my own presents, if you don't mind.' He laughed. My agreement over signing players was clear. I would pick the players and I would choose who we bought. I had been warned that if the president believed he could find players and force them on his manager, it would weaken my influence and power over all my players.

Señor Nuñez was trying to be helpful and I also think he was in some way trying to be helpful also to the smaller club. I must say that had Nuñez bought me Hugo Sanchez to go with Steve Archibald, he would have received a different response, but there was no possibility of us being able to afford the Mexican, who signed for Real Madrid that summer. I still had no regrets over choosing Steve a year earlier, though I had studied Hugo's style and importance while he'd been at Atlético Madrid. Before we took on Real that season, Steve asked me what Sanchez did that made him so special.

'You're going to find it difficult to believe,' I began to explain to him. 'But at a corner he will run in, spin round the back, the kicker will knock it over the top and Sanchez will hit an overhead kick when not facing the goal. There is every chance he will score. He has done that on quite a few occasions.'

'You are having a laugh,' Steve said.

'No way, he will try it.'

The game started and Real soon had a corner. As predicted, Sanchez spun round and in an instant directed an overhead kick against our post. Frame by frame he did what I had watched him do so often in the videos I had studied. Steve said afterwards that at least he had known what to expect, even if he had been unable to do anything about it.

My life became even more hectic. I had been able to move around the city without too many people recognising me, but now it was never going to be the same for me again. I didn't have a problem with harassment. They would say hello, ask how you were and carry on walking. I was also sensible enough to realise that no matter what I did, they would eventually become fed up with me and it would all end in the sack. Very few are allowed the time Alex Ferguson was given at the beginning of his career at Old Trafford, or given the chance to rebuild the club without picking up any trophies, as Arsène Wenger has been doing at Arsenal. I went into the job with both eyes wide open, but determined to make as much of a success of the job as I could. The longer I was involved, the more I wanted to ensure that when my time came I would at least leave behind some sort of worthwhile legacy.

I hoped that the European Cup could provide the answer in 1985-86. For all their Catalan pride, there was open resentment that they were very much second best to Real Madrid, especially in Europe's premier competition. Barcelona had never won it up to the time I arrived. They had been finalists once, losing to Benfica in 1961, and had won both the European Cup-Winners' Cup and the Fairs Cup, but never the European Cup. When you compare that with the greater success of Real, who had been the pacesetters of the competition, winning it for the first five years of its existence playing breathtaking football, it was a void I realised I would be expected to fill. I will rephrase that; they hoped I might come up with the answer. Past failures destroyed previous incumbents, such as World Cup winner César Menotti and Helenio Herrera, the Argentine coach who gave the world the defensive *catenaccio* system. The first manager to present the Camp Nou with 'the cup with big ears' could surely pick the place for his statue.

My second season did not go as smoothly as I had planned. It wasn't bad, but disappointing after what we had achieved during my first year, and it was eventually dominated by our European campaign. Sadly the season was to coincide with the totally unacceptable behaviour of Schuster. The German's form was in and out, and perhaps as a result he became a pain. His poor attitude was to prove crucial.

There were problems, too, of a much different sort for someone who had been such a wonderful player for me in the previous season. Poor Rojo sustained a knee injury which kept him out of the side. He thought he was on the sidelines because I had finished with him and became upset with me. However, I had nothing but good thoughts about him. He fitted our system like a glove, and was one of our key players, but there was no way I could go against the medical advice that he shouldn't play. He would subsequently face a tragedy far worse than not playing as a regular when his daughter was killed in an air crash.

We finished second in La Liga but were a long way behind Real Madrid, who had spent big, bringing in others as well as Sanchez. Instead we focused on the European Cup. In the first round we saw off Sparta Prague, but on the away-goals ruling. Porto came next and we played well enough at the Camp Nou to take a two-goal lead into the return, thanks to goals from Marcos and Schuster. We looked settled in Porto, until they scored twice to level the aggregate score, only for Archibald to strike the goal that saw us through. Porto scored again, but once more we went through on away goals. These were grinding ties but we did what we had to do: we came out on top.

Holders Juventus were next in the quarter-finals, and that meant facing an Italian defensive system that had to be painstakingly unpicked. They were superbly efficient at stopping you and we had to be prepared for that, but also aware of their lethal counter-attacking. The mood in Barcelona was developing into what would soon become a frenzy of anticipation. The fans were more and more demanding as we progressed. I thought that was good for us: the more they demand, the more the team has to stretch themselves. The media was whipping it up as the event of the season.

The only person who didn't give a damn for the game, or certainly gave that impression, was Schuster. He asked to be transferred prior to the tie. Unbelievable but true. His attitude was intolerable, but I had to find a way of consoling him, as he was such a talent. It is no exaggeration to say we needed him and his formidable self-esteem. I had nothing against him and was anxious to solve the problem. I could enjoy his company and thought we understood each other, but I was less than sympathetic at his timing in demanding a transfer. It would have been acceptable only if Schuster had serious family reasons he could no longer face. Wouldn't a true professional have wanted to be part of a major European tie that offered a face-to-face with Juve's top player Michel Platini? You would think so, but this was an occasion when his shallow, selfish quality – the one flaw in a supremely talented footballer – surfaced. He did not appear to give a damn about anything or anybody other than himself and, as I would learn, his wife.

We met and I said: 'You want out? What are you talking about?

We've got the quarter-finals in a couple of weeks against Juventus. You can't do that.'

'Well, I'm not happy.'

'At the moment, you can't go. But I'll do a deal with you: I promise you that I'll let you go at the end of the season. See this season out and we'll sort something out.'

He was in a mood and not for compromise, insisting that he was not happy. I was genuinely trying to find a solution. It was my role as coach to ensure my club has the best players available for every match, whether I like them or not. If there are problems they have to be solved in favour of the club, provided the player is under contract.

'Look, I'll tell you what to do, you can play ... Let's get this game behind us first.'

So, finally he agreed to play, while I confirmed I would make certain I'd let him go at the end of the season. I would even put it in writing, and he accepted our deal before heading home. The next day he knocked on my door again.

'I want to leave. I want to leave straightaway.' I was sure he had been tapped up, so I said to him: 'Well, Bernd, I don't understand it. We had a talk yesterday, quite a long chat, and I eventually said I'd let you go.'

'Yes.'

'Well, there's only one thing's happened, Bernd. You went home and you spoke to your wife.' We all knew his wife played a key part in his decision-making. She was older and appeared to have a big influence on him. I felt sure his wife had told him he had to leave.

'Bernd,' I said, 'if you've got trouble at home over this, and it is obvious she calls the shots, why not send your wife in?'

'What? You won't mind?'

'No, no, I don't mind. That's okay. Send your wife in. Tell her to come in after training.'

Now, I had a tiny manager's office in this huge subterranean area big enough to land a jumbo on, close to the dressing rooms and an area where the players used to play head tennis. When she came in after training, she walked through the place where all the boys were getting undressed, and I could see her having a little look at who are the big boys and who's not. It was ridiculous. She eventually swept into my office and I asked her what the problem was.

'Bernd's not happy.'

'Yes, but he was happy a couple of days ago and now he is not. Why?'

She spoke some English and explained it to me, coming up with a list of issues, but I told her it was surely impossible to be so unsettled with a club before a European Cup quarter-final. They had to see it from other people's point of view. I added: 'We've got the most important game in this club's history and it could go on from there to a final. I will guarantee you, as I have guaranteed Bernd, that he can leave after it's over.' She wasn't happy, but he stayed although he seemed very grudging with it.

We had to win and did so on 5 March 1986 at the Camp Nou, despite being without the injured Schuster, Rojo and Caldere in midfield, or Marcos and Clos up front. To make matters worse, Carrasco was injured in the warm-up and that had to be dealt with calmly. He started the tie but was subbed just after the interval, when I replaced him and Esteban Vigo Benitez in a double substitution with Manolo and Jose Moratalla. Julio Alberto scored the only goal of the first meeting eight minutes from time in front of a 120,000 crowd close to collective hysteria.

We had the narrowest of leads and were prepared for a desperate night at the Stadio Comunale two weeks later in Turin. Steve Archibald, who a year earlier was dismissed by Schuster as a passenger, gave us the lead after the half hour with a goal which I dared to hope would be the tie-winner and which certainly reduced the crowd to silence. The richly talented and stylish footballer Platini equalised before half time to leave things back in the balance. We stayed cool, we knew what we had to do and that saw us through, despite the fact that Schuster once more did not play, because he was still not fit enough. Fortunately, he recovered in time to play in both our semi-final ties against Gothenburg.

While I was in Turin I was approached by Gianni Agnelli, Juve owner and the family boss of Fiat. He asked if I would consider joining them as manager/coach. I kept that approach at the back of my mind as I wondered if my future might lie in that direction. We returned from Italy to the sort of praise you enjoy reading and watching and listening to.

Barcelona was by now in the throes of mass excitement bordering on frenzy. Who were the Swedes of Gothenburg to stand in our way, was the general opinion. The final looked a certainty to some, though not to me or Allan as we both knew the pitfalls, as the Swedes are an athletic nation and have always presented the world with good footballers. We watched them to work out the problems they could cause us. We recognised you do not reach the semi-final of Europe's premier club competition just by being lucky. They were there on merit. To get past them we would need players of the highest quality on form and knowing their role. It was up to me to tell them what their role would be.

However, there was always a danger among Spanish players that they will want to perform as individuals rather than be part of a team. If we were to lose our team ethic, and turn back to being individuals, we could be in trouble. I am not saying that did happen in the first leg, but even with Schuster back in the side we lost 3-0. It was a considerable deficit to recover from and we could only do it as a team.

To anyone who has never watched a match at the Camp Nou, I recommend they find a ticket for a major European night, or when

Real are in town, when it is full of anticipation and prepare to be amazed by one of the great sporting occasions. The second leg was one of those occasions. I knew it would be a full house and there was no way we would be able to stop Gothenburg from attacking us or to stem the cries from our fans for us to attack.

I didn't want our players getting caught up in the emotion of it all, as I knew we had 90 minutes to score three goals, which was plenty of time, so I changed our normal preparations. The players expected us to concentrate on shooting practice, but we didn't do any. After a couple of days of this, it got back to me that the players had been asking one another why they were not doing any shooting practice. If they had asked me directly, I would have replied: if you can't shoot and score now you never will, so what's the point of spending three or four days working on that aspect of the game? Now was the time to make sure we prepared our defence, as we couldn't afford to concede otherwise we would have to score five goals to go through.

I had worked the players day after day in training to prepare for any points of the tie when we would be exposed, as we would be. We trained with five attackers against four defenders, or four against three and so on. I emphasised to our midfield players that they would have to get back quickly when Gothenburg attacked. We needed to score goals, but at the same time we had to protect ourselves. We would have to defend well, but not through weight of numbers as that would cut our attacking options.

We also had a couple of La Liga matches in which to practise these new tactics, which I would also use later on with England. On that night against Gothenburg, the crowd was pushing us to attack for that first goal, as I knew they would, but after eight minutes, it was the Swedes who broke away, shot and hit the post. They claimed Michael Andersson had followed through to touch the ball over the line, but our keeper Urruti persuaded the referee to check with his assistant and it was rightly disallowed as being out of play. If they had scored we really would have been in trouble.

From then on we dominated proceedings. When we pushed up we were compact, the players knew exactly what they had to do, with our midfield always recovering to help out in defence. After 60 minutes, when we were still only 1-0 up, I subbed Bernd, but in the last half-hour our patience finally wore them down, as we got to 3-0, with all three scored by the experienced Pichi Alonso. There were no more goals scored in extra time, so it went to penalties, which we won 5-2. At the end the players hoisted me high in what they saw a triumphant gesture. As I sat aloft, I looked down and into the face of an exultant ball boy. I recognised him instantly – it was the young Pep Guardiola. Only the best ball boys were good enough at FC Barcelona.

We had made the European Cup final, where we would face Steaua Bucharest, who had beaten Anderlecht. There were so many dangers to us, but the biggest was complacency, or rather a false sense of superiority about meeting a Romanian team. I kept hearing it was a final made for us, the assumption being that it was all but over, and we simply had to turn up to win. It was both stupid and disrespectful. If the players thought that way we would sink. Playing the Romanian champions may have looked better for us than facing a Milan side or Bayern Munich, and it may have appeared to be to our further advantage that we would be playing the final on Spanish soil in Seville, but I saw it differently.

Steaua had competed exceptionally well to reach this point and they would be hugely motivated by having the chance to become the first Romanian side to win the European Cup. That would be their inspiration. If anything the venue, the Estadio Ramón Sánchez Pizjuán, added to the pressure on us, because we had the local advantage.

The match itself was a major disappointment. They defended in depth, and I do not blame them for that. Too many of my players didn't turn up. Steve Archibald had an injury but played when perhaps it would have been better had he not. I thought Schuster was a disgrace as he didn't appear to put a bit of effort into it. Even now, all these years later, I still rage inwardly when I think of his contribution that day. How can a player endowed with his talent not rise to the occasion of a European Cup final with the world looking on? His performance would not have been worse if we had sent him out on crutches.

We had made it to Seville with him in a mood, Archibald carrying an injury and Rojo not fit. In the circumstances, it was vital to get the German on our side and in the right frame of mind. I was trying to get him going and he seemed comfortable enough in training, so I selected him. I thought to myself that at least he could take a penalty if it went that far, but then I began to worry about us not making it to extra time because Steaua were stretching us, and he seemed to be treading water. I felt we would struggle to make it to a shootout, so I took him off after 85 minutes.

It might have been a game to forget, but it was still there to be won and the prize was the biggest on offer in European football. A penalty shootout is not so much player v goalkeeper as man v fear. It is about players standing up to their fears and overcoming them. There are any number of ways to score from the spot, but score you must. My players that day lost it.

I have never actually replayed the ending, but it is seared in my memory. The Romanians took the first kick and missed. That was us in the driving seat. Alexanco, who had scored in the shootout against the Swedes, placed the ball, stood back, shot and missed. Oh my God! It was Steaua's turn. They missed. We were being looked after from above. Pedraza, who like Alexanco had scored in the previous shootout, picked up the ball, placed it, paced back and missed. I was helpless. There is nothing a coach can do in these circumstances.

Bucharest scored their next two penalties, and when Pichi Alonso and Marcos both missed I had to walk away with as much dignity as I could muster. If we had become the first Barcelona side to lift the European Cup we would have been Catalan heroes, all of us who had taken part. The players failed to grasp that chance to make history and denied themselves the one and only opportunity they would get. I despaired.

Schuster played one last trick on the club, as his team-mates went through the intensity of the remaining minutes, the anxiety of extra time and then the penalty shootout. I had specifically warned them that all should be available in the dressing room until the anti-drugs people had decided who they would test. I made it clear that should any players singled out for the test not be available, we would automatically be banned from next season's European Cup, which I assume applied to all of UEFA's competitions. That is why I was enraged when I found out that he had got dressed and left the stadium.

Looking back now, I still feel Schuster's attitude reduced our chances. He abandoned his responsibility. He was highly talented and could be a nice man one-to-one, intelligent and a good talker. I don't know why he did so little to help us. Perhaps he was unsettled by his family situation and determined to be transferred. I felt sure that something had got to him, but he should not have allowed it to affect so many other people. When next we met, he had the audacity to repeat his demand to leave. I replied: 'Why should I help? You reneged on our deal. You should have stayed if needed for the drug test. Why not? I spoke to you; I spoke to your wife. We had an agreement. You have messed it up. Anyway, how did you know you wouldn't be tested? You didn't have a clue.'

In my mind there was only one appropriate punishment: I suspended him for the length of time we would have been banned by

UEFA if he had been named for a drug test – one whole year. I don't know if a player has ever been banned for as long as I banned Bernd. He trained every day of his suspension in my third season, and to his credit he trained well, but I never played him. He would still come over to ask for something or other, like a bit of time to take his children to the hospital or whether he could have an early day. We did not talk directly and Graham was the go-between, with any message or request coming via Graham. It didn't do much for us having him out of action, because we could have done with him, but I couldn't let it go, so we carried on regardless. When we eventually parted company, as I left he shook my hand and said: 'It was great being here.' That was a fine gesture, but I wish he had felt that way in Seville.

The board had arranged a reception for after the final. It wasn't exactly a bundle of laughs, as we were all unhappy and sickened by the experience. When we approached the banqueting area at our hotel, we had to pass a large cake they had made for us with the message in icing: 'To the winners.' It remained uncut. There was no hiding place. It was the president, the board and the fans who had my deepest sympathy that evening.

If there was disappointment and criticism after the Seville business, then I was prepared to face it head on. I was enjoying the job immensely, bar the obvious setback. The hurt of Seville turned to tragedy over the years. Urruti, a marvellous character, was killed in a car crash and Angel Pedraza, who missed one of our penalties, through an illness that crept up on him and found him defenceless. Both my former players were ridiculously young at 48 years when they died.

My excellent working relationship with President Nuñez and Señor Gaspart continued, and the players gave the impression through the majority of their performances they believed we were moving in the right direction. I made several new signings prior to the 1986-87 season, as I hoped we could again challenge for the title. I brought in goalkeeper Andoni Zubizarreta and midfielder Roberto, both Spanish internationals.

I had spoken to the president about our needs for the season ahead and that involved a new goalkeeper. Urruti was a terrific member of our squad and truly excellent goalkeeper, but time was against him. Nuñez and Señor Gaspart moved straight in for Andoni Zubizarreta, who joined us in a record-breaking deal for a keeper of £1.4 million from Athletic Bilbao. Neither his signing nor Roberto's from Valencia were considered major. Only foreign signings were described as that, but both played a big part in the future after me. Zubi broke every record possible and is now FC Barcelona's Sports Director.

I also returned to England to buy Gary Lineker from Everton for £2.75 million and Mark Hughes for £2 million from Manchester United. They were exact opposites. Gary was 25 years old and already a major player. He had been part of England's World Cup campaign in Mexico and ended up as the tournament's top scorer, winning the Golden Boot award. He took the move to Barcelona in his stride. There are players who blend easily into a new life, coping with a new culture and being determined to learn the language and integrate. It means they can concentrate on their football without being constantly homesick and wondering where they can find a restaurant that serves a full English breakfast with tomato sauce.

Our early overseas transfer pioneers, such as Denis Law and Jimmy Greaves, found the experience difficult in the 1960s when they moved to Italy, yet John Charles revelled in it. Ian Rush was another, like Denis and Jimmy, who couldn't cope and returned home. Sadly, Mark was a big disappointment. He was only 22, and I think his age and a certain immaturity were responsible for his lacklustre performances as much as anything. His physical style of play also caused problems, as he was unable to use his robust approach in the same way he could in England.

He feared nobody and that included the Butcher of Bilbao, Goikoetxea, who had made his terrible mark on both Maradona and Schuster. When he ran up against Mark and tried to intimidate him, he quickly learned that here was a player best left alone. Mark tamed him the first time they came toe to toe. Some players get away with a highly physical game all the time, but some don't. Mark would rarely do other than defend himself, but the match officials saw his name before an incident and kept pulling him up and showing him the yellow card. Mark never moaned once to me, but that was influencing his game. It got so distressing for him, I had to drop him. Steve Archibald was more than ready for a return. He had been in the reserves since the arrival of the new signings because we could play only two foreigners.

Hughes's inability to make an impression placed a question mark on my judgement. The Welshman, a gem of a man, was as powerful a player as I have worked with. He was a naturally quiet lad who took it and got on with it, until the decision was made to loan him out to Bayern Munich. Eventually, he returned to Manchester United where his ability continued to develop. In 1991, he gave Barcelona his response when he scored twice against them in the European Cup-Winners' Cup final. The Barcelona board had eventually seen Mark at his best just when they least wanted to.

Gary scored goals and he did that better and more consistently than 99 per cent of his fellow strikers and had proved that in Mexico. It took him time to find his game and when he was doing that Mark took an awful lot of the pressure on his behalf, but once Gary got going, he was hard to stop. In his first season, he scored 21 goals without checking his stride. He was a remarkable player and very single-minded. Gary thought about everything he did during a match. He nearly always found the target and was always intent on making the goalkeeper work. I always said to my strikers: 'Hit the target, do not shoot over the bar because there is no one there to deal with it. If you shoot and it goes wide, either left or right, there may just be a chance of someone coming in on it.' I would tell them to be considered in attack, always to give themselves a chance of changing direction to allow for the movement of the goalkeeper, as when a player is flat out, there is only one way he can go. Gary worked that way.

His goals came from inside the six-yard box with hardly any variation. If the keeper parried the ball, he would often be there to pick up the rebound. For corners, he would go to the near post and get in front of the defender to score. If I compared his style with that of Alan Shearer, then Alan would be at the far post to climb above the centre-half. Alan scored from a variety of positions, long and short; not Gary, who was a prowler in the box. He never worried about how simple the strike was, so long as it was a goal. It was the secret to his prolific record. Gary made few mistakes, but the biggest was the opportunity he had, in a friendly against Brazil at Wembley, to equal Sir Bobby Charlton's 49 goals for England. Graham Taylor was manager and this was prior to the 1992 European Championship finals. England were awarded a penalty, and Gary stepped up to take it. The record would be equalled, or so we thought. What did he do? He was far too clever and tried to chip Branco, the goalkeeper, who saved it. I never asked him to be clever.

Zubi was on the receiving end of one of Gary's more memorable goalscoring nights when he caused a considerable stir in Spain by scoring all four of England's goals in a 4-2 win midway through the 1986-87 season. In doing so, he was not only biting the hand of the country paying him a not inconsiderable salary at Barça, but also doing it against his club and Spain's number one goalkeeper Zubizarreta. Gary recalled that when he came face to face with Zubi in the dressing room area after the match, they looked at each other, Zubi shook his head and said: 'Fucking 'ell, Gary.' Zubi must have picked up some Anglo-Saxon phrases in the short few months since he had joined us.

We did not have as good a season as I expected in 1986-87. Losing the European Cup the way we did had an effect on team morale. There was certain to be a backlash from what was a bitterly disappointing experience. We had our new signings, and that should have helped, but we particularly missed the influence of little Rojo. We were trailing in La Liga and were not going to win the title. There was one particularly poor match that ended with the team desperate and upset. By contrast, Gary bounced into the dressing room all smiles, looked around and shouted: 'Come on, cheer up! It's not the end of the world.'

I rounded on him: 'It might not be the end for you, Gary, but maybe it is for them. Why don't you shut it?' That was a prime example of how he could be, as part of his character. Gary found Johan Cruyff, who would eventually succeed me, far less than sympathetic towards him. When he came in, Johan changed the way Barcelona played. He lined up with one striker, Julio Salinas, who was big, strong and excellent in the air, and two wide players. This meant there was no place for Lineker, unless he played wide and that is what Cruyff asked him to do.

When the end came for me, it was quick. It has been said Hughes's lack of form weakened me in the eyes of the fans and the directors. Maybe. I had intended to leave when my contract expired after three years, as Nancy and Tracey had seen much less of me than I would have wanted, and I thought it was time to return home. I had meetings with the two senior men, Nuñez and Gaspart, and explained that to them. They persuaded me to stay for an extra year, but I was doubtful and told them I did not think it was the right thing to do.

We got off to a bad start in 1987-88 – one win in the first five matches – and the crowd began to demand a change at the top. Señor Nuñez asked me what I thought. I said it was not going well, it did not look as if our form was going to improve quickly and it would be best if I left. It was amicable. I used to meet the president on a Monday, and on this occasion said to him: 'If you are concerned about this, I have had three wonderful years and I do want to go back to England.'

That was it. I'd had the thrill of a lifetime, and I still have great contacts at the club. There was never any animosity between me and the senior members of the club hierarchy, or ever with any of my players, including Maradona. The only serious disciplinary problem I had to deal with was Schuster. The rest of us were there for each other. I take pride in being considered by some as modern Barcelona's enabler and appreciate the Catalans who say I started the ball rolling towards a new era. But I take no credit for the great teams and huge success of those who succeeded me as coach. I had my time and they would have theirs. When you grow to love a city and its people and its football, even the bad times are good. That is how I remember Barcelona.

I am pleased to say that the goodwill has survived the years. When Barcelona were in London for the Champions League final against Manchester United in May 2011, I was at Wembley as a guest. It was a magnificent performance from Barcelona, who hit the very peak of greatness. They were literally unplayable and, for all United's efforts, it was obvious there was nothing they could do to contain them. To do it on such an occasion could not have been more satisfying for their coach, Pep Guardiola. United lost 3-1 and it could have been more, such was the gulf between the two.

On that occasion, a number of people from the club paid me the highest compliment possible when they said I was the coach who established their 'pressing game'. It wasn't solely me, of course; Allan was there, too. I feel good about being told by them that they thought I played my bit, before the Dutch influence of Cruyff, Louis van Gaal and Frank Rijkaard and before them Luis Aragonés, who took charge immediately I left and went on to manage Spain and died at the age of 75 years in February 2014.

So yes, when we talk about legacies, it would be nice to think that title of 1984-85, coming after so many barren years, helped Barça on their road to recovery and stopped the domination of Real Madrid. They have progressed marvellously since then, and I am so fond of that part of Spain – and particularly that great metropolis – that I would love to think I had indeed put down a marker for them.

But now, I was coming back to England, ready to start a new chapter in my career and be closer to my girls, Nancy and Tracey, and my mum and dad.

# 13

# MANAGING GAZZA

ON BALANCE, when I consider my five years as manager, coach, chief executive and 50 per cent owner of Tottenham Hotspur FC, there is more good than bad to reflect on. That may be difficult to believe when I remember the animosity that eventually created an atmosphere more toxic than I have experienced inside any football club. However, what we achieved overshadows memories of the madness.

I would much rather recall the professional satisfaction of building two outstanding teams: the first was inspired by Paul Gascoigne's flowing football and Gary Lineker's prolific goalscoring, which took us to third in the league, a feat that has yet to be beaten by any Tottenham team since. That same team went on to win the FA Cup in one of the most dramatic and (for Gazza) traumatic of Wembley finals. The second team I built was led by the intuition and timing of Teddy Sheringham plus the skill and marathon-runner stamina of Darren Anderton. I am certain that side could have gone on to be champions by the mid-1990s.

I also look back with pleasure at having worked with so many other wonderfully talented footballers we either bought or developed: Chris Waddle (who was my predecessor David Pleat's key signing), Paul Stewart, Erik Thorstvedt, Nayim, David Howells, Vinny Samways, Sol Campbell, Pat van den Hauwe, Gary Mabbutt, Paul Allen, Justin Edinburgh and Dean Austin. The list is not endless, but it is certainly substantial. These players were what mattered, not the controversies of the boardroom and the never-ending talk about money or the lack of it. It is far more consoling to remember those things than to dwell on the hassle, disruption and misery caused by Tottenham's massive debt and the acrimony created in trying to deal with it. It is a depressing thought that too many people in English football may remember only the rows and not what my players produced.

I have to admit to finding a touch of vindication in our success, after the disappointment I felt at not producing my best form during my years with the club as a player. Sadly, the club's progress came to a halt a step or two from the summit, which left me with a sense that there was still unfinished business.

However, the truth of the matter was that my time at Spurs became dominated by confrontations with the board, initially with Irving Scholar, who convinced me I had to become manager, and then with Alan Sugar, my eventual partner. I should have recognised my partnership with Sugar was doomed to fail, yet I believe that had we managed to come to terms with each other's temperament and settled our differences, the title would have returned to Spurs. Of that I am certain. I do not wish to dwell on my rows with both men, but I cannot ignore them and they were a major factor in my story at Spurs between 1987 and my sacking as CEO by Sugar in 1993. Nor can I ignore the accusations and falsehoods from outsiders that were aimed at me and eventually threatened to engulf me. I could take the barbs, but my family had to live with me being vilified as the stereotype tricky cockney.

When I left Barcelona in late September 1987, Yvette and I decided to have a year off so we could travel, rest and I could recharge my batteries. I also wanted to spend more time with my daughters after the peculiar rigours of managing Barcelona. Our first stop was Florida, but within five days of arriving there I was contacted by Irving Scholar, the up-front, urbane chairman of Spurs. He had been given my phone number by the football agent Dennis Roach, a neighbour of ours in West London, who was trying to sort out a deal to stage a Frank Bruno–Joe Bugner fight at White Hart Lane. Scholar, a wealthy property developer in his day job, was ready to fly out to speak to me and present his offer.

I had turned down a firm and very lucrative invite to join Juventus and a similar one from Roma. Arsenal had also approached me again, after the departure of Don Howe, but for the second time I turned them down. With my Spurs connections, I felt it would have been impossible for me to accept the job. However, all three were enticing proposals. They made me feel good, confident that what we had done at Barça was recognised outside Spain.

It was the lure of returning to a former club, I guess, which turned my head and made me accept Irving's offer to join him at Tottenham. Yet again in my career, it had nothing to do with money. Irving's offer was half of what I had been paid at Barcelona and far less than the other ones. Irving is persuasive and very charming, but it was the prospects the job offered, not his charm, that impressed me. He talked enthusiastically about his ambitions for the club and there was no doubting his sincerity. Irving was a man who liked to be associated with big names. He was also obsessed with football trivia, often driving me to distraction with irritating questions only fellow enthusiasts would be able to answer. But there was no denying that he wanted his club to be the best and I have no doubt he would have competed relentlessly to sign the greatest footballers, if his finances had allowed. Even when the financial pressures grew, and we became less close and then icily distant, his ambition for Tottenham was genuine. Irving was like various people you meet in football – he would talk endlessly about football, which clearly was his passion, but without the intimate knowledge of a coach.

As soon as Irving made his move to bring me in, I researched as much as I could about the club. I gave myself time to do this, and we agreed I would postpone my arrival until the beginning of December, though events brought that date forward. I wanted to know if they had the money to be serious players in the transfer market. He told me I would have control of our transfer policy and said that there would be a fund of £4 million to bring in new recruits, as long as half of it was raised through selling players. I analysed the players in the squad and tried to understand who were the most influential figures at the club. At first assessment, the players looked better than good, though sadly a number of the best ones were not going to be mine. I hadn't realised, and was not told, that Tottenham was in the throes of a player sale and was struggling financially. They were running out of pots to pee in, and the funds that were supposedly on offer never fully materialised.

I studied hours of videotapes in the final few days of our 'long' break in the West Palm Beach Resort unaware of the extent of the crisis. I watched how Tottenham lost the FA Cup final to Coventry City in the previous May, which taught me a lot, not least how very good players can blow it. You can learn as much, if not more, from a defeat as from a victory.

What I had not anticipated was that most of the quality players in that final had been given assurances they could leave or were coming to the end of their careers. Glenn Hoddle had already gone to Monaco, while Richard Gough had just returned to Scotland with Rangers for a record fee between the two countries of £1.5

million. The Argentine world champion Ossie Ardiles was on the way out, his playing career all but over at 35. Ray Clemence's Achilles' was shredded badly enough to make him a doubt to continue with his career. At 39, he would join our coaching staff instead. Clive Allen, who played for me at QPR and Crystal Palace, took his goals to Bordeaux in the summer after I joined. His fellow England star Steve Hodge would also be on his way that summer, to Nottingham Forest, following an agreement made between him and my predecessor, David Pleat.

The players I was left with were good but not gold, and the departures meant the dressing room had lost some of its most influential characters. Having started the season well, things had begun to fall apart and when I eventually took charge they had gone seven games without a win. I knew I had to create a survival spirit as I'd realised that relegation was a very real possibility. The short-term target was simple: stay up. If we could survive my first season back, we would then have to find a way of living up to the good football Spurs supporters had been used to through the decades. My first recruit was Allan Harris, who joined as my assistant, exactly the role he had at Barcelona, and between us we set out a plan for what remained of the season.

We worked hard on the playing side and were able to bring in Terry Fenwick and Paul Walsh. They were made of the right stuff – tough and experienced men. Paul's transfer from Liverpool was not a problem. He would be ideal for us. Irving wasn't keen on the signing of Terry from QPR, as he wanted bigger names on board, not those he considered less than glamorous. I thought Terry's England status would have been good enough to make Irving change his mind, but it took time for me to persuade him Terry was what I wanted and would give me vital strength in defence. But essentially there was no more money for new players, at least for the moment.

For all Irving's enthusiasm and his astuteness as a businessman, he sometimes appeared weak to me and seemed all too willing to make his views widely known if we disagreed. But he was in charge of a football club where too little money was going into our reserves. Despite the financial pressures, which had forced the sale of some players, he made sure we initially kept hold of one big star: Chris Waddle. Having Chris to work with was an invaluable asset, but we would need a number of other high-quality signings if we were to move up the table. I doubted we would have the cash to buy unless we sold, which would have been one step forward and who knows how many back.

My first match was against Liverpool at home in front of a full White Hart Lane at the end of November 1987. Hodge was sent off very early in the match, which did not help my mood, and we went on to lose 2-0. It was obvious there was considerable work to be done and that was confirmed when we lost to Charlton in our next match. It was going to be a battling season and I kept saying we would get out of it, if for no other reason than we simply had to. It was down to us.

Having worked with the supremely talented and highly technical footballers of Spain, it came as a shock to realise just how far below that standard were the skills of the players I was now coaching. It was not their fault, but a great deal to do with the English system that stopped good coaches from being able to work with players before the bad habits were formed. I could not make that my problem. What I had to do was find ways of exploiting the commitment we had in bundles.

Thankfully Chris Waddle was available to us. We know every player who gives 100 per cent is a worthy member of the team, but you also need others with exceptional talent and game-changing ability. They win matches for you. Chris came into that category. He was a provider but there were no restrictions on where he went or what he did. I would let him roam where his instinct took him; to the right, the left, the centre. It was up to him and it worked. Chris was in majestic form that first season. Would we have survived without him? Possibly, but he was the example to the rest of the squad; he gave us all hope. With his presence we would progress if we could find the right players to place around him. We owed him that. We finished 13th, which was a relief and the best outcome I could have wished for.

At this point of my time at Spurs, I would not say I was a disinterested spectator of boardroom anxiety, but my responsibility was to produce a team that would be successful and capable of recovering our position at the top of the English game. The realisation we were as good as broke, with the banks watching our every move, made me constantly on alert. When I joined, I had asked Irving for a precise job specification: was I to be head coach, as I had been at Barça, or a manager with the extra responsibilities that goes with the role? 'You will be our manager,' was his reply. A short time into the job and you could have fooled me. From the outset, Irving did not seem to want me in the boardroom.

A number of meetings took place before I was invited to attend, and even then I was asked to leave when the discussion got round to finance, though perhaps the reason for that was that he did not want me to know the state of the club's finances. It would not have made pleasant listening, but it would not have prompted me to walk out of the club now I was in charge of team matters. Even though not normally on the board himself, a manager would expect to be involved in regular board sub-committees and to be called to full board meetings to explain team matters or called in to discuss what he thought was an important matter to the club. Obviously, when I became a 50 per cent owner with Alan Sugar, I attended meetings as a director.

On the plus side, and this is what attracted me, the club had an enviable tradition, some excellent players and fantastic support, even if they did not take any prisoners if they were unhappy with the players for whatever reason. But all that was irrelevant unless we could bring in some quality signings and find the money to buy them. If I had realised how bad the situation was, I probably would not have accepted the job.

The club's credit rating must still have been good enough, as somehow Irving found the money to buy some players for my second season, 1988-89, but only if we sold. As a consequence, Clive Allen, Nico Claesen, Steve Hodge, Johnny Metgod and a young Neil Ruddock were moved on during the summer, but in came two spectacular signings: Paul Gascoigne joined us for a record fee of around £2 million from Newcastle, while Paul Stewart came from Manchester City for £1.7 million. The debts might have been piling up, but at least we had spent wisely on real talent, and in Gazza we had acquired a genius.

He had turned down Manchester United and Liverpool to join us after listening to his fellow Geordie, friend and mentor Chris Waddle. The best judges, including Geordie idols such as Jackie Milburn, were agreed in their assessment that Gazza was the finest young English talent any of them could remember. Chris took the line of least resistance with Paul; he told him how we would look after him, what a great club we were, and how he had to forget what he had probably been reading in the press about us and our rowing board. Come and join us was his message. Gazza only ever wanted to be around people who made him feel good and comfortable and who liked him.

The season was a success when compared with the one before. The effort we had put in and the quality introduced by our two new players was bound to be in our favour. They understood what I wanted from them. I told our team that, more than anything else, they had to enjoy what they were doing, not be scared of facing up to a crowd or making mistakes; be aware of the players around them, use the ball, think smart, be confident. They had to know how good they were, which was not a problem for one or two players who thought they were much better than I did. The application of these basics, coupled with Chris's wonderfully intelligent football, earned us results. It didn't happen immediately, as after ten games we were bottom with just one win, but soon the results began to improve.

Mid-season we found the wherewithal to buy Erik Thorstvedt from IFK Gothenburg, for £400,000. Erik was to prove equal to our demands for a top goalkeeper and did so way into the 1990s. He got off to the worst possible start when he let one slip through on his televised debut at White Hart Lane. You could sense the crowd wondering if we had bought a dud, and the *Sun* saw the funny side labelling him 'ERIK THE UNREADY'. It was to improve for him. We'd also found another £100,000 to buy the Icelandic defender Gudni Bergsson from Valur, and like Erik he was to serve Spurs well.

That season, we won 15 league matches and drew 12 without beating Manchester United, Liverpool or Arsenal. Instead, we had good draws against Man U and Liverpool, though Arsenal did us home and away. We were building confidence, had formed a good team and finished in sixth place. It was a dramatic improvement in a short time. We let ourselves down in the FA Cup when we lost to Bradford City. It was a repeat of the shocking FA Cup defeat in my first season, when we were knocked out by Port Vale. Cup competitions can make fools of the best or the unwary, and there was no way we should have been turned over by either of these teams. It was the manner of the defeats which angered me – a lack of professionalism I would not tolerate or allow to develop.

It was a considerable loss to me when Allan Harris took the decision to strike out on his own. He was offered the manager's job with

Español, the club based on the outskirts of Barcelona and one we both knew well from our time there. He deserved the opportunity and, although I would miss his influence and experience, I was delighted for him. It turned out to be a fiasco. Almost as soon as he had returned to Spain, the president who signed him was forced out of the club and his successor wanted his own man, not Allan. He went on to be a successful pioneering manager in the Middle East, where he worked in Kuwait and Egypt. It was there a club victory cost another Briton his job – the opposing manager was the great Dave Mackay, who had himself turned to the east for work when it was far less fashionable than it is now.

I felt that we were building a new and better team, but I worried that the never-ending rumours about the club's financial position might affect the players. It was difficult to believe we would ever face the terrifying possibility of administration, but the warning was there and you can never be too big to avoid corporate collapse. As we have seen recently, an even bigger club, Glasgow Rangers, has had to fight for its existence, so it could easily have happened to us at that time. No one who is involved in a football club can dismiss boardroom troubles as an irrelevance and believe it has nothing to do with them; in truth it affects everybody.

Things were made worse when stories about our problems were leaked from inside the club to the national press. I have good friends in the media, but I have never volunteered stories to them or anyone else. I have always made that my strict policy since an early age. Yet at Tottenham stories were constantly finding their way to the national press. I was pretty certain who the source was, so when news about a player we had agreed to sell to another English club was leaked, I pointed out how wrong it was to leak transfer stories when a deal had been struck. I was told it was nothing to worry about, and that if we sneaked it out that a player was for sale then it would alert others and possibly push up the price.

I believed that way of working was disgraceful, and I did not like being associated with it.

I was all too aware that no matter what we did on the field, the board was close to pushing the panic alert. They were not the best of circumstances to go into the 1989-90 season. We still needed to compete in the transfer market, despite the club's precarious financial position. My priority was for a top striker, and I cast my mind back to the Camp Nou and Gary Lineker. He was open to a move, especially after Johan Cruyff's decision to play him out wide, a decision that neutered one of the world's top goalscorers. I flew over to Barcelona and they were happy to deal with their former coach and offload a player now more or less surplus to their requirements.

I thought it might also be the time to show an interest in a young Barça midfield player I had worked with. I had learned to admire the skill and dedication of Nayim, and he became part of the transfer package that cost us £2 million for both of them, with £600,000 as a down payment and the balance to be paid a year on. Even before Gary had kicked a ball for us, I knew we had signed the bargain of the season, while the acquisition of little Nayim was an added bonus.

In less than two seasons, we had risen from a relegation-threatened side to potential contenders, with more expected in the months ahead. The thought of Gary being fed by Chris Waddle and Gazza was as good as it gets for a coach. Sadly, it was to remain just that: a thought. Not long after the deal had been completed, Irving told me excitedly that Olympique Marseille had made contact and wanted to buy Chris. I did not want to sell, but Irving had to help reduce the club's overdraft. But even without Chris for the future, I still had to be pleased with our progress. We had improved because we had good players who knew exactly what was required of them and what I wanted from them. Their fitness was improved and that makes even the best players more effective. There was still the pain of selling Chris. It had to be done according to Irving and his board.

Bernard Tapie, Marseille's extraordinary owner, a mega-rich businessman, politician and personality in France, took control of the negotiations for his club. You couldn't make up characters like Tapie, who as time was to prove had no great respect for the law of his land. He was accused of match-fixing at Olympique and has since spent a short spell in a French jail having been convicted of corruption. I found him to be a gentle negotiator. His original offer for Chris was £2 million, which was pushed up to over £5 million if we included Paul Walsh. That part of the deal collapsed and we ended up with a British record fee of £4.5 million for Chris. It was a lot of cash, but it would have been better for the team (if not Tottenham Hotspur plc) had we been able to keep Chris. It wasn't to be and I had to get on with it.

I expected to be able to use much of the Waddle money for signings, but only around a third was allocated. There were two other much-needed buys available to me: Steve Sedgley, a fine young defender who had sat on the bench as a Coventry City sub during the club's FA Cup victory against Tottenham in 1987, plus Pat van den Hauwe. At Everton, Pat had earned a reputation for himself as a young buck difficult to handle off and on the field, but what interested me about Pat was his ability as a forceful defender, not his lust for life or talent for attracting trouble. He gave me 100 per cent on the field. There was the occasional problem with him, but nothing I could not cope with.

We had put together a team I believed was capable of pushing us up the league and potentially winning something, perhaps the League Cup or maybe even the FA Cup. However, the debts were still piling up, and Irving was not reacting well to my constant prodding for new signings. I looked at it differently, as a manager perhaps should. I reasoned that if new signings improved the team

and brought success to the club, then that would improve atten-
dances which would mean more money in the bank and therefore
more money to sign the best players.

We had worked for a good start and duffed our lines after winning our opening match against Luton. Three of our next four
games were defeats. Questions were being asked, but after that
shaky start we went on to play our way through the season. My
hopes for a decent cup run were ended when we were knocked out
of the FA Cup in the third round by Southampton and then from
the League Cup by Nottingham Forest. By the end of January, we
could (as all beaten cup managers say) concentrate on the league,
which we did, finishing with a fabulous run, winning eight of our
last ten matches. It left us delighted in third place, behind champions Liverpool and Aston Villa.

Gary Lineker easily paid off his transfer fee, though embarrassingly we took our time about paying what we owed Barcelona, who
were left to chase the balance. He scored 24 times in the league
and ended up as the First Division's top goalscorer. Gary knew
what he was worth and what he could do, and the single-minded-
ness I saw in him when we were both at Barcelona was what
continued to make him such an effective striker.

For us to finish where we did was the first highlight of my term
with the club. To sustain a league campaign is hugely satisfying to
everyone involved, but especially to the coach when players follow
instructions and make it work. And if the fans enjoy the way you
win, it can be doubly pleasing. We were not trying to emulate
former Tottenham teams as such, but we respected the tradition of
always trying to play football that would not only satisfy us as professionals but entertain and satisfy the expectations of our
supporters. It should be the meeting of minds on the pitch and off
it. Our aim was no more complicated than that. We would set ourselves out to cope with each game as it arose.

The challenge would be to find the resolve to do it all over again and try for an even better finish in 1990-91. I genuinely thought it was possible we could be title runners-up; having finished 16 points behind the champions, I felt that was too big a margin to expect us to make up in one season. It would take a little longer and probably more new faces.

In the aftermath of the World Cup, when England had lost the chance to reach the final in a penalty shootout, this Spurs team will be remembered as the Gazza/Lineker side. Undoubtedly they played their part – the stars if you like – but it was not a two-man team. Others regularly produced 100 per cent performances without attracting the same media interest. After his tears in Italia 90, Gazza had become the most famous player in the country, with everything he did getting more attention than the rest of the team combined. The World Cup did not change him. He returned the same Gazza, wanting to play, win and be loved. He took it all in his stride. There were occasions when he was a little anti-social, but we had come to realise that whatever he did it was meant to make us laugh.

My confidence in the team to take one step closer to the title never materialised. Sadly, the bad vibes from the boardroom I believe impacted on our league form, which was poor. After a bright start, we won just twice after Christmas and finished the season in tenth place. I knew from an early stage that I would be losing Gazza and Gary at the end of the season. That in itself caused ripples throughout the team, which again affected our performances. I was also working through a hectic work schedule, which involved all sorts of meetings designed to try to secure the financial backing the club needed. That workload would increase dramatically towards the end of the season, with me flying for so-called 'secret' meetings in Rome with Lazio. In the circumstances, tenth was a reasonable position considering what we had to confront.

But against that we settled into an FA Cup run that took us all the way to Wembley. It would be Gazza's Cup one way or the other. We saw off Blackpool and Oxford United in January. Portsmouth were next in line and Gazza gave a master class. There was a pre-match scare with Gazza. Doug Livermore, who had replaced Allan Harris as my assistant manager, said I wouldn't want to hear what he was about to tell me in our South Coast hotel the night before the tie. 'What is it? Tell me now,' I said.

He hesitated: 'Gazza has been playing squash non-stop.'

It was not exactly a crime, but hardly sensible so soon before a match. I found out Gazza had been playing for a couple of hours, but knew he would be fine. If it had been someone else, I would have been much more worried, but Gazza always had so much energy. I was more concerned to find out who Gazza had taken on, because I would have no option but to drop them. After an hour or two with Gazza, they would surely be wrecked and unable to play their best. Meanwhile, Gazza was so brilliant the next day it was freaky, as he scored both goals in our 2-1 win.

Second Division Notts County looked relatively easy on paper as quarter-final opposition, but only for the unwary, and I did all I could to make sure we were ready. Despite my warnings, they took the lead, and White Hart Lane fell quiet as we went in at half time 1-0 down. With Gazza carrying an injury, I had to try to persuade him to conserve his energy, getting him to spend some time playing up front, where he would have less running to do than in the centre of midfield. In the second half, a Nayim strike was deflected in by County defender Craig Short, then with just over five minutes remaining Gazza blasted home the winner.

Our reward was an all-London semi-final against Arsenal at Wembley. There is a longstanding North London rivalry between our two clubs – everyone in football is aware of that. Beating them had become a very special mission though, ever since the

Gunners had thrashed us 4-0 in the pre-season Makita Cup a couple of summers ago. It was no friendly to be dismissed. We had just signed Gazza and Paul Stewart, but both had turned up well overweight. Losing like that and playing the way we did in front of my friend George Graham's Arsenal was hard for me to take, hard for the players to accept and difficult for our supporters to live with. Now we had the chance to grab back the bragging rights.

We would have far preferred either of the other semi-finalists, West Ham or Nottingham Forest, as we knew George Graham's tactics would not give us an inch. Furthermore, Arsenal were closing in on the league title, having lost just once all season and earning a reputation for a miserly defence. In both our league encounters, we had drawn 0-0, but having studied them closely I believed I had found a way to play against them that would give us a chance. It would mean changing the way we played, and I knew that would not go down well with the squad so close to battle.

When I explained I wanted something from them we had not tried before, the squad looked uneasy. I believed our best option was to make the Arsenal full-backs Lee Dixon and Nigel Winterburn push forward, the nearer to us the better. I put David Howells way out on the left, not his favourite position, against Dixon while Paul Allen was moved onto the right, forcing Winterburn to get close. Howells and Allen would then retreat, encouraging the full-backs to push up, and that would leave gaps for Gary Lineker in the centre and our trio of midfield players – Paul Stewart, Vinny Samways and Gazza – to exploit. We had a few days to rehearse this approach and I knew the team would work like hell to give it a chance.

I had one other ploy up my sleeve: we asked the doctor to give Gazza a tranquiliser shot the night before the game. This had two benefits: it would keep him quiet and give everyone else a restful night. However, on the day of the match he was hyped up, wilder than I had seen. He was like a caged animal, literally screaming: 'We've got to win this game – we've got to win this game! We must beat them, we can't let them win!'

On and on he went. He appeared obsessed and mad, as he whirled round the dressing room. He was eyeballing the rest of the team, shouting in their faces. I had to keep my eyes on him in case he went too far. Whatever inspired him, it produced one helluva pre-match show. I could have sat in the corner, lit up a cigar and had a coffee and just watched him do my job for me. When he went on the field, he was back to normal, hardly tranquil, but playing brilliant football, one of his greatest performances. He scored with a stunning free-kick from about 35 yards in the fifth minute. It is one thing to target the goal from that distance, but something else to bend and hit it with unstoppable power. Gazza did. It left David Seaman, a great keeper, helpless.

After he scored Gazza ran over to me, eyes staring, with the rest of the team following him, put his arms round and bellowed in my ear: 'The silly bastard only tried to save it, didn't he?' They were such big mates from their time together in the England squad, and they were both mad on fishing. It was an unlikely partnership and fishing seemed such an unlikely hobby for Paul. I have never been able to imagine Gazza sitting quietly with David on a river bank or by the side of a lake, though I had it explained to me how serious Gazza was when it came to fishing. If anyone came to join them and started fooling around, he would become agitated and then really angry if they persisted.

That goal was enough to knock the momentum out of any side, even Arsenal. Our second goal came from a graceful build-up. Gazza set it in motion through Allen and Howells, whose shot rebounded off an Arsenal defender to Gary Lineker, who scored. Arsenal did not give up and Alan Smith pulled one back to make it 2-1 at half time. Having put in so much effort, Gazza eventually ran out of energy, so I subbed him late on, before Lineker made it three to secure our passage to the final.

The delight we all felt at reaching Wembley did not seem to filter through to the boardroom. The financial position had continued to deteriorate, and with our debts and search for new owners being widely known, it was inevitable other clubs would want to sign Gazza. Knowing we could hardly turn down their offer, Italian club Lazio were determined to recruit our prize asset, and negotiations to sell Gazza continued as the season wore on. Our bankers were equally determined we should reach a deal to reduce our debts. Meanwhile, I was switching from football to takeovers, back to football and on to finding a 'benefactor' on a daily basis. I felt I managed to compartmentalise my duties pretty well: I was with the players in the morning and then spent the rest of the day hunting for backers or other corporate business, but it was hardly an ideal way to prepare for an FA Cup final.

We could have done without all the aggravation before what was the most important match of our season. I had played in the winning Spurs FA Cup team that beat Chelsea in 1967 and still regarded the final as the greatest of all English sporting occasions. It was an afternoon for the country and most of the rest of the world, not just the two clubs, to enjoy. I wanted to focus on that, not the sale of the club or the transfer of Gazza. However, on the eve of the final, Paul signed a contract with Lazio agreeing to pay him a £2 million signing-on fee plus a salary of £1 million a year – not bad for a 24-year-old. It was a justifiable price for a unique talent, but the whole deal was subject to a medical arranged for a few days after Wembley.

Brian Clough's Nottingham Forest were the favourites to win him his first FA Cup on 18 May 1991, and he certainly gained the neutrals' sympathy vote. We thought differently. The final demanded 100 per cent from all of us, so for a few days we had to forget all the rest of the turmoil surrounding us.

Sadly, it turned out to be an occasion remembered for all the wrong reasons: not because of the great football we played but for the sheer drama of the occasion, starting with the bloody reckless, madman tackling of Gazza. As well as that, there was a disallowed goal which TV replays proved was perfectly legal; a missed Lineker penalty and then an own-goal winner for us from Des Walker in extra time.

There was no excuse for Paul's behaviour. It has been assumed by many that he had worked himself into a frenzy pre-match. But was there any indication before the match that a storm was brewing around Gazza and about his off-the-wall behaviour on the pitch? No. There was no repeat of the hysteria that had transfixed the dressing room before the semi. This time he was the opposite, eerily subdued in a way that was perhaps equally strange. Gazza would mouth a couple of things then move on, as if he was thinking about it all. The only way I can describe it is that he was in his own world. There was no reason to believe he was anything other than keyed up but in control and ready to perform.

Inside a few minutes of the kick-off, he had lashed out with two murderous tackles. The first went high into the chest of Garry Parker and the second was a scything challenge as Gary Charles ran across the 18-yard area. The referee was Roger Milford, and to everyone's surprise – and my relief – he decided not to send off Gazza for either tackle. He didn't need to. Paul was stretchered off, unable to put weight on his leg after damaging his cruciate ligaments. The horrific damage was caused by Charles falling heavily on top of Gazza's leg, leaving Paul badly injured and in agony. Was his apparent pre-match self-control the lull before the storm? I think so. Strange behaviour was nothing new from Gazza. I did not think there was a problem, but I was wrong.

It was to have been Gazza's final, but it turned out to be a very successful one for his replacement, Nayim. I'd had to make a difficult selection decision between Nayim and Vinny Samways in the starting line-up, and had decided on Vinny, who I asked to play on the left. He hated playing there, but at least he was happier than Nayim who was stuck on the bench and hating that more. With Gazza self-destructing, I was able to switch Vinny to take Paul's place in the centre and play Nayim on the left, which worked out perfectly. It had been clear that I had got the balance of the team wrong when Vinny kept on wandering into the middle, making it easy for the Forest right-back Gary Crosby to exploit the space.

Gazza's brainstorm gave me the opportunity to rectify the problem. The plan I'd devised was to block the supply to Clough's son Nigel, who was such a devastatingly talented player, by playing Howells in front of our two central defenders where he could keep a close eye on him. If he did that, it would give us a winning chance. With Forest playing their wingers very wide, which occupied our full-backs (Edinburgh and van den Hauwe), this left Sedgley and Gary Mabbutt to tie up their centre-forward. All of which was fine until Forest took the lead with a great Stuart Pearce free kick, awarded for Gazza's second tackle, if we can dignify it with that word.

The final swung decisively our way when Paul Stewart equalised early in the second half. By then we were playing good football. Paul had never quite won over the affection of a section of our support after missing a penalty on his debut. The criticism they gave him was prolonged and unjustified, but he came away from Wembley a hero.

The winner just would not come in 90 minutes, so we prepared for the extra-time decider. We got it with an own goal from England defender Des Walker, an unfortunate way to end such a showpiece event, but I thought we deserved it. I felt the football we played that day was vastly underrated. We had won a major prize that would have been thought impossible, or highly unlikely, when I arrived three and a half years before, one that had enthralled players and fans alike.

We came away from Wembley with the trophy but also with the sad realisation that Paul was out of football for the foreseeable future. We went to visit him in the hospital, bringing with us the cup that he had done so much to help us win. We knew he would be playing in Italy next season as soon as the medics gave him the all clear. Lazio, who had been expecting to parade Gazza in front of their supporters, were as stunned as us at the seriousness of his injury, but they remained determined to sign him. For all our concern about Gazza, I had to remember that this had been a team effort, and I was pleased for the players, staff and the people who ran the club day to day, all of whom deserved this moment after all the pressure we'd been under.

With so much going on at boardroom level, there was little time to enjoy the celebrations. A big concern for Tottenham was finalising the Lazio multi-million pound deal for Gazza. I simply wanted to see Paul fit again and then to push Lazio to the limit for the maximum fee, as the figure we had previously agreed was up in the air because of the injury. Eventually, the deal was done and we began to prepare for life after Gazza.

Even now, more than 20 years on from that day, people still ask me about him, and what it was like to work with him in those days before his problems started to multiply. I spent a lot of time with Paul, liked him and appreciated his precious and unique talent. Spurs owed Paul more than they could ever repay him. Of all the great players I managed for the club, none had his sublime talent or a greater winning attitude. And none did I feel more warmth towards. It was Paul's brilliance that so often proved decisive and helped me lift Spurs to respectability from the bottom of the old

First Division, and his series of virtuoso performances had led us to a Wembley final. Yet that day came frighteningly close to ruining his career.

Of the many things that occurred in my life at Spurs, the most memorable incidents tend to revolve round Paul and what then seemed to be an eccentric, quirky streak in his character. I had no clue he would be overtaken by the alcoholism that for too long has controlled his life, though his behaviour over the years made it clear there were reasons for serious concern about his health. If it was my privilege to manage arguably the finest talent England has produced, certainly the greatest in the modern era, then his fall from grace has been of the deepest concern. That's not because I have a guilty conscience that I could have done more for him, but simply because however hard I and others close to him have tried when we realised the extent of his health problem, we have failed to make him reverse the process.

I can't think of another former player who, long after he last kicked a ball, still has the affection of the national population in the same way as Paul. Fans love to remember the man in his pomp, scoring goals of awesome quality and entertaining us all. They know about his generosity – he was like Maradona in that way. Latterly, I suspect the majority feel his pain when they see him portrayed as a hopeless drunk.

We all hope he can be saved, but there are some things so shocking you turn away from them, not in disgust but in the realisation there is nothing you can do, that you are helpless. It is how I felt in the summer of 2013 when I saw a picture of Paul slumped against a wall in a hotel lobby, his casual shirt unzipped, his leg strapped and a crutch by his side. His head had twisted to the left. The picture of his distress is imprinted on my mind. He might have seemed to be asleep, but in fact he was drunk and incapable, doubly incapable because of his leg. People were trying to help, but what do you do with a dead weight? What do you say to a person who is insensible, who wants another drink not your help even if he could unravel what you are saying? For an alcoholic, anything that feeds the craving comes before wasting money on food and the time it takes to eat it, so Paul has no physical strength and lies where he falls.

I had been warned in a phone call to our home in Spain that Paul was back on the booze. This latest call was to advise me that the *Sun* had a picture of the man who once was our country's hero, now driven by drink to public humiliation. And it was all there in the *Sun*. I went down to our store and bought a copy and had to steady myself. I just hope Paul is still with us by the time this memoir is published. The terrible shape he was in that day made me fear he might not be.

But I'd rather devote space here to the charismatic 'daft as a brush' youngster I bought for Tottenham and watched perform as the very best of his generation for my England team in 1996. Few people know him much better than I do, and I'd rather recall the great things he achieved as a player and his almost skittish sense of humour. I keep hoping that the next news item with his name on it will say he has found the cure and a nice woman and is settled. Sadly, there seems to be little reason for optimism as there have been so many false dawns. My concern for him did not end when he was no longer in my charge. Like everybody else in whose life he became entangled, you wanted him to find some peace.

He never caused me trouble I couldn't cope with at Spurs. I was not witness to a man I believed to be destroying himself. Maybe I just didn't see it in him. But if I didn't, then neither did those I worked with, including the psychiatrists and medical consultants that are part of the modern football club's staff. He was never perfect, and his behaviour could be in poor taste, even anti-social, but we just learned to accept him as he was, and hope we could control his 'awkward days'. To me, it wasn't until he went to Italy that his life first showed signs of serious disarray and this became increasingly obvious on his return, when he began to hang out with the celebrities who befriended him, most with good intentions. After he retired from the game, his inability to cope without the closeness of his former wife and the children he adores has surely accelerated his spiral to the point where alcoholism leads to a catastrophe.

It was a coup for me to sign him for Tottenham when so many other clubs, including Manchester United, were desperate to buy him. It annoyed me when I read Alex Ferguson saying what a pity it was he had not signed Gazza as he believed his United set-up would have made him a better player. What Alex was suggesting was that he, being the managerial master (and no one can argue with that assessment), would have solved the problem with Gazza, but I doubt that. Alex argued that London would have been the problem. Wrong. Gazza lived in a London suburb near our training area where we could look after him. In the heart of London, Gazza could go about his business relatively undisturbed. It is in the small towns and residential areas that trouble can be found, and that would apply to playing for Manchester United and living in the wealthy suburbs. Nobody other than Gazza himself is capable of solving his problem. Alex and Manchester United saw how difficult it was to deal with Paul McGrath's drink problem. It is extraordinarily sensitive.

No club could have devoted more time and energy, or consulted more experts, to see him through his problems than Tottenham. It was overseen by me and my staff, with a lot of extra help from Ted Buxton, whom Gazza trusted like a member of his family. We did it not to make him a better player, because you can't make the best better. We did it because we recognised the inconsistencies in his character and feared they would be exploited, as they were, and in time induce even more problems for him, as has been the case.

Despite those problems, and his pranks, I have never spoken to a player, team-mate or rival who has bad-mouthed him. They love him like you would love a brother. There were many occasions when his behaviour would irritate, but we always forgave him because there was never anything malicious in what he did. He might have been mischievous for sure, but he would never set out to hurt. And he displayed a vulnerability that was endearing. If he was getting a bit out of hand, I knew how to bring him back into line by saying something like: 'Ah, so you're a big shot now.' Or: 'You don't want to do what the others do; you don't want to be a team player.'

'I do, I do, I do,' he would say. 'I'm not a big shot.'

He would like a joke to perk him up. The thing about Gazza is you couldn't help laughing with him. One day when I was walking out from my office as the players began warming up he asked if he could see me: 'Can I go back to my hotel?'

'What do you mean? We've got training, starting now.'

'I'm serious,' he said. 'My towels are not in the right position.'

'Are you round the twist or what?'

'No, you know that I can't walk on lines.'

I was genuinely astonished, though we have since learned he has the medical condition OCD (obsessive compulsive disorder), so I replied: 'Isn't your life complicated enough without worrying about towels and cracks in the road? Towels? I thought you'd be throw-ing them on the floor.'

I was winding him up, but I relented and told him: 'The boys are starting training; you've got five minutes.' He jumped in the car and was back in a few minutes having sorted out his towels, placed them in the right order, neatly folded.

When he returned, he started to talk with me and as we ambled to where the players were getting ready I asked if he could help me out.

'Anything boss, anything. What is it?'

I explained to him that Yvette and I were having a dinner party that night. 'You know a bit about cooking, don't you, Gazza?' I asked.

'Yeah, boss, a little. What do you want to know?' he said eagerly.

'I wanted to know how long you can keep a chicken in the freezer for.'

'Oh, that's easy,' he replied. 'At least a couple of months.'

'That's odd, because that's what I thought,' I said, puzzled.

'Why boss?'

'Well, I put one in the freezer last night and it was dead this morning,' I said, scratching my head.

I don't think it's a particularly good joke – unless you are under 12 – but he fell to the floor, banged the turf with his hands, jumped up and ran what must have been all of 600 yards to where the youth team and the reserves were playing, catching all the players out with that joke. That was typical of Paul.

He was so committed to the game and so exceptionally talented that after training he would join up with the reserves. He would even turn up to work with the kids. Everybody else would be knackered, but not him. It was as if he always wanted to show people what he could do, but the truth was no one could do what he could with the ball, and few could compete with his energy levels. He appeared to be faster with a ball at his feet than he was without it. It was like he had glue on the end of his boots, so good was his control.

I have no doubt that he was the most naturally gifted player I have worked with. Bernd Schuster was special, a great talent at Barcelona, but Gazza could do everything on the field. He could score goals and make them and he would do things that were spectacular. He would also take incredible chances and I would shout at him never to try it again, but even that didn't stop him.

I remember how there would be times when, rather than clearing the ball further upfield when we were under pressure at the back and the ball was headed out to him, he would often head it straight back over our defence and into the hands of the keeper, with the opposition strikers lurking in case it fell short. But it never did. He did it so often, but afterwards he would just run past me and wink while we were all still catching our breath that he'd got away with it.

In some ways, if I was to compare him to anyone, I would say there was a lot of Dave Mackay in Gazza. He had Dave's craggy chin, barrel chest and power. If he had a flaw it was that he had Bryan Robson's reckless tackling style, often overstretching when going in to make a tackle. When a player does that, his leg does not have the strength to withstand impact. I tried to advise him: 'Stand up when you're tackling. If you stand up and keep low you won't get hurt because you'll have your whole body behind you.' When he broke his leg playing for Lazio it was because he had been overstretching.

Normally when one player gets all the accolades, the others can become a bit jealous, but with Paul all they wanted was for him to do well. The kids at the club were so concerned for him when Lazio were in the process of buying him, they waited behind an extra five days when they could have been on holiday, just so they could learn the outcome of the fitness test that would decide if he went to Italy or not.

After he left us and the decade wore on, Gazza became increasingly notorious for his behaviour. It was no longer simple lads' night out stuff, but much more worrying than that. My concern grew when I saw some of the people he was hanging out with. As his career drew to a close, they were involved on numerous occasions and although I wanted to help, it was depressing in the extreme to watch Paul in a world of booze that was endangering his life.

One Sunday morning I found out just how far things had gone for Gazza when I received the most distressing of calls from the police at Kensington.

'Terry Venables?'

'Yes.'

'This is the inspector at the station down the road from you. Gazza's here. You have got to come down. If we don't do something, he will be dead by tomorrow.'

I went straight there and into a room. The inspector was facing me. Gazza had his back to me with a cigarette in one hand and a slice of toast in the other. He was looking down at his feet.

'What's going on?' I asked.

'We have to get food down him.'

I put my hand on Gazza's shoulder, which startled him. He was trying to focus and when he saw it was me, he shouted: 'Gaffer, Gaffer. What are you doing here? I'm okay.'

He was anything but. He looked dreadful. I asked the inspector if I could speak to Paul privately.

'What's happening, Paul?'

'I don't know,' he said.

'Look at me Paul, look at me. If you don't react to what I am saying, you'll be dead.'

Paul looked me straight in the eyes. 'I want to be dead,' he said. It was chilling. I had to get him out of there, which is exactly what the police wanted from me. They were as concerned as I was about Gazza's health. This wasn't a man on a booze-up, but an alcoholic close to falling into a coma, with all the consequences that might follow.

What can you say to a man in the state he was in? It wouldn't register anyway. I had to get him out of there, which is what the police also wanted. They were clearly concerned, but what could they do except lock him in the cell until he sobered up and then what? He needed professional help, not a night in the cells. The best place for him was the Priory and that's where I decided to take him. I informed the inspector, who then arranged for a police car to take us down to the Royal Garden Hotel, where Paul had been staying, to collect his things. As we got to his room, Gazza pulled out a bag of money from under the bed. 'Pay the bill for me, Gaffer,' he said, handing me the bag.

I asked the officers to stay with him while I went downstairs to sort it out, but when I returned they were standing outside the room. 'Why are you out here? He shouldn't be left alone ... The state he's in he could be doing *anything*!' I shouted.

We opened the door and there he was sitting in a chair guzzling from a bottle of vodka; it was then obvious why he had tried to get rid of me and the police. We booked him into the Priory for as long as was needed. 'I'm only going to be here for a day, Gaffer,' he told me.

'Gazza, stay as long as you need to get better. Don't start rushing out, *promise* me you'll stay,' I said. He didn't answer, but muttered something incoherent under his breath as he slowly shook his head. I went with him to his room and got him settled. I pulled down the blankets and he got into bed, turning away from me as I covered him up. 'You all right?' I asked.

'Gaffer,' he said. I stood looking down at him. I'd known him since he was a young man and at that precise moment I felt as if I was putting a child to bed. I kissed his head, it just felt the right thing to do.

'Get some sleep. I'll see you in the morning,' I said.

When I got home I called the clinic and they told me he was still sleeping, which I was happy about. I hoped I would then be able to try to talk some sense into him in the morning when he was sober, but I never got the chance as when I returned the following morning he had gone. Later that day, I called Gary Mabbutt, who

Malcolm Allison suggests the likely number of goals that Palace were going to score against Chelsea during the side's 1976 FA Cup run. I learned so much from him.

When Malcolm left, I took charge of the team, and led the club all the way to the First Division. Here I am in training with Kenny Sansom and Vince Hilaire.

We had lots of ideas for what we wanted to do at Queens Park Rangers, and installing an artificial pitch for the 1981-82 season was one of the more controversial moves.

Jim Gregory was a wonderful mentor to me, and I found him almost the perfect football chairman.

Barcelona's president Josep Lluis Nuñez is blessed by the priest in the chapel in the Camp Nou ahead of my first season in charge of the club.

Allan Harris and I pose with new signing Steve Archibald, who was to prove such a key figure in our La Liga title triumph, and Bernd Schuster, the talented but challenging German midfielder.

Urging on my players ahead of extra time in the hugely disappointing European Cup final of 1986. History beckoned for that team, but we fell short against Steaua Bucharest.

Welcomed to White Hart Lane by Irving Scholar in November 1987, our working relationship would eventually be soured by the increasingly poor financial position of the club.

But when I had the opportunity to work with players as good as Chris Waddle, it was too good a chance to turn down.

We did find enough money to sign up Gazza and Paul Stewart for the start of the 1988-89 season, and they helped set the club on its way to success.

Celebrating winning the FA Cup in 1991, despite the horrific loss of Gazza to injury early on. That summer, however, was all about saving the club.

Happier times: Alan Sugar, Gazza, me, Gary Lineker and Tony Berry line up together. My partnership with Sugar did not last long.

After I was sacked by Sugar, the fans protested against my removal, but there was no way back, and a series of court cases soon followed.

I'd had an early taste of working in the England set-up during the 1982 World Cup finals, with Ron Greenwood and Bobby Robson.

Getting my dream job: England coach. Despite the misgivings of one or two at the FA, I was thrilled to have my chance to lead my country in a major tournament that we would be hosting.

A moment of pure genius from Gazza against Scotland set our Euro 96 campaign flying.

Steve McManaman and Alan Shearer celebrate a goal during our 4-1 thrashing of the Netherlands in Euro 96. It was my perfect match.

Me with Yvette and Pelé at Umbro Star Chamber in 1996.

I hadn't expected to have another chance to work with the England side, but when Steve McClaren took charge, he invited me to play a role in the set-up, and I could not turn down the opportunity.

A moment of madness. Leaving the field at the MCG after a lone pitch invader had upset Australia's rhythm against Iran, when we seemed destined to go to the 1998 World Cup finals.

On the sidelines with Bryan Robson and Viv Anderson during my spell working at Middlesbrough, when I was brought in to help keep the side in the Premier League.

You can tell from this picture just how close Peter Ridsdale and I were during my spell at Leeds United. I would never have taken on the job if I'd known how many players we would have to sell.

has also spent a lot of time over the years trying to help him, and he too had not heard a word. It would be weeks before either of us had any further contact with him. When he did call it would be late at night, and he would leave a message asking me to call him back in the morning, which I did, but he never picked up. It was the most frustrating time as all you wanted to do was help him. What added to the frustration was that he constantly changed his number, which made him more elusive.

The sad truth is that alcoholics have to make their own decision about cure or be damned. It has become increasingly clear to me that Paul no longer has the capacity to think straight about this issue. There have been golden moments when I thought he has finally seen the light and stopped drinking. A month or two later, he would be splashed over the front of our newspapers, in the gutter somewhere. You can never give up on him – and I never will – but he has ignored so many chances. So many people have said they will help rehabilitate him – a new agent, a new friend, but so far no one has managed it. It has got to the stage when I just don't know what to do. Everything has been tried, time and time again. We all live in hope that in the end he will find a way, as he still has so much to give.

# THE SUGAR YEARS

Nobody likes to admit they are broke. It is usually revealed bit by bit, when you can't afford the players you need and can't keep up the payments of the ones you have bought. That's how I learned the truth about the state of the finances at Spurs. One of English football's great institutions was running out of money and running out of it fast. The debts would become mountainous and while the football side was fine and improving, it was the investments of chairman Irving Scholar and the board, on behalf of the stock market-listed leisure company Tottenham Hotspur plc, that were haemorrhaging cash.

You don't expect a club with Tottenham's pedigree ever having to consider the possibility of going out of business. There have always been arguments inside clubs about the money available for signing new players and the financing of other team matters, so that was not new to me. It was the scale of our problem that was so shocking. I can think of few things professionally worse than the embarrassment of managing a club that was struggling to pay its bills. Can you imagine how upset I felt when Barcelona demanded the return of Gary Lineker because we hadn't cleared the balance of his transfer fee? I was unaware of the debt to my old club for some time, then discovered we were £1.1 million short, which the chairman arranged to pay off only after obtaining a loan from an outside source.

That source turned out to be Robert Maxwell, the bombastic, untrustworthy publisher of the *Daily Mirror*. Maxwell, in his cynical way, must have seen it as some sort of down payment on a buy-out of the club. To him, Spurs was ripe for plucking and he planned to add it to the stable of clubs (Oxford and Derby) he had dipped into and out of as owner.

The problems we faced were numerous. How was I expected to react as a professional when we had to postpone the first home match of the season, against Coventry City, because builders' rubble surrounding the new East Stand was designated unsafe to our supporters? The cost of the building work had doubled from the original estimate to £9 million. That was a bad enough drain on our finances, but we also lost many hundreds of thousands of pounds of revenue before we were issued with a safety certificate so we could admit the fans.

I could go on. We had to pay Tranmere Rovers £500 in compensation because we took so long to pay their gate money share from a cup tie. How could we do that to a little club? Others also had to prise shared gate money out of us, with one – Southampton – threatening legal action long after they were due to be paid. We turned up late for one match because our team coach had been towed away as an obstruction in London's West End while we were having our pre-match lunch. It cost us a £20,000 fine from the football authorities. That was down to bad parking and contributed to the belief that the club was unprofessional, a shambles waiting to become a crisis.

The compensation for me was the pleasure of working with outstanding players. First there was the Gazza/Lineker axis, then the prospect of what Teddy Sheringham, Darren Anderton and Nick Barmby would produce in the future, when I got them together as a unit, not to mention a very young Sol Campbell. That excited me. They kept me believing, maybe they even kept me sane in all the troubles that were to come.

The relationship between Irving and myself, chairman and manager, I never considered less than full of good intentions when we began what we were both determined would be a highly successful era. He was a Spurs nut who seemed to have been rendered virtually helpless as his plan for the club headed towards financial meltdown. As I have said, nobody likes to admit they are running on empty. Spurs was hit with two recessions in the early 1980s and early 1990s. That did not help overall, but the mistake Irving and the board made, again I must say with good intentions, was to diversify.

Firstly, they had floated the club on the stock market as a leisure company, Tottenham Hotspur plc. They believed that would give them a number of financial benefits. There were now two separate companies, the plc and the football club, which was my employer. The trouble began when the plc bought into a series of companies, Martex, Stumps and Synchro Systems among them. They had one thing in common – they made losses after bright starts. The money from the football side was used to support some of the plc's other interests, which forced me further into an already tight corner.

Despite those costs, the club still found the money to sign Waddle for David Pleat, then Gascoigne, Stewart, Lineker and Nayim, for an outlay of over £6 million. Scholar also backed less glamorous signings, so his heart, if not always his business head, was in the right place. I will admit that I did put him under pressure to keep buying players to improve the squad. I was promised that the money we received from the sale of Chris Waddle could be used to bring in new players, rather than going to pay off debts, so in that sense I helped contribute to the club's debt. But my primary responsibility was to build a team that could challenge for, then win, the title, which meant buying the best we could afford. The problem was we could afford virtually nothing, unless we went further into debt. That dilemma led to some very heated meetings with Irving, which led to us falling out – not a good state of affairs between the chairman and the manager.

Everywhere Irving turned, it cost us. We were tied up with kit suppliers and manufacturers Hummel, but they were struggling badly enough to be declared bankrupt. The situation had become so desperate there was a real possibility of the unthinkable, that we would go under. The very thought intensified Irving's desperation to find a new backer. I was willing to help in any way I could. On reflection, it would have been better for me to steer clear, isolate myself and focus purely on the football side.

However, when Irving gave me clearance to seek a backer, I set about looking for an individual or a group willing to invest £11 million in the club. It was an opportunity for me, too. If I found the right people, it could help me fulfil my ambition to own or part-own a club. I had come close to it at QPR, but that was a much smaller business than Spurs. I set myself a crazy schedule of coaching in the morning, dealing with player problems, talking to the media and then meeting people who could bring money to the club. Some of these meetings went on until four in the morning. It would then be home, some sleep and the cycle would begin again. I had kept myself fit and my health never suffered. Dare I say it, I was enjoying the challenge, and that helped me see it through.

No matter what we did on the field, the shouts and screams from the boardroom warned us we were heading for the high dependency ward. It was essential the club found a money man, preferably someone who knew and understood football. The situation was so precarious that it seemed almost anyone would do, if they were prepared to come up with the much-needed cash. The days were over when football clubs would be backed by wealthy men who did not care if there was a profit, provided their club was stable.

I was close to tying up one deal that looked potentially strong, but when it came to the crunch I was told it just wasn't a viable business proposition. I contacted Jim Gregory, who had taken his money out of Queens Park Rangers. He was all for it and I knew it would interest him as he was always up for a battle. I actually thought a deal was on the point of being finalised when his sons persuaded him against it.

There was another possible saviour. I was introduced to Larry Gillick, an extremely wealthy and very interested investor. Larry was an enthusiast with big plans, but unfortunately he was not sufficiently persuasive to close a deal. After months of talks and the signing of documents, the time came when we shook hands and went our different ways, me still hanging on to the hope of finding a way to take over the club.

There was so much going on behind the scenes, which was plain nasty and very disturbing for all of us. Maxwell was one of those involved in the bidding, with all the charm of a snake-oil salesman. There was no way I wanted to see him working with Irving. Some felt the media mogul would give the club the sort of financial clout it needed, and his own newspaper certainly presented it that way. Fortunately he was chased off, and to my relief a proposed deal never took place. We were soon to discover what a lucky escape we had had, as he was using his company pension fund to bale out his debt-ridden companies.

I did what I could to help out Irving, and there was much to like about him. When Irving knew my mum was terminally ill in a hospital in Wales, he went out of his way to ensure I had all the time and help you need in these circumstances. I have never believed, like Bill Shankly, that football was the single most important thing in the world and for all our fall-outs his kindness to me and therefore to my family was a comfort. The medics had said the treatment was working in Mum's favour, she seemed to recover and that gave us hope. We even made plans to bring her back to London to stay with us, where we could have nursed her, but the outcome was inevitable. I remember sitting outside with her at the hospital in Wales after she had just had her hair done. It was a hot day and cricket was being played on the green in front of us. I saw but took nothing in about the match. Even today, when the cricket is on, that picture of her having her hair combed comes into my mind. We stayed in her room, my dad, Yvette and myself, and I was beside her at the end.

If I appreciated Irving's kindness then, I wasn't best pleased when he decided that one way to solve the club's debt problem was to reduce my salary by £25,000 when he offered me a new contract. The AGM of February 1991 showed the scale of the problem, revealing debts of £13.6 million, an enormous sum then. By now, Irving and I were almost trying to avoid each other. When we did get together, I often had rows with him that regularly turned into shouting matches over the availability of money to buy players. The pressure was increased by our failure to find the right investor. It became more and more alarming as everybody we approached said the same thing – it was not a good investment.

Then, finally, we had someone who was interested. I had met Alan Sugar briefly when I was involved in a couple of small promotional deals for him. One of them was an advert for his Amstrad company with the tagline: 'The Best Player I Ever Signed'. He had made contact with me after reading that I was trying to find investors for Tottenham and he suggested that we meet. I knew he was a good family man and extremely wealthy, so there was no question he would have the money we would need as a partnership. I also knew that if he said he would do something it would happen. He believed that the club was worth investing in.

Meanwhile, Irving hoped the board would find the cash necessary for survival. There was no chance of that. They did not have the money to pay off the debts, so barring a miracle they would have to step aside. It was the one thing Irving did not want to do. He had been hoping for some time that somebody would come up with the funds and the problems would be solved. That way, if he had to sell most of his shares, he could still be left with some and a seat on the board. The attitude of the Midland Bank was crucial, too. If they called in the money they were owed then it was all over. Maxwell was still expressing interest in coming in, while I hoped I could secure backing from Sugar. All these options were under consideration as Spurs headed towards slipping over the edge.

One important factor in how this would resolve itself was the profitability of the football club. Sugar recognised, as I did, that not only could Tottenham Hotspur FC be saved but it could also have a very profitable future. I was exhausted after the FA Cup final and so took off for a break with Yvette. On my return, batteries recharged, Sugar and I met the two key shareholders on the board: Irving and Paul Bobroff. Irving held 26 per cent of the shares, while Bobroff had 11 per cent and with the shares of another director, Tony Berry, we would hold 45 per cent. The Spurs supporters held some shares and their group of shareholders backed us too, which meant we had control of the company and the sale was agreed at 70 pence a share, which meant I had to drain my resources to find the £3 million necessary to buy an equal share in the club.

Irving agreed to stand down so Sugar and I could take control. There were still a couple of interjections from Maxwell before he was beaten out of sight, and Scholar tried to keep some of his shares. Sugar's take-no-prisoners style in the final act of the deal was exactly what was needed. He was impressive as the clock ticked. The arrangement was confirmed in July when Sugar and I officially announced the takeover, with him as chairman and me as chief executive. He would look after the business side of the club while my responsibility was the football. I had no illusions about what I had let myself in for. I was going to be working with one of the toughest guys the City of London has dealt with.

We were never close and never tried to be. Initially, I could not work out why he wanted to be involved in football when other major businessmen saw investment in a club like Tottenham as not viable. However, he saw the possibilities offered by the new Premiership, which was due to come into being a year later, and which would eventually develop into a massive revenue generator. I remember sitting in a Harry's Bar with Sugar, Rupert Murdoch and Sam Chisholm (a tough little man in charge of Murdoch's Sky set-up). Murdoch's Sky Sports channel was on the verge of bankrolling the game by acquiring the exclusive rights to show live league football. Meanwhile, Sugar's company was involved in aspects of television technology, including the production of the satellite dishes required to connect with Sky. Previously, football had been financed by marvellous but reckless benefactors, local businessmen or long-time fans like Scholar, who enhanced the game for over a century. That would all change once hundreds of millions of pounds began to gush from Sky.

From the start, I believe Sugar felt I was ill-suited to the job as CEO and that I had no experience, when in fact I had a similar role with Jim at QPR. I had been the one who signed the cheques then. Sugar has a way of dealing with people that must have worked brilliantly well for him in his business contacts, but I didn't find it easy to adapt to his style. It was difficult for me, his partner, to work out what he wanted. Some have commented that we were both too stubborn in our dealings with each other, but I have never considered myself stubborn. I can fight my corner and am ready to do so, but our failure to respond to each other was not down to a similarity in our natures. I would say we were very much opposites, in my experience. We just did not gel as a chairman and CEO. It is not a crime, it happens. I found him very much a dominant figure, again no crime but an irritant.

I knew Sugar had been one of the entrepreneurial successes of the time, with his Amstrad company making him many millions from the manufacture and sale of computers. He did not have much of a public persona at the time, certainly nothing like the profile he now has. It would be up to us to work out a partnership, a way of going forward. He said he was a long-time Spurs fan who was taken to White Hart Lane by a relative when he was a youngster. I wouldn't know about that.

It is difficult to give an idea of what I was going through at Tottenham and thereafter without mentioning my former partner. I can only think that where it went wrong between us, and remember we were supposed to be equal partners, was his apparent inability to share control with me. He was used to being in sole charge. I also believe he may have hoped he would get more praise from the fans, as it was his wealth that ensured the club's survival, but it was my name the fans chanted during our first season after we had rescued the club. The majority of people who turn up to football matches couldn't care less about the owners.

Highly successful businessmen too easily confuse sport with business. I accept the need for business acumen of a high order, but the normal rules that apply in business do not always sit well on the shoulders of sports people. Sugar came to Tottenham to lift the club financially, in partnership with my contribution. He has claimed he's the only man who's made money out of football and I certainly wouldn't argue with that, but a question that must be asked is where that took Spurs. They are way behind Manchester

United, Manchester City and Chelsea and have been living in the shadow of Arsenal for decades, though that may be about to change. In the time he ran the club after my departure, they lifted one trophy in nine years, the League Cup. A club may be perfectly organised as a business, but if the team does not achieve as a major club is expected to then questions will be asked about why. That is inevitable and normal.

There was an extraordinary difference of opinion between me and Sugar over Gazza's transfer to Italy. Even now I cannot offer a rational explanation for it. In its way it highlights the failure of Sugar and me to find common ground to work for the benefit of Spurs. The proposed transfer was put on hold to assess Gazza's fitness after his cruciate injury. I was told he would be fit and I knew he was a tough Geordie, but it was still one of the more damaging injuries a footballer could suffer. However, Paul did recover and the final negotiations took place in London.

I went along there with Tony Berry from the club (presumably representing Sugar) and Gino Santin, a successful restaurateur in London and Milan whom Sugar called the 'café owner', who with his Italian connections had laid so much of the groundwork in securing the deal. Lazio had brought a surgeon to the Hyde Park Hotel who my research told me was the best in Italy. The details of that deal would form part of the battles that would follow, played out in the media and the courts, as Sugar and I explained our understanding of what happened. I don't propose to go over the details yet again, but I still maintain that not only did we help to get a better deal for the club than had been on offer, more importantly football was my side of the business, which included selling and buying of players, so I felt my decision was the one to go with.

When Gary Lineker's agent fixed him up with a big-money move to Nagoya in Japan after the 1991-92 season, Sugar and I fell out again. I was surprised Gary was prepared to play on, suffering as he was with a big toe problem. If that sounds comical then it was a deadly serious handicap for a player like Gary. We had paid £2 million for him and now his agent had arranged, I was assured, a £2 million transfer fee to Japan, which seemed great business. I was happy, Gary was happy but Sugar was furious. Gary had done brilliantly for us with his goals – 80 in three seasons – and that included two of the goals that swept us through in our semi-final win against Arsenal, but he was getting on at 32 years and struggling with that chronic injury. Sugar believed we should have received double that, as Lineker was one of the world's great strikers, but that didn't allow for his age.

The loss of Chris Waddle then Gazza meant new players would have to be found for the start of the 1991-92 season, the first under our new ownership. I would have a say in the club's future and from where I was working it appeared to be full of promise. I had to decide was how much time I could devote to coaching and management, given my new CEO duties. I felt my position as chief executive would be demanding enough without the added responsibility of working daily with the players. For that reason, I appointed Peter Shreeves, a former manager and coach at the club and a very popular figure at White Hart Lane, as the man in charge of the team. There was a fine list of youngsters coming through, including two of the very best in Nick Barmby and Sol Campbell, both of whom were exceptional and wanted by every top club. Manchester United were particularly interested in Nick and were very upset when they did not get him and he signed for us.

Sol was a giant of a player, who was shy and reticent off the field and a natural leader on it. We started him further up front, but it was clear that central defence would be where he'd flourish. When I was able to buy Gordon Durie from Chelsea in August, I was adding a powerful talent and a renowned goalscorer to our squad strength, but I needed players to work with him and these would take until the next summer to sign. This would be a year for bedding down. But as in the previous season, when our charge on Wembley had tangled up our league performances, this time it was the European Cup-Winners' Cup, a prestigious competition second only to the European Cup.

We were good enough to eliminate two excellent teams in Hajduk Split and Porto before Feyenoord managed to edge us out over two legs. What we could have done without was surrendering the FA Cup at the first hurdle after a replay against Aston Villa in January 1992. We had done the hard part at Villa Park, but then lost at home to the only goal. In the league we lost to Manchester United, Chelsea and Everton, but more positively beat Nottingham Forest, West Ham and QPR. We drew with future Champions Leeds at Elland Road, which was very encouraging, and then lost to them 3-1 in London. We finished in 15th place and Peter was sacked, but even in a disappointing season I could sense a good team in development.

Meanwhile, I was starting to have to learn to live with often ferocious media attention. This was a time when the way football conducted its business was coming under increasing media scrutiny, and I was at the centre of their attention. It seemed that a campaign of harassment against me was conducted by a few in the press corps and other sections of the media, including the country's two major television channels, BBC and ITV. I could cope with the nastiness that a lack of cash can cause, but I could not understand – and to a degree still cannot – why I was the subject of so many stories about me that were hugely damaging. The stories were not about my teams or my selections or my buys or anything to do with football, but about my business life.

When you have played and managed at the highest level, as I did, then you are accustomed to criticism even when you feel it is unjust. I do not think anybody in our game, and that includes the late Sir Bobby Robson who took it flush on the chin as England manager from every section of the media, or Graham Taylor who was lampooned as a 'Turnip', or Glenn Hoddle and his healer lady, suffered the same incessant abuse as I did. I cannot possibly forget the bad ones and the apparently concerted attacks on my integrity. Whatever I was to face on the training pitch, and however difficult it was to compete for the best players with shallow pockets, was nothing compared to the pain a small group of journalists, written and broadcast, inflicted on me.

When you have been compared to the Kray twins, murderers, some things need explaining, because so much that has happened to me I have found inexplicable. The blasts I took on a regular basis were designed to destroy my reputation. People who didn't know me and what I was about were sure to be influenced by what they saw or read, and I have no doubt that members of the Football Association were affected by all the stories when the England job was on offer.

The portrait that was drawn suggested I was a cheeky cockney and, worse, I was tricky. It became much more serious than printed banter from media men, some of whom clearly lined themselves up against me. For years, one newspaper writer, Patrick Collins of the *Mail on Sunday*, criticised me in a relentless way. Harry Harris, then of the *Daily Mirror*, was another who seemed to spend his days collating information, presumably from a Spurs source, to sustain a campaign against me. Richard Littlejohn, the *Daily Mail* columnist and a friend of Tottenham, gave me a very rough time and then must have become bored by it all and stopped. We met latterly and by chance in Sheekey's restaurant off Leicester Square and shook hands.

There were a few others who seemed to take every opportunity to fire shots in my direction. Fair enough. This is not about apportioning blame, but trying to explain what can happen when reason appears to be replaced by bias. Not one of them knew me as a coach/manager or as a man. I used to guest on Chris Evans's radio show on Saturdays and suggested Collins and Harris might wish to join me and exchange views. Not a chance. We were told it was impossible as Collins had a match to cover. I bumped into Harris, at another of these accidental meetings, who told me we should forget what had gone before and make up; he even suggested we might have dinner together with our wives. I presumed he was joking. I did appear on the same television programme as Sugar, but not together as we were interviewed separately.

I would regularly wake up to headlines that were depressing. They confounded me with their venom. One of the country's leading broadsheet newspapers, the *Independent*, ran attacks on me calling for police action against me. The articles were full of unsubstantiated rubbish. I have always wondered why that particular paper took the aggressive line it did. My own investigation showed that it came from a source on another newspaper, who had been feeding the broadsheet with information against me. Ken Jones, chief sports writer for the *Independent* and an old friend, had no input on the articles. He approached his editor, Simon Kelner, with concerns about the substance of them, which the police almost immediately said bore no truth and therefore there would be no investigation, but there was no apology from the paper for running them in the first place.

Mihir Bose, who reported on sport for the *Sunday Times* and *Daily Telegraph*, and was for a time the sports editor of the BBC, was another who wrote a series of critical articles about me. When we met, again accidentally, he said he hoped I did not think there was anything personal in what he had done. Of course not! He later wrote a book called *False Messiah: Life and Times of Terry Venables* in which he referred to a court case I originally lost against a London businessman who claimed I had not paid him for work I had asked him to undertake on behalf of Scribes West, my London club. I had to pay compensation of some £19,000 when the original case went against me, but it was subsequently proved in my favour. In legal terms the judgment was set aside. Now it was his turn to pay, much more than I'd had to, £120,000. An apology from Bose should have been the least I expected. When Nick Trainer, our lawyer, met up with Bose, Nick said to him: 'So, Terry was right after all.' The reply was: 'Oh, yes, Terry is always right, isn't he?' There still has been no apology.

MP Kate Hoey used parliamentary privilege to savage me from a witness statement that was subsequently set aside. I asked her to repeat what she said without privilege but she did not. Most staggering for me was *Panorama* producing two investigations into my business life. These were in the days when *Panorama* was reckoned to be the main investigative programme on the BBC, yet they decided on making two programmes looking into the business life of a football manager! Why? I can't offer an answer, nor why ITV's *Dispatches* programme also attempted to delve into my business affairs.

I can offer an example of how these flagship programmes operated when trying to put together a programme on me. I had set out to buy what was then a members' club in Kensington, Scribes West. It was owned by a hyperactive man by the name of Geoffrey Van Hay, but for whatever reason it was running at a loss and he was prepared to sell. However, he didn't appear to be keen on selling to me, an East Londoner. I saw Scribes as an investment for the future, as it is well situated in a busy area in the West End, a brisk walk from the Albert Hall, and near the *Mail* newspaper offices. The paper had recently moved there from Fleet Street and the occupants were known to entertain and imbibe.

I never considered myself as the flavour of his month. I had a use and that was to dig him out of a financial hole, but he kept on digging. I had given him absolute instructions not to buy anything new while I was out of town at one stage during the takeover. When I returned it was to see an addition to the club's furniture, a coffee table. I asked him where it came from and he replied he had bought it because it looked good. It did look good and it did not cost thousands, but it cost money I did not want to spend, so I bought out Van Hay and cleared his debts. To do so I had to deal with 16 Scribes shareholders individually.

I contacted each one and paid them what they were due as shareholders. It was not a huge amount of money involved. One of them was John Chalk, a highly successful businessman. I knew him and phoned and asked if I could meet him at his home in the West End to pay him what was due, which I did. A little later he contacted me to tell me an interviewer from a flagship television programme had contacted him and gone to his home. They wanted to talk about me. He was asked if we had ever done business and he said yes. They then asked John what it was like to deal with me and he said it was fine – perfectly normal, straightforward and above board. He asked them when they would film the interview and he was told they wouldn't as it was not what they wanted. Presumably they wanted something far more damning than a vote of approval.

Before I took over, Scribes was the meeting place for a number of snobs and poseurs, some of whom had trouble paying for their drinks. They had a worldly bar manager in Nick who stayed on to work for me. Nick would tell the story of the night Prime Minister Margaret Thatcher was guest of honour at the opening. The prime minister was quite a coup and all credit to Van Hay for pulling that one off. Nick was approached at the bar by two wives of members. While they fussed around, one said: 'Nick, you must be so proud, indeed honoured, to serve so many famous people tonight.'

Nick told me afterwards it had crossed his mind to give the only reply possible and tell them to fuck off. He resisted and thought of the truly great men he had served behind the bar at London's most prestigious hotels over many years. Yvette and I came to call Scribes 'the Bunker', the place we could go and forget what was going on above ground. There were a few niggles involving footballers or former players and others caught by the paparazzi, but generally it was a business we enjoyed running.

Saturday night was the highlight. Apart from being a good, fun night (we had karaoke after a fine dinner), it paid for the rest of the week. It would not be Van Hay's idea of a perfect night, but my clientele paid for their food and drink. On this particular Saturday, I told Nick that a writer (from Associated Newspapers) was coming to do a piece on the club. Nick knew how important it was to have the nationwide publicity an article would produce. My long-time friend Eric Hall would be master of ceremonies. Eric always had two ambitions, neither of which was making money. He wanted to be the funniest man in the world and the best agent.

That evening I saw a man and woman sitting at a table next to the bar, and I asked them if they wanted a drink. 'That would be very kind,' the man said as he stood up. He was so tiny he didn't come up to my shoulder.

'I like you, Terry,' he said in a low voice.

'Thanks,' I replied.

Then he added: 'There's one thing I don't like about you.'

'What's that?'

'You're Tottenham and I'm Arsenal.'

'That's nothing to worry about,' I replied. 'Enjoy your evening.'

'Thanks, we will. It's karaoke and my wife and me like to sing.'

As I began to walk to our office, Nick ushered me to the side and whispered: 'You know who that is, don't you?'

'No.'

'He's "Mad" Frankie Fraser.'

I immediately had a vision of the writer coming in and spotting 'Mad' Frankie. I had further visions of headlines like 'Tel And His

Gangster Friends'. I told Nick to seat the writer and his wife in one corner and Frankie in the other, and to take the lighting down beside Frankie's table so he couldn't be seen. I then went to find Eric to warn him that 'Mad' Frankie, who had spent most of his life locked up for many violent crimes, who was a friend of the Krays and the enforcer for the Richardson gang, was having dinner in my place and would be joining the karaoke. Eric was already aware of our notorious guest, but less appreciative when I told him on no account was he to mention 'Mad' Frankie's name.

'But...'

No buts I told him. You draw attention to him and you will be fired on the spot and out the door. He seemed to take it in and I knew he loved the job so he would not want to lose it. There were no problems. The dinner went well. 'Mad' Frankie was a quiet little figure in the corner, who appeared to be enjoying himself. Nobody had recognised him or if they had they kept quiet.

Eric took the stage. 'Ladies and gentlemen,' he began. 'Welcome to Scribes. You have had a wonderful dinner, now for the karaoke. A special big welcome to one of our guests, "Mad" Frankie Fraser, who is going to sing for us tonight [pause] "If I had a Hammer" [another pause] and then "Knees Up Mother Brown".'

I grabbed Eric, bundled him round a corner and sacked him.

'Get out!'

'But, it was funny.'

'Eric, it was hysterical. Get out and don't come back!'

He phoned me every week for three months before I let him back into Scribes and his old job as MC. Eric was funny and there was no real comeback from 'Mad' Frankie or the newspaper. Some time later, Frankie returned with a group of eight men. They drank our best champagne, bottle after bottle then argued the bill of £1800. They claimed they were overcharged. Why would I do that? They were certainly not the people I would choose to argue with, but I did. After a time, they slammed £600 on the bar and said they would come back with the balance in a few days. They did, though not quite the full amount. Honour was preserved all round.

Back at my other club, Spurs, Doug Livermore and Ray Clemence succeeded Peter Shreeves for the 1992-93 season, but they agreed to take charge only if I returned as coach. I said it was difficult to balance both roles, but in the end I did. It was almost as before: I would supervise the coaching, deal with the media more often than not, but then instead of looking for investors as I did under the Scholar regime I attended meetings of the Premier League and the Football Association in my role of chief executive. We made progress as a team, but I didn't know it was going to be my last season.

My main concern was being able to make the best use of our new signings. I just knew Teddy Sheringham was going to be a wonderful buy. Nottingham Forest eventually agreed the deal, though as you would expect Brian Clough was very reluctant to sell such an important player to a rival, even at £2.1 million, which I thought was a fair price. His reluctance was understandable. Others wanted him and Alex Ferguson was eventually able to sign him in 1997 when Teddy still had enough guile left to make class contributions for Manchester United, including helping them win the Champions League in Barcelona in 1999. He joined us in August, having scored the first live televised goal of the Premier League era. How did we get him? It was simple enough: Teddy wanted to play for a London club and was happy to join me at Spurs. That transfer eventually became caught up in my court case with Spurs over my dismissal, when a statement from Alan Sugar claimed I had told Sugar that Clough 'likes a bung'. That comment has been discussed at length, and for the last and final time I will say it must have been a misunderstanding between me and Sugar.

Teddy is one of the best players I have ever worked with. I know players are only too happy to work alongside him. Jürgen Klinsmann had a fabulously successful career in Germany, France and Italy before joining Spurs after I had left. I was interested to read that Jürgen thought that of all the many players he partnered for his clubs and the German national side, including Rudi Völler, none was better or easier to play alongside than Teddy. Partnering Gordon Durie, with Nick Barmby and Paul Allen also playing their part, Teddy's deftness and intuition were vital. He might not have had much pace, but he knew how to maximise the powerful runs of Durie.

You can do so much work in training with a partnership, but every so often (as with Gerry Francis and Stan Bowles at QPR) one comes along that you expect to fit perfectly. This is how I saw Teddy and Gordon developing. When we added Darren Anderton, who joined us from Portsmouth and was so tireless, I knew we had someone who would supply a lot of the ammunition. We worked on their fitness, and that gave them confidence, but we still needed to work. It was not perfect but the development of the team was obvious to me.

Sadly, Gordon did not match his Chelsea goalscoring rate, ending up with just four, but Teddy finished as the Premiership's top goalscorer, with 21 goals, and 28 in all competitions. Gordon was clearly worried about a family problem and he wanted to return to Scotland because of his wife. That was acceptable, though a considerable body blow for my team plans. The club sold him to Rangers in Glasgow, where he went on to win a clutch of Scottish titles in the days before it became the one-horse race it currently is.

It was wonderful to be working with talented footballers. We finished eighth, which was good, but more importantly I felt the team we had now was destined for the very top. Teddy and Darren were outstanding, but we were strong in every department, with Gary

Mabbutt and Neil Ruddock forming an excellent central defensive pairing, though Neil was sold on to Liverpool at the end of the season. Add to that Justin Edinburgh, Dean Austin, David Howells, Pat Van Den Hauwe, Jason Cundy, Dave Tuttle and Stuart Nethercott and we had a strong squad. Youngsters Barmby and Campbell were only going to get better. I could see where we were going and felt that, given two seasons, we could win the title or at worst be serious challengers.

Fate decided otherwise. Sugar sacked me, his partner, despite the wishes of many of the club's minority shareholders who contacted me and said it was imperative for the well-being of the club that the team continued to improve. They knew that clever businessmen do not make successful teams, coaches do.

I faced my partner in the club boardroom in an extremely unpleasant meeting. Sugar berated director Jonathan Crystal and then emptied his briefcase on the table before reaching for an envelope which he passed over to me. The letter told me I had been sacked, claiming I was not up to the job. The club's offer of compensation for my dismissal was slightly less than my original £3 million investment, plus £450,000 for ending my contract. I'm not sure if Sugar thought I would jump at his offer, but there was no possibility of that.

I wanted a minimum of £5 million to leave, which I felt was reasonable. I had invested in a football club that had been failing, which was an enormous risk in my circumstances compared with the level of risk Sugar faced, with his many millions. Philip Green, the billionaire retailer, tried to broker some understanding between us without success. In his autobiography, I am told Sugar denies he would have ever offered me more than he had done in compensation, which confirms my own feeling at the time. In fact, I never believed he would sanction me a dime.

I was contacted by Igal Yawetz, an architect I had introduced to

Tottenham, who told me that the club wanted to negotiate, but apparently Sugar was not going to be involved. I felt there was no point in meeting if Sugar was not there. Good friends told me to take whatever was offered and maybe I was stupid to turn down even the prospect of a deal, but looking back I'm pleased I did because I think had I agreed it would have sickened me inside. It would have saved me financially, as I was in a weak position, not pot-less but seriously reduced. A year after my departure, the club was apparently valued at a minimum of £100 million, which gives some sort of idea of what I felt I lost out on.

I cannot say I came through my return to Tottenham unscathed, but I am grateful there were people in football who were prepared to judge me on my value as a coach and manager, and to ignore the untruths and exaggerations that were written about me. I believe the team I left behind for Ossie Ardiles was talented and committed, and I am certain that would have made them winners. We had come a long way from that worrying first season when I flew in from Florida and relegation was a distinct possibility. What started as a sort of a love affair ended in divorce, with me walking away without any alimony, but at least the revival of the team was a very tangible satisfaction.

I have flashbacks, moments when I say I wish I had done this or that, but though I carried scars out of Tottenham I was ready for the next job. Happily it was to be the role I had always dreamed of attaining: England head coach.

# 15

# AUSSIE DOWNER

THE FLIGHT FROM London to Sydney is normally a test of endurance – intimidating, physically and mentally draining. Not on this occasion. I was preoccupied, full of thoughts about what I would be taking on when we landed in Australia. I had agreed a contract to be national coach of the Australian national side, the Socceroos. It was an exciting new challenge that would keep me involved with the international scene, which I enjoyed and felt comfortable with, and it offered me the chance to coach a team to the finals of a World Cup. It would be France 1998 or bust.

While I was flying, I had to work out my strategy, learn about my staff and my players (some of whom I knew but most of whom I did not), and research our immediate opponents whom I knew neither by name nor reputation. That kept me from being bored throughout the near 24 hours we had in the air. What I did not account for in my calculations, and could never have imagined possible, was that so much hard work, so many fine players and an entire nation would be denied the chance of taking part in the France finals largely because of a mentally disturbed loner, who should have been locked up and never have had the chance of spoiling a major sporting event by running on to the field and stopping play.

Remembering the scene and its heartbreaking conclusion has given me nightmares since. None of my players had been involved in such a high-level occasion before, and perhaps that was a factor in our failure to qualify for the finals. But having said that, their inexperience would not have been challenged but for the publicity seeker and his unforgiveable behaviour.

My Australian experience had all started with a phone call in November 1996 from the man who would inspire me to quit England for a job on the other side of the planet. He introduced himself as the head of Soccer Australia, and admitted he was taking a chance, as he did not know how I would respond, but he told me they were looking for a new national manager/coach. He laid on the charm. He wanted a coach good enough to offer his country success, with a considerable track record. He would not even mind one with a London accent. He went further: they would offer me the job if I said I was interested. My answer was thanks and yes I was intrigued; more than that, I would be honoured. Having agreed to take on the role on 17 November, I confirmed I would travel to join the Socceroos in Sydney in January 1997.

I was impressed with a man I did not know, but I instantly decided he was my type and that we could work in tandem. Within a couple of days, the extraordinary David Hill was in London with his assistant Basil Scarsellar and a contract. I was to learn that David was English-born and been brought up by his single mum and three brothers in Eastbourne on the south coast. It was the 1950s and life was tough, so his mother decided to take advantage of the Fairbridge Farm Scheme, which was set up to transport British kids to Australia where, they were told, they would have a better life. That was not the case for him and his two brothers (one stayed behind), and when they arrived they were subjected to deprivation and abuse.

David's mother was able to join him a year later and that allowed him to forge ahead as a scholar and eventually carve out a successful career in the Australian business world. David, who is an Aussie to his core in all but the country of his birth, felt that UK officialdom had all but abandoned him and his brothers to unsupervised servility. Such early problems did not stop him rising to the very top. He took on the system and beat it, and that appealed to me after all my recent challenges.

David became known as a great trouble-shooter. They would call him in when major national industries, such as the railways and the national broadcaster ABC, needed sorting out. Now he was in charge of making football a success in a country better known for its love of cricket, Aussie rules, swimming and track and field. He was upfront about what he wanted for Australian international football and what he would pay for the right man. He explained they could not afford the sort of pay a national coach would get in a European country. The salary was just A$200,000, but that did not bother me.

I genuinely didn't take the job for the money, which was worth around £80,000 at the time, way below what I could have earned in Europe. I had been taken by surprise by the number of job offers, or potential offers, I received in the aftermath of England's relative success in Euro 96. The Turks were very keen to have me as their national coach and flew to London to meet me the weekend after the European Championship final. Their arrival came just two days after the death of my friend Bobby Keetch. In the circumstances, it was impossible for me to think about a new job, far less take one on. I attended the meeting, but only to explain how sorry I was that I could not discuss football in the circumstances. They understood and left.

It wasn't just a case of receiving international offers, there were opportunities in England as well, which I'll talk about in the next chapter. There were other offers, not all of which I took seriously, but I knew at the back of my mind exactly what sort of job I wanted. By sheer coincidence, the Australians offered me exactly what I wanted from my next job after England: to remain in the international scene and to have the chance to take a team to the World Cup, which had been denied me by the FA. The bigger and better the occasion, the more I enjoyed it. If the money was less than I'd been used to, it was hardly poor and there were compensations. Dave promised I would have a wonderful lifestyle and a job I would find satisfying beyond compare. In the very short time I had to consider the opportunity, I knew it was for me.

Deciding what to do after managing England was a problem that others had faced before. I only had to think of what happened to Sir Alf Ramsey in the aftermath of his becoming the first and so far only England manager to win the World Cup. He should have been retained in some capacity by the Football Association. Instead he was virtually ignored, as Bobby Moore was, and sent out to pick up whatever crumbs were offered him. In his case it was Birmingham City, where he was appointed a director. It did not work out. How could it? He then had a role as technical director in Greece with Panathinaikos, who were willing to tap into his knowledge, but again it was not a role that would last. Neither job was a humiliation, but both were insubstantial rewards for a man who had done so much for the country.

Alf was incomparable, but with few exceptions that is the way it has worked out over the decades for former England bosses. What do you do afterwards? You have to live. Don Revie went to the United Arab Emirates, Ron Greenwood did a lot of work on radio, while Bobby Robson, Graham Taylor, Glenn Hoddle, Kevin Keegan and Steve McClaren all moved back to club football, as I did eventually. I also had the media to fall back on. Working for one of the big television channels could be extremely well paid, while some work on radio stations was useful for little more than to keep my name before the public.

We had taken off from an icy, freezing cold Heathrow and were heading for high summer in Australia, with the memories of Euro 96 still taking up space in my head. The way we had exited the finals six months earlier continued to hurt and I was constantly being hounded on all fronts. That's the way it seemed to be, so removing myself from it all would be a pleasure.

When you are approached as a manager, the first thing you look at are the players you will be responsible for. In Australia's case there was a lot of talent, some of whom we knew in the UK, like Harry Kewell and Mark Viduka, both highly capable and, in the case of big Mark, a touch perverse. When he was in the mood, anything was possible, but there were times when nothing would move him. Those two, on form, were good ones to start with. In addition, there was goalkeeper Mark Bosnich, West Ham's Stan Lazaridis, Aurelio Vidmar and John Aloisi (then of Cremonese in Italy), all first-class footballers. Maybe they lacked familiarity with high-level competition, but I would enjoy working with them.

What so impressed me about David was his directness. He didn't mess about like the amateur fudgers on the FA committees, who would talk round a problem rather than address it. Before I arrived, he had been embroiled in a nationwide project that turned into a major controversy over his decision to set up a merchandising plan for football. He realised that there was big interest in the game in Australia, and there were clubs running successfully among the migrant communities. But he was worried that you would see young guys walking about in Manchester United or Real Madrid outfits, or else wearing the shirts of their local clubs with their associations with various exiled communities, the Croats and Serbs,

Italians and French and the Brits. David simply wanted them to wear Australian colours. He tried to change it and in the process was accused of bias and a racist policy, all of which was nonsense.

I was part of his plan to raise the profile of the national team. You cannot sell merchandise if there isn't a reason to buy it. He wanted a strong and successful national team, and I was to provide it. My role was therefore twofold: I had to get Australian soccer on to the back pages and, crucially, produce a squad that would qualify for France.

The welcome Yvette and I received was exceptional. We lived in a well-appointed apartment – one of the benefits I have talked about – overlooking one of Sydney's bays, with yachts by the dozen moored up and waiting to sail at the weekends. From our main lounge window and our balcony, we could see the Sydney Harbour Bridge and the Opera House behind Circular Quay. Our apartment was situated in a very pleasant residential area, with easy access to shops and restaurants. We were comfortable and when you are comfortable you can concentrate on the job.

Although I knew some of my players, I still had to meet the others and assess my chances of success from the early matches that were arranged. I would be working with two very experienced football men, my assistant Raul Blanco, an Argentine who had emigrated to Australia some 30 years before, and Les Scheinflug, a German who had moved to the country in the early 1950s. Their knowledge of the Australian scene and the friendship we built between us were vital.

The Australian Federation had organised a four-country tournament for just a few weeks after my arrival, involving New Zealand, South Korea and Norway, who were enjoying life having left the snow and ice behind. The tournament had been designed to try out our home-based players, leaving the others based in Europe to be assessed during the World Cup qualifiers. The

Norwegians and their coach Egil Olsen perked up when they saw I was in charge. They liked to rumble the English, and you could see they thought it was a certainty they would be able to take apart my rather lightweight and inexperienced Australian team.

We had won my debut match 1-0 against New Zealand at Melbourne's Lakeside Stadium then flown north-east to Brisbane where we beat the South Koreans 2-1. We faced the Norwegians in the Sydney Football Stadium and beat them 1-0, to the great credit of our team of local players. Egil was not happy as he stood there on the touchline in the wellington boots that were his bizarre trademark.

My main concern now was working with the Australians playing with clubs worldwide, so two matches were scheduled for them before our opening World Cup qualifier, against the Solomon Islands. We beat Macedonia in Skopje and Hungary in Budapest's Nepstadion, and this gave me the chance to assess those players who were based in Europe.

The qualification process for Australia was more complicated than we were used to in England. First of all, we had the Oceania group stage where we were drawn with the Solomon Islands and Tahiti. We beat them all convincingly, scoring 26 goals in our four wins. The main danger to us qualifying for a play-off decider with a team from Asia would be New Zealand, who had won their group. First of all we beat them 3-0 in Auckland and then won 2-0 in the return in Sydney.

That result meant we would play either Japan or Iran for the right to go to France, depending on which side from Asia lost out on automatic qualification. It was to be Iran, and I realised how difficult it would be in a country that always seemed to be in turmoil. To prepare, we played a final warm-up match in Tunisia, which we won with virtually a full squad to select from. One of the joys of working with the Australians was their willingness to travel wherever they were needed without complaint. They would happily fly halfway round the globe to appear for their country in a friendly. They would also listen and learn, and were happy to try new ideas about how the team could be set out.

My focus was now on the play-off and there had been many positives from our run of results. Our success had had the impact David Hill wanted, as we were on the back pages throughout the country, with the Australians more and more impressed with their team and the possibility of performing in front of the world in France. We were being backed by massive interest now we were within two matches of qualification.

We had also sorted out Soccer Australia's administrative problems. My London base became the HQ for Soccer Australia. Everything was planned from my office and dealt with by my business partner Joe Pawlikowski and our PA Zoki Kuzmancevic. They conducted business so successfully that Joe was invited to take over as Soccer Australia's chief executive. He organised everything the team required – travel, hotels, visas – often getting great deals into the bargain. They did all the admin work, sending letters to all the players setting out our arrangements. It took the weight off the Australian side of the administration, who were particularly delighted with the money saved when Joe set up a deal with an air carrier that saved them many thousands of dollars – for instance when we flew from London to Dubai, where we trained before we faced Iran.

Tehran is a beautiful city, if a mad-house of a place. We knew we would be playing in front of a capacity crowd with an atmosphere as passionately nationalistic as anything my players had experienced. Having been warned what to expect, I believed if we could survive the intimidation, and the players had the character not to be overwhelmed by it, then I was confident we would qualify. The attendance figure was officially 128,000, but it had all the intensity

I had been warned about. The Azadi Stadium was packed two hours before kick-off, I learned later, and the noise when our team coach pulled up was incredible. We made it to our dressing room, but there was no soundproofing or peace – it sounded like bedlam coming from the fans.

I decided to take the team on to the pitch to test the reaction of the crowd, and when the noise in the dressing room became just about unbearable we made our way out. None of us could believe the level of noise, a screeching, ear-piercing sound that went on unremittingly – how, I do not know – until the end of the match. When we emerged to acclimatise, the crowd were screaming at us and we had to shout at each other just to be heard. I kept them out there for three-quarters of an hour, so when we returned to our dressing room they had become as accustomed to it as was possible. It was not going to be a shock when the game started. In those circumstances, not only did we take them on, we shut them up when Harry Kewell gave us an early lead after 19 minutes. They equalised just before half time through Khodadad Azizi and the game ended 1-1.

The scene was now set for the Melbourne Cricket Ground one week later, on 29 November 1997. The players were confident, not overly so, but in tune with the situation. We had been undefeated in 13 matches since I took over, so there was every reason for them to believe in themselves. There is always the lingering doubt in my mind: players must be aware of the dangers, but not fearful and so scared they tighten up. Some 85,000 tickets had been sold – a record for a football match in Australia – and it was going to be a full house and this time the atmosphere would be to our advantage. Only international football can produce an unmatchable support for one of the two teams on the field.

We had actually played well enough in Iran to make them feel inferior in front of their own supporters. Everything was in our favour for the return. The Iranians were out of their comfort zone, we were in ours. They would face crowd hostility this time, we would not. We had the advantage of an away goal, they would have to score. Our strategy had been worked on, the players were geared up and ready. We took control of the game and then took the lead when Kewell scored on 32 minutes. We should have added to that before Aurelio Vidmar hit our second three minutes into the second half. We were not exactly coasting, but we were in control. The team had performed, the crowd were in raptures and the big celebration was not so far away.

It was at this point when someone decided it was time for him to act. I have no great memory of him running on to the pitch. I did not see him jump at the goal netting, or ripping a section of it down, but in that instant he was about to destroy everything we had worked for. The referee, Sandor Puhl of Hungary, had to stop play and the groundstaff were called to fix the netting. I kept asking myself what the hell was going on, because I was not certain of what had happened. The game was halted, but why did it take so long to restart? How many men does it take to fix a goal net? The crowd were howling. I remember it as a half-hour stoppage, but in fact it was no more ten minutes. It was enough for Iran, and too much for us. It lifted them, and gave them an opportunity they should not have had. They were rejuvenated while my players lost their rhythm. It was terrible to watch.

You have to ask questions of security at the stadium. The man involved was a schizophrenic known as SHOK, but whose real name I never knew and would rather not find out. He had already been involved in two separate, highly publicised incidents that month. First, he had interfered with the Melbourne Cup at Flemington, then he made an appearance at the funeral for the rock star Michael Hutchence where he shouted at Hutchence's friend Paula Yates. I do not know the details of these incidents, but

I find it hard to believe that security were not on to him. I know from my friends in Australia that since the MCG incident, he has been involved in many other cases of disruption.

For our part, we should not have succumbed at that point, but we did. We were like a runner brought down in a middle-distance race. It is invariably a lost cause even if he can run on. We could have had a penalty, and I made that point to the referee. He replied by saying: 'You should have scored more goals.' There was no question we were in control after Kewell and Vidmar had given us what should have been an uncatchable lead. The Iranians were close to being demoralised, a beaten side. We had shown them what we were capable of in Tehran, where we had overcome the crowd hostility and took the game to them. Now we could rub it in. Instead, because of that intervention, we did not have the experience to hold on to what we had. Iran were inspired to attack us, which they did. I tried to tighten us up, but could only watch as Iran scored twice in a matter of minutes, with Karim Bagheri hitting home after 75 minutes (I thought he looked offside) and Azizi scoring again four minutes later. It was 3-3 on aggregate, but they now had the away-goal advantage.

To me there was a clear case for having the match replayed. If it had happened to one of the big countries, I am sure FIFA would have taken a much closer look, but not when little Australia was the victim. I have had a long career in football, but I have still never seen anything like it. I was completely stunned. What could I say – it was surreal? It felt as if I had been hit on the jaw with a sledge-hammer. I couldn't talk about it for a long time.

It was heartbreaking, not just for the players and me, but for the whole country. The players had been with me and backed how I was preparing them. We had gone from a team that had not been winning to one that was. We achieved what we did because they were intent on listening. They were outdoor sportsmen who chose to play football in a country where it was not generally popular. They took in tactics it would have been hard enough to impress on European players. They were a joy to work with and we achieved remarkable things in a short time. The Australians knew that football had become so big worldwide that they had to find a way to be involved, and those players had opened the door to a wide audience at home.

When I was in charge they had excellent players, but none with the know-how at international level and that was the big factor when we were leading against the Iranians and couldn't kill the game. Our players were not able to close out the game, but then who could have foreseen the ugly way it ended? I keep going back to the pitch invader, of being in charge and losing it all after his intervention. I still cannot understand how a disturbed individual, famous for causing trouble at major events, was allowed to stroll about unhindered. How the hell did he even get in? How can security allow it to happen on the very night your country can qualify for the World Cup finals?

Our qualification attempt had ended in catastrophe, but we had touched the heart of a lot more Australians than before. David Hill was determined to build on the goodwill we had created and believed I had a part to play in developing the squad further. He offered me a new four-year contract that would have taken me to the next World Cup. It was a generous offer, but it did not seem workable to me. We had the Confederations Cup to come in a matter of weeks, but after that there was nothing. There was no Asian or Arabic competition as there is today. Basically, there would have been more than two years with nothing competitive to work for, and I did not want to do that.

I explained to David how I believed the lack of experience, exposed against Iran, had to be resolved whoever was in charge in the future. For now, after that terrible blow, I had the tough challenge to get the players to refresh themselves quickly enough to be ready for the Confederations Cup. We had only a couple of weeks, a ridiculously short time, to prepare for the trip to Saudi Arabia, who were hosting the competition.

It was a big ask for a young, fast-learning but still inexperienced squad. Imagine the situation: most of my players had to return to their clubs in Europe after Melbourne, visit their families and go through the training process with me, before playing two lots of South Americans. As if that wasn't enough, there was also a dispute with the players over payments, who even began to threaten to take strike action. At one stage it came close to us not taking part. The players were down and felt they had not been given enough recognition for what they had done in coming so close to qualification for the World Cup, and bringing the game its highest-ever profile in the country. After doing so well, were we now on the point of imploding?

It was less than ideal preparation and the payment row had not been resolved by the time we flew out. We had difficult ties to consider, starting with one against Mexico, followed by a match against world champions Brazil two days later, then finally 48 hours after that we took on the hosts Saudi Arabia.

The players knew what bonuses the Brazilians were on for competing, so there was friction in our camp before the tournament. It was up to David to deal with that. What I admired about the players was their attitude to work. Sure, they were having a row over bonuses, which was something we could have done without, but as soon as they were on the training pitch they did not allow it to interfere with the preparations. We would get the balls out, warm up and start some small-sided games to see how they looked. They were fine. They were going to haggle for what they deserved, but that never stopped them working flat out.

Mexico came into the competition with a good record, so we did superbly to win 3-1. It was a major thrill for me. It showed what the team were capable of when they were committed and enjoying themselves. We had watched Brazil's match against Saudi Arabia (they won 3-0) and I knew that if we did not present them with something special, they could and probably would give us a good hiding. We had to do something different to occupy them.

I wanted Brazil to go out wide when they attacked us. I did not know who their coach Mario Zagalo would select, but he could call on brilliant forwards such as Romario and Ronaldo. We knew with the players they had, they would go through the centre with quick passing moves, therefore I had to have a defence that would stop that happening and make them go the long way round to produce crosses. We could deal with those. What we needed to do was defend well, but not just defend; I wanted us to be able to break out from the back.

I decided to play three central defenders to make it as difficult as possible for them in the middle, but allowed one of them to break forward when we had the ball. If they did that, we still had enough to defend in case we lost it. They had to be organised and know what they were doing; they couldn't move haphazardly without ensuring there was proper cover. If we just sat back to defend, I feared they would wear us down, so I tried to give them something to worry about by having one wing-back, Stan Lazaridis, who would play up and down on our left covering the man on their right. I then had four defenders, including a more traditional right-back, with Harry Kewell playing up front with Mark Viduka, but playing wide. I'd tried something similar before, but never against opposition as strong as this. We surprised them and stopped them scoring. Our plan had worked.

We might not have scored ourselves, but a 0-0 result against Brazil was highly creditable. Unfortunately, after that, the Saudis were more difficult than we had anticipated and we did not have quite enough time to be ready, so we lost 1-0. But the Brazil result gave us the confidence and self-belief to beat Uruguay in the semi-final, thanks to another Kewell goal in extra time. It was a hugely creditable result for a team which a month before had been on its knees.

We were now in the final, but having surprised the Brazilians once it was not going to happen again. They swamped us 6-0. It was a big defeat, but the players could learn even from that. It was my last match and only my second defeat in the 19 matches I had as national coach. When I took charge we were about 45th in the FIFA world rankings, but when I left we were close to single figures.

I am proud of my Australian connection. I do not doubt that the Australians will be powerful contenders for the world title in time. They have the mentality to succeed, with players who want to improve and will accept help to become better, but they need their own stars. Their youngsters need a national hero to emulate. Someone like Andre Agassi or Shane Warne will have kids follow them, watch what they do and try to copy them. If you have a Pelé or a Messi, they will be watched and copied. The right man for Australia will emerge, of that I am certain. But for now, it was time for me to return to England and to the project I had been working on there during my time in Australia.

# 16

# SPARE A POUND, GUV?

IT WASN'T GREED but necessity after I'd finished with England that drove me into what turned out to be a series of short-term projects that ranged from satisfying to frustrating, all the way to embarrassing. Having lost so much ground financially during my 'difficulties' at Spurs, I had to make a living. More or less everything I had saved from Barcelona and before had been used either buying into Tottenham or in the legal battles that followed. I was not broke, but I was drifting closer than I wanted to troubled financial waters. I was on the lookout for anything. And anything turned up in the shape of Martin Gregory, son of Jim, the owner of Portsmouth FC.

They were in trouble deep enough to cover Martin's head. He had had frequent talks with me when I was with England about the desperate situation he found himself in at Portsmouth. He had wanted me to get involved then, but while I was contracted to the national team there was no chance of me being able to do anything but give advice and support. Martin quickly put together a deal he knew I would be unlikely to resist, the chance to continue pursuing my ambition to own or be a part-owner of a club. When he told me the details it really was an offer I could hardly refuse. It made so much sense as a way of securing my future.

It was this: he would give me a three-year option to buy a controlling interest in Pompey; I would have absolute control of the playing side, working with a manager/team coach; and I would be able to nominate a majority of the directors on the board. It was my chance to be involved in football again, with far greater responsibility than simply coaching the side. To make a living was paramount, I do not disguise that, but a compelling reason was my bond with his father Jim. I simply found it impossible to ignore a crisis threatening the club he had bought after he quit Queens Park Rangers, following his long reign there.

I was back in business and up to my neck at Pompey less than one month after I had finished with England in June 1996. Pompey was not the most glamorous of clubs, but I knew it as a vibrant one from my travels there as player, coach and manager. By the end of July, I had agreed with Martin that I would have a nominal title as director of football, working with a manager/coach. At the same time, I would be a director with input into the running of the club. My position also allowed me to look at any other business opportunities if and when they arose.

There was one, vastly superior, offer made to me when I was invited to take over at Blackburn Rovers by club owner Jack Walker. He asked me to replace Ray Harford, one of the good guys, a very well-respected coach and an extremely pleasant man who would later die tragically young. Harford had resigned in late October 1996, with the club bottom of the table only 18 months after winning the Premier League.

Jack's offer was so generous I doubt any club in the country could have bettered it. I had a number of discussions with him, so he was less than happy when I declined the offer after so much effort had been made trying to convince me how good the job was. I had to explain that although it was very much appreciated, and the set-up meant there would have been no interference on team matters, after England I did not feel right about making a quick return to club football as a manager.

So Portsmouth it was. There were those who worried about my sanity when I accepted and I could understand their concern. Pompey had been a troubled club for years and now they were asking me to help steer them out of a mess that looked terminal. I could have walked away from what was a potential disaster, and if Jim had not been involved in the background, I would have, believe me. He had passed on the rights to run the club to his son Martin, and it was with Martin that I eventually agreed to pay one pound for having 51 per cent of the shares in my name. The club, with all its debts and all the problems that had to be resolved, would be my responsibility as the new chairman.

Jim was aware of Martin's approach, though his health was deteriorating to the point where it was distressing to watch. I visited him as often as I could, regularly accompanied by Yvette, and it was a harrowing experience as he entered the final stages of his life. We would drive to the home of this once dynamic man, and Jim would be sitting there in his own world, looking straight ahead. There would be no acknowledgment of us. I have no recollection of him saying anything to either of us that could be classified as conversation; he would just be sitting there. It was disconcerting, especially when you consider he was a relatively young man of just 70 years old when he died in 1998.

While I was never going to say no to Martin, because of my high regard for his father, there was also a professional, business reason for me taking on the challenge at Portsmouth: I would be my own boss and that was very appealing. My Australian adventure was being negotiated at the same time and would be under way, but I believed I could cope with both roles. With the right people in charge during my absences with the Australian national side, I really believed it would work.

I saw Pompey as the club I would return to when my time in Australia was over. It is a club with a long history, but that had been abused for decades. I am not saying those who had run things at Fratton Park in the past had deliberately set out to cripple the club; far better to say they were ill-advised over certain financial matters and the intricacies of running a football club so that it would be capable of competing and therefore surviving. For all the talk and big ideas that emanated from the mouths of club officials, the vast majority of the money they had spent had managed to trickle down the drain.

To those of us who were Second World War babies, Portsmouth was a club of some significance. It was the senior service club of the English leagues, one that built its strength and support from the armed forces, most notably the Royal Navy. There was a romantic appeal about them and their exploits. They had won the FA Cup in 1939, the year war broke out, and were twice league champions soon after it had ended. Somehow that seemed fitting. My dad served in the Royal Navy and maybe his interest in the club made me more aware of them than would have been normal for a Dagenham boy. I can't say he sat me on his knee and told me story after story about the club's exploits, but when he mentioned them you could detect his respect for them and what they meant to someone of his background.

By the time I arrived at Fratton Park, they were on death row. It was my job to pump life into them, if there was enough left to save. It was still a business and it had to be run as such, although that would be more complex because of my absences in Australia. I appointed my people and they looked after things on a day-to-day basis. Terry Fenwick remained as coach, employing the ideas that had become second nature to us during the years we worked together as player and coach.

Terry had come through a tough season before my arrival, when Portsmouth had managed to avoid relegation only by the thinnest of margins, on goal difference ahead of Millwall, though that in itself could be regarded as an achievement when you consider the state of the club. He had to take the criticism and took it well enough. I had the highest regard for him and was particularly impressed by his enthusiasm for wanting to learn. I guess, like me, he had been one of those 'irritating' players who constantly asked questions.

He had been a member of Bobby Robson's England squad for the World Cup finals in Mexico in 1986, and he was the one prepared to give his opinion when it was clear Bobby would have to make some changes if England were to emerge from the opening group. At a meeting after the first two uninspiring performances – a defeat to Portugal and a draw against Morocco – he argued what other good judges were expressing. I cannot say just how much Terry and others influenced him, but Bobby made a number of changes including the risky one of dropping Chris Waddle. He teamed Peter Beardsley and Gary Lineker as his attack and named Peter Reid, Steve Hodge and Trevor Stevens for the final group match against Poland. From a team that had been below par, they went on to sweep the Poles aside with England's first positive performance, they then beat Paraguay 3-0 before the fateful confrontation with Argentina, when both the virtuosity of Diego Maradona and his Hand of God goal prevented England from reaching the semi-finals.

To me, that showed the sort of initiative that is impressive. I had no doubts about telling him to carry on, though I realised it would still be a difficult task on our resources. We agreed a plan to see us through the first season and then we would look to build from there. The club was keen to make an impact in the First Division, after what had been such a miserable season. We had to be resourceful about signing new players, though no more so than 90 per cent of the clubs in the Football League who also struggle along financially.

Initially we spent £985,000 on players, the most obviously successful being Matt Svensson from IF Elfsborg. Against that we sold four players, generating £650,000. Furthermore, in Lee Bradbury and Deon Burton, we had players who were very definitely assets that other clubs wanted to sign. These two made their contribution throughout 1996-97, but it was the effort put in by Svensson that was near superhuman. You could never say about the Swede that he was stylish or even our best player in every match, but you would want him beside you in the trenches. He gave everything and that inspired performances from others. It also had the same effect on our supporters, who acknowledged him as a club hero.

After all, how many other players are red carded as they are stretchered off? That happened to Matt in a league match against Tranmere Rovers. Matt was injured in a clash with the goalkeeper when they had both gone in high, but Matt took a heavy knock to the head and had to be carried off, only to be shown red.

We battled to the very last week for a chance to return to the top league and finished in seventh place, one place short of a play-off spot. We were so unlucky not to make it, as our performances had been so much better than the year before: we won 24 matches, drew nine and lost 21 in all competitions. We also had a promising FA Cup run, beating Wolves and Reading before facing Leeds United, who were then managed by George Graham. With the tie at Elland Road, we were the big outsiders. It was a classic, with us winning 3-2 against a Leeds team led by Ian Rush and also including Lee Bowyer, Tony Dorigo, Brian Deane, Lucas Radebe and keeper Nigel Martyn. George was gutted.

There is nothing quite like a run in the FA Cup to inspire the players and the support, but Chelsea showed us no mercy in the quarter-finals. They paid us the compliment of selecting their strongest team, which featured Italy's Gianfranco Zola and Roberto di Matteo, Frank Leboeuf of France, Dan Petrescu of Romania, plus top Brits Dennis Wise, Steve Clarke, Scott Minto, Frank Sinclair and Mark Hughes. They were formidable and we lost 4-1.

When I had to be in Australia, I kept in regular touch with Terry in conference calls. He gave me his on-the-spot rundown of each game; while I studied the videos that were sent out to me. We analysed the matches together, and I would occasionally make suggestions which he would work on if he agreed. Terry was strong-minded enough to say no if he felt something would not work. I also kept in contact with Nick Trainer, our lawyer who was acting chairman in my absence and making administrative decisions on the spot if and when needed.

We had been helped in our progress by the loyalty of the Pompey fans. They were the best thing about the club and I decided we had to offer them something, not just on the pitch but off it. Fratton Park had been magnificent in its pomp, but it now appeared ancient and grubby and in need of revamping. Ideally, the club should have built a new stadium on a new site, as neighbours Southampton were to do when they left The Dell for St Mary's in 2001. Sadly, the local council seemed to me at the time to be less than helpful, though they have since played a part in rescuing the club. Perhaps if they had helped us then, the club might have progressed and not been passed from one foreign owner to another.

Portsmouth fans had learned long before our arrival not to hold their breath for any improvements, though I am pleased to say that our little group found the way to build a new stand. It was planned as the first step in what admittedly would have been a long road to producing a stadium worthy of our support. The only downer about it was that we had to sell players to raise the finance. We could have borrowed more money from a bank, but that would have been too risky for us – debt on top of debt is not good business.

Manchester City manager Frank Clark approached us about the possibility of buying Lee Bradbury. Frank must have realised how difficult it would have been for us to sell such an important player. Would the support understand? If we had sold Lee and the money had disappeared towards unknown costs, I reckon we would have lost their trust. But if we used it to buy the fans shelter from the wind and the rain, with a bit of comfort, it would be more acceptable. I managed to push the price up to just on £3.5 million, which City accepted, and that covered the £2.7 million cost of construction. We also sold Deon Burton to Derby for £1 million, which gave us a little respite at the bank.

I was ensconced in my new life Down Under and delighted at the way Pompey appeared to be recovering. I was confident about the forthcoming 1997-98 season, and with my new inside knowledge of Australian football I was able to arrange the transfer of four players to Pompey, the most successful being John Aloisi from Italy. The deal cost us just £300,000, which was excellent value for money. It was a pleasure to be associated with John, who scored 25 goals in 60 league matches for us before he was sold on to Coventry in a £650,000 transfer long after I had left.

After such a fulfilling debut season, the second term proved far more difficult. Terry was not able get the players to dig out results. As chairman I take the blame; I should have spotted quicker than I did that the squad was not responding to him as they should have. My absences with the Socceroos did not help, but I wanted us to hang on and see it through until I returned when I hoped to set out a new strategy with Terry.

To make things more complicated, the club's financial problems had increased and we were soon openly (and publicly) in crisis. The Co-op Bank halved our overdraft facility from £2 million to less than £1 million. At the time, Martin was listening to overtures from prospective buyers from abroad, but in order to sell the club, he had to buy me out as I had ownership of the majority shareholding. What emerged, however, was that because of the club's debts the bank had control of the shares, which effectively meant I owned 51 per cent of nothing, as I shouldn't have been 'sold' them in the first place, even for a pound. If he wanted my shares back so that he could sell the club, I am afraid he would have to pay for the privilege. It is quite true what they say – something is only worth what someone else is prepared to pay. In January 1998 he paid me £200,000 for my shares and my time at the club was over.

I have never had any trouble with the Portsmouth fans, apart from the disappointment caused by poor results in my second season there. I was sorry to leave in mid-season when the team was struggling, but at least they avoided relegation. That did not stop the fans baying for Terry Fenwick's dismissal, and he eventually lost his job. Although I made a good profit on the shares, I never had a salary at Portsmouth, and neither did Nick Trainer for his work as a director and deputy chairman. The arrangement we had agreed with Martin was that if there were any profits from transfers, then he and I would decide how they would be shared, which meant my company received a percentage of the money from the sale of Bradbury and Burton, after the cost of the new stand had been deducted.

Martin was now clear to reap the benefits of any takeover. The one very big mistake he made during this time when the club was financially struggling was not listing the money he had previously invested in the club as a loan. When the club went into administration in December 1998, he would have been legally entitled to be repaid, but as it was not registered as a loan he lost it. At that time, Milan Mandarić was able to step in and take control of the club.

Martin angered me with comments he made around the time of my departure. He was quoted as saying: 'The time is right for Venables to go. He should walk away. I realise I am not the most popular person in Portsmouth, but things were never this bad. We thought we were pulling one of the world's top coaches, but it has not worked out.' I thought this was graceless. He had been desperate for me to come in, so much so that he effectively gave me 51 per cent of the shares, and as a result of my time there the club built a fine new stand.

While my time at Portsmouth ended badly for me, it was nowhere near the worst career decision I have made. My return to Crystal Palace would certainly be worse. Time doesn't always explain why you became entangled in events you had been wary of from the start. For me, working with Mark Goldberg, or trying to, was one of those.

Mark was a successful businessman who had amassed a fortune at a young age through his IT recruitment company. He was a South Londoner and a Crystal Palace fan of a special breed. In fact, I doubt there has ever been a Palace supporter quite like him. Mark remembered the good days when I was coach and Malcolm Allison was manager, and he decided he wanted to buy the club from Ron Noades and then employ me to run the football side. There was no way I wanted to be involved.

He first made contact when I was still contracted to the Australian national side. My mind was set: nothing was going to drag me back to Palace as manager, but he kept coming up with different possible roles for me. Completing the deal to take control of the club took him longer than expected, while he got the financial package in place with the help of various backers. He officially took over in the early summer of 1998 and came across as charming, persuasive and full of energy, but the more we talked the more bizarre I thought it was.

The rumour was that he had £40 million set aside to spend on the club. I do not know how accurate that figure was, but money seemed to be no object when it came to securing my services. I asked Leon Angel, a friend and business associate who is an expert in finance, to establish if he could make sense of Mark's proposal. His report back said that Mark was genuine and that he was committed to making Crystal Palace great. I was told his company was incredibly successful and that he had made enough money to pursue his dream for the club.

I should have been more concerned as, for all his supposed business acumen, Mark had been unwise to buy the football club from Ron Noades without also securing the freehold. How could a man with his experience do that? In the circumstances, Leon suggested that if I was going to do business with him, it would be best if I was paid up front, in case some of the promised backing or sponsors did not materialise.

I still wasn't interested. However, the more I said no, the more incentives Mark would offer: pre-payment, an executive car, a house to live in, and a high salary. Eventually, I succumbed and was appointed head coach at the start of the 1998-99 season, following relegation the previous campaign. Looking back, I realise that I must have been weakened in my resolve by the failure of Australia to qualify for the World Cup finals. I hadn't realised just how much that had affected me. Listening to Mark talk, sometimes my mind would drift and so one day I said okay – and that was it.

Leon conducted the contract negotiations, which gave me a lump sum in advance of, I believe, £300,000. There has been criticism levelled at the cost of employing me, but it was no more than a top-level international coach/manager would receive. I had people I wanted around me, like Terry Fenwick (as first team coach) and Ted Buxton, and they also needed to be paid. Meanwhile, Steve Coppell who had been stood down as manager had stayed on as director of football. My arrival at the club was delayed because of the World Cup in France, as I had a contract with ITV to work with them for the duration of the finals, but Mark voiced no objections about that.

I was mindful, as was Mark, of the great days when we played in front of 52,000 at Selhurst and of course I would have loved to see that support return. I worked hard to make it happen, but it was never going to be an overnight transformation after such a poor season before. There were moments of light from the team and then there were periods without a win. People might have accepted that, but for the stories that appeared in the press about the money being spent in a profligate way. Agents were involved, mainly through Mark, and there was no harm in that if they came up with the right players. What you don't want are duffers flying in from South America.

I was supposed to be in control of the playing side, but I learned Mark was himself talking to agents about players and arranging deals. Morale was dropping fast throughout the club, created by Mark's misdirected energy and ambition. It affected every section of the club, with the office staff changing and new people being brought in. I should have argued more strongly against what I can only describe as Mark's scattergun approach. He was intent on giving us the best, so I am not criticising him for that. It is just that there has to be a limit. He surely had to listen more to the views of his fellow directors, even when he controlled the money. Mark was like a kid in a candy shop, as fitness experts and personal trainers suddenly appeared, while players came and went. Despite it all, our results continued to be way below expectations. Perhaps, given time, we would have turned the corner, but there was so much going on. Then something happened that put it all into perspective for me.

I was in Sunderland with the team on 16 December 1998 when I took a call from Yvette to inform me my dad had suffered a heart attack. I left immediately for the station at Darlington to board the London train. I have caught the service on numerous occasions over the years and it is always packed in the morning. I had a first-class ticket so I knew I had a seat, but I was astonished that the first-class carriage I was in was empty. Indeed, there was not another person in that section of the train. The eerie emptiness took me back to the death of Bobby Keetch days after Euro 96 and that empty bar in the Hilton. Yvette was there to meet me at the station to tell me that Dad had died earlier, but she had waited until I arrived home before letting me know.

In my mind, it was the end for me at Palace. I was not prepared for the grief as well as the madness. I would leave as best I could. I was unaware that Mark's supply of money was drying up, but this was a period when it was difficult even for thriving companies like Mark's to compete. The first signs of a financial crisis at Palace came in the first two weeks of January 1999. One critic claimed it was the expense of meeting my demands that was such a drain on Mark's finances. Apparently I was signing players on big salaries. In actual fact, I was recommending some signings and it was Mark who was agreeing their money. It was not my budget, I felt, but his. It was his final decision to buy or sell, not mine. I am not shifting blame – I accept my responsibility – but stating facts.

My recommendations could not have been so bad. Whatever transfer figures you look at for my time there – and it is not easy to find a definitive list – Crystal Palace came out with a profit, perhaps as much as £8 million between players bought and players sold. Yes,

I was expensive, but then so was Attilio Lombardo, the little Italian who had been signed by Steve Coppell from Juventus the season before I arrived. We were virtually the first two out because the club could not afford our wages. My instinct had been right from the start: I should have stayed away. Soon after, Mark's finances took a turn for the worse, and he was eventually declared bankrupt in 2000. We walked away from the house in Oxted that was to be ours, leaving behind all the brand new goods and furniture Yvette had bought. I wanted out; enough was enough.

I had a fairytale contract that gave me specific rights, in the event of my leaving. Did I pursue it in court? No. I was paid up front, as Leon Angel had originally suggested. It was my security, and I was glad for it. Those who say I was paid the remainder of my contract are wrong. In the event of my leaving the club, either through dismissal or by my choice, I should have received a considerable settlement, including that house, but in fact I came away with just £12,000.

I have not spoken to Mark since, but I read about him from time to time and know he is manager of non-League side Bromley. He lost a lot, but he did it his way. He has had the occasional moan but has generally accepted his fall as one of those things. I liked him, despite my bewilderment at what he was doing. I could understand his love for Crystal Palace, but not when I learned of his undoubted passion to make the club great by throwing every penny he had at it. If only he had taken his time and listened to others he might have made it. Good luck to him if he ever fulfils his dream. Either way, no one can accuse him of not trying.

Soon it would be my turn to try again, and next time I was going somewhere that was on a much steadier financial footing.

# 17

# CONTRASTS

BRYAN ROBSON WAS destined to become as successful and assured a manager as he had been a player at Manchester United and for England. The man was different class. He was one of the new breed heading for the top in the summer of 2000, only for the team he had built at Middlesbrough to show signs of imploding. Within a couple of months of the start of the new season, it became worrying enough for him to ask me for some help and advice, as you would do with people you have worked with and trust. Could I provide an answer?

Bryan had been part of my coaching team with England from the start to the finish of our Euro 96 campaign. He had moved from Manchester United to Middlesbrough, initially as player-manager, where he led his side to promotion to the Premier League in his first campaign. When he felt his legs had gone and it was time to quit playing, he switched to full-time management. In just over six exceptional years, he had led Middlesbrough to three Wembley cup finals, two of them in 1996-97. It all happened so quickly, there should have been little surprise when the club was relegated at the end of that campaign, only for Bryan to lead them straight back to the top league yet again.

You could argue it was inevitable there would be a slump, possibly even a dramatic one, at a club without the limitless resources of the elite, but one who had nevertheless brought in high-quality players from around the world. Bryan gave us a global team featuring some famous names: Juninho, Fabrizio Ravanelli, Gianluca Festa, Emerson, Christian Ziege, Marco Branca and Carlos Marinelli, plus quality British players Paul Gascoigne, Gary Pallister, Nick Barmby, Paul Merson, Paul Ince and the Republic of Ireland's Andy Townsend. He bought well, often brilliantly.

In the summer of 2000, the club chairman Steve Gibson sanctioned a batch of expensive new signings, high-quality ones as before: Christian Karembeu of France, Ugo Ehiogu, Noel Whelan, Alen Bokšić and Joseph-Désiré Job. That little lot, I was to find out, cost not far off £20 million, which confirmed the bond of trust and respect manager and owner had for each other, absolutely essential between the two most important men at any football club. It was a brave decision by Gibson to back his manager with another considerable investment – they had finished an unspectacular 12th the season before – though the sell-on profits could be considerable; in the case of Juninho the club had made something like £7 million profit when they sold him to Atlético Madrid in 1997. In such a case, it was good business.

But, despite the new names and fresh blood, Middlesbrough had been nowhere near as successful as Bryan had demanded as the new season got under way, and by November they were in one of the relegation places. Words were said, and the situation got no better. If the collapse of confidence and poor results continued, relegation would be unavoidable. Having talked things through with Gibson, Bryan got in touch, though it must have been extremely difficult for him to ask me to join him as head coach. It takes a big man to ask for help in this way. He must have known there would be those saying he was fighting for his professional life, and that he had messed up.

His request took me by surprise and I recognised there could be a problem with having us both there. My initial reaction was to turn Bryan down, as I didn't want to be seen to be taking over from him. He suggested I talked to Keith Lamb, the club's chief executive, and then I spoke to Steve Gibson. The more we talked, the more I warmed to the idea. Had Steve contacted me on his own, without Bryan's say-so, I would have dismissed it, but since the contact came direct from Bryan, and we had worked closely together with England, and since I was certain he was not under pressure to seek me out, I said yes.

My contract would run until the end of the season. I had studied Middlesbrough's performances on video, and it was clear from those that this was a group of high-quality footballers whose confidence would often evaporate when they conceded a goal. With discussions still ongoing, I watched them live on television at West Ham, who were in mid-table at the time. Middlesbrough lost; dire hardly described their position. My mother-in-law Dolly looked at Bryan's face on television and remarked how sad he looked. He had put such a lot of himself into the team, and here they were losing matches they could have won and certainly should not have lost.

On the strength of what I saw of the players available, I believed relegation was avoidable, though many viewed them as dead certs for the drop. Soon after that game, I finally agreed to accept Middlesbrough's offer. The job was easily defined: keep Boro in the Premier League. It was a big decision for me professionally, as I had a lot of television commitments, as well as my column in the *Sun*, but also personally, as we had to pack our bags and head north. In fact, I had been feeling restless, licking my wounds after the

Palace debacle, and so it felt good to be back in action on the training ground.

I had kept up to date with a game that never stops changing. I didn't want to wander too far from its heart, if for no other reason than I needed to be informed for my media work. Our new lifestyle in the North East fitted us like a glove. As Londoners used to the 'Big City', we were to love just about every minute of my seven months with the club. It was going to be a full-time operation, with Yvette, Dolly, our dog Boo and me finding a house and putting London out of our minds. We had our walks along a river, wonderful countryside to roam in, and peace of mind.

The club, from Steve Gibson to Keith Lamb, a thoroughly professional administrator, to Bryan plus his staff, Gordon McQueen and Viv Anderson, could not have been more welcoming. It might have been awkward, and there were initially moments when we all felt a little uncomfortable. Happily, there was nothing that could not be resolved amicably. Steve continued to support Bryan with good positive statements, saying how Bryan needed to catch his breath after six and a half years of intensive work.

We agreed a pathway to survival. There were arguments about the team system we would adopt, but as I was brought in to offer my experience that had to prevail. I had expected to be confronted with a team very much in the doldrums – they were in 19th place, and had earned just one point in eight games – but rather than feeling sorry for themselves, they exuded a determination not to be relegated. They wanted to know what they had to do to get out of it. Confidence was the missing factor, certainly at the outset. Players with their experience knew they should have been nowhere near the relegation zone. They just required help to rid them of the uncertainty that had been dragging them down. It was up to me to show them what to do, and to highlight flaws I had already spotted on videos. They had to stop conceding as easily as they had been, because going behind hits the confidence of a struggling team. They had to understand there was no magic formula. If we were to survive we had to work hard together.

What I was looking for was a quick win. If we lost our first couple of games, our recovery would be doubly hard. We had a very good defence in front of a brilliant goalkeeper in Mark Schwarzer, who I always thought Arsenal would have been smart enough to sign. Mark had not played for me with Australia, as Mark Bosnich was the keeper, but I knew Schwarzer was excellent and his performances would be vital. He would need extra cover and we found that for him. There were small things to sort out in our game which may have appeared relatively trivial, but could be crucial in a match. For example, I had noticed how, when we were defending free kicks, the defence was too close to the goalkeeper, making it more difficult for him to come for the ball. That was changed.

We worked on our free kicks and corners, as these were two situations which could produce us a winning goal, maybe the only goal of the match. I was looking for a defiant mood, and what I saw I liked. If we were short as a squad it was up front, where we needed more power, so we signed Dean Windass – the only recruit in my time – who had seen it all and carried the scars of numerous battles.

A coach knows when a group of players respond to him. It was clear to me they wanted to learn and that if I had the answer then they were ready to listen. Our first home match was on 16 December 2000, against Chelsea at the Riverside. I was told the crowd would be big and passionate, and they did not disappoint. We knew we must not lose a goal, and we didn't. We had to score, please the gods, and we did with a Dean Gordon strike. Three points! It not only renewed the confidence of the players but gave the support hope that their team could and would be saved.

It was the launching pad for the rest of the season. We drew 0-0 at Tottenham next, then came back to the Riverside to face Liverpool: no goals conceded and we scored with a Christian Karembeu strike before the interval to earn a superb victory. We were then unbeaten for the next seven Premier League matches, which saw us move out of the relegation places, so we felt that, barring a collapse of morale, we would see out the season still as part of the Premiership.

It needed positive coaching from the four of us – Bryan, Gordon, Viv and me – and a defence mean enough to give nothing away without a battle. When I look back at the results, my immediate thought is that we had so many drawn matches, but that is what saw us through. We had learned how to survive and continued our work with the players. Every session had a purpose. I talked to them; I told them how well they had done and how much better they could be. Above all, it was their sheer will to go for it, to take on board what they were told that worked for us. For me it was a joy, a pleasure to train every day, to be with the players and be part of such a special set-up.

I seem to remember reading I was forever popping back to London like a man in need of a big-city 'fix'. I do not remember making any trip back south, except with the team and definitely not to my home, in all the time I was with Middlesbrough from December 2000 until the summer of 2001. I had decided not to have any sort of break, just as I had decided not to return to London from Barcelona, unless it was unavoidable. One London sortie to Arsenal's home at Highbury was particularly memorable when we won 3-0 against a full-strength team of David Seaman, Lee Dixon, Martin Keown, Tony Adams, Patrick Vieira, Thierry Henry et al. Our first two goals that day may have been own goals, but even if we discount them we would still have won with a Hamilton Ricard strike.

We seriously thought of staying on in Middlesbrough after the end of the season, and I was offered the chance to do so by Steve Gibson, who was keen on my taking a more permanent role at the club. It was very tempting, and as a family we loved the lifestyle. With Keith Lamb present, Steve had a discussion with me about the possibility of my overseeing the playing side in more of a board-room role, as he had tried to do, but couldn't with much regularity because of his business commitments.

When I considered my other previously agreed commitments, it was clear it was too complicated. I had a contract with ITV, from which they had released me to join Boro. They were under no obligation to do so, and with the World Cup finals a year away, they asked me to renew my contract to cover that, and I agreed. I thought a good job had been done: everybody was happy, we had beaten the threat of relegation, the team had been terrific to work with. In the circumstances, I thought the best thing I could do was to leave.

My last match as head coach was against West Ham at the Riverside, which we won 2-1. The end could not have been better. We were 19th in the Premier League when I arrived and we finished in 14th spot. We deserved an open-topped tour of Middlesbrough, and the relief in the boardroom from Steve Gibson was genuine. I never thought I would enjoy my life as much as I did at Middlesbrough. The players and all those I worked with daily made it special for me. It was the pick-me-up I needed after what had gone before, and I was left alone to get on with what I love doing. Bryan decided to leave at about the same time I did, as he felt his time had run its course, and he had been receiving some criticism from the fans. He went on to manage various clubs, but he is now back at Old Trafford in an ambassadorial role. No club could have a more accomplished representative.

If my time working with Steve and Bryan at Middlesbrough had been a happy one, the same cannot be said of my next job. Leeds United was my bad day at the office. Some day! It lasted all of nine months from July 2002, when I succeeded David O'Leary, until I left in March 2003. There were moments when the clouds parted long enough to let in a glint of sunlight, but for the rest of the time it was infuriating, frustrating and desperately disappointing. Joining Leeds United as manager was my misjudgement, my poor decision and one that still hurts like hell.

I had spent the season after leaving Middlesbrough as an analyst on ITV in the build-up to the World Cup finals and then at the finals themselves, shared between South Korea and Japan. I had time to do other things: after-dinner speaking, working on Chris Evans' Saturday morning Virgin Radio programme and helping with business promotions. I indulged myself by buying a season ticket with hospitality at Chelsea – it was very expensive but worth it. You could say I was a happy man. I loved watching the matches as a spectator at Stamford Bridge, plus going to games wherever ITV or the *Sun* wanted to send me. I could enjoy myself without any managerial responsibilities or concerns.

Always there was this compulsion within me to go back to being involved in the game in a hands-on role. And that is when Peter Ridsdale made his approach. He turned up at our home in Spain all bells and whistles and full of hot air. Ridsdale was, I felt, a disaster for Leeds. I felt I was used as a scapegoat for the storm that was about to engulf the club. I will never forgive him for that. I am prepared to admit my mistakes; not Ridsdale, unless he is talking about my appointment in a disparaging way as his one and only major blunder. Ridsdale is a good talker, I will give him that.

I listened to his plans and I accepted his word. At the time I did not realise I had been hired when in reality he wanted to appoint Martin O'Neill as his manager. Indeed, they had wanted him before they appointed David O'Leary in 1998.

When David left the club, Ridsdale came to me. Being second or third choice, and seen as no more than an emergency stop-gap, was not an ideal start, but it can happen in football, so I got on with it. To say it was my monumental error to go there should not be taken as a slur on Leeds United, who had been rightly considered a leading club for decades since the ruthlessly professional one established by Don Revie. Good guys have managed them since: Jimmy Armfield had a spell at Elland Road, Howard Wilkinson won the last title of the old First Division in 1992, George Graham took them forward and David O'Leary had shot them into the very top bracket as unlikely but worthy contenders for the title. For the previous five seasons, they had always finished in the top five, and in 2001 they had reached the semi-finals of the Champions League.

The price of that had been high. Ridsdale's soaring ambition for Leeds United sadly outstripped the club's ability to cope financially. It was a classic blunder from a man unwise enough to claim he was 'living the dream', when in truth Leeds were living dangerously. By all means buy the best, but you must make certain you can pay for it. To 'live the dream', they needed the money from the Champions League to help service the debt, so when they just missed out on qualification in 2001, having spent only one season since 1993 in the competition, they faced financial meltdown.

I did not see it as clearly as I should have when I was approached a year later, and certainly had no warning of a financial collapse. All I had asked for when the job was discussed was to have money to buy if needed after I had assessed at first hand the players available to me; I also insisted that no one should be sold without my knowledge. That is a normal condition for a manager. I realised that finance would be a major factor. If you have money, fine, but if there is nothing in the kitty, you have to sell to buy. There was no way any new manager would want to lose quality players such as Rio Ferdinand, Jonathan Woodgate, Lee Bowyer, Robbie Fowler, Robbie Keane and others. I did not, but they were all sold.

It is pointless walking into a club to learn there is no money and knowing you are going to be blamed for poor results. I would have steered clear if I had been aware the debts were so colossal that all those players would have to be sold to stave off bankruptcy and to please the financiers of the City of London. There is a line you do not cross when selling and that is when it becomes suicidal to the team's prospects.

My remit was straightforward: I had to produce a winning team to finish in the top four or at worst fifth place, where they had finished the previous season, to qualify for the UEFA Cup. My contract was for two years, and I certainly could not complain about the squad I inherited from David. There were fine players available to me: Rio, Jonathan, Robbie Keane and Robbie Fowler, who I was pleased to work with again after he had been in my Euro 96 squad. However, I quickly learned that I had inherited a team that would soon be moving on either through their own choice or to generate cash.

Too many of the players who remained did not want to know or were past listening to what I was trying to tell them. The culture was all wrong. Maybe they had been sated by too much success, performing in the Champions League and becoming used to the highest level of European football. That was no longer available to them, which was not my fault but their own. They were back in the secondary UEFA Cup and too many felt that was not worthy of them.

Ridsdale's decisions often left me baffled. I was battling to hold on to players from the very start, when Rio Ferdinand left for Manchester United within a fortnight of my arrival, after I had been led to believe he would not be transferred. The fee of over £29 million was huge, and perhaps impossible to turn down for a club with debts of £78 million, but that was not the point. I did not want him to go and had been told that he would not be leaving us. The only star player I willingly agreed to sell was Robbie Keane, who went to Spurs for £7 million. Robbie wanted out and we were well supplied with strikers, so that was not a major problem.

Then, in quick succession I lost Lee Bowyer to West Ham and Olivier Dacourt to Roma on loan. I didn't see the latter's departure as a great loss; he was a player who never came to terms with the physicality of the Premiership and I had no time for his poor attitude. As I saw it, he was not worth the money Ridsdale was paying him when I considered his contribution to the team. He is the only player I fined as a manager, and I did so only after witnessing what I believed to be the cynicism of the man.

At the time we were a team trying to find our form. Too many were underperforming to make any appropriate impact on our season. In my eyes, Dacourt seemed to be treating it all with a shrug. However, his laissez-faire behaviour can be infectious. I admit I was struggling in very difficult circumstances to fix the overall problem, but when I saw him trip up in training I decided to act. At the time I thought it was deliberate. I was watching the players warm up in groups, and Dacourt's group was far enough away to think they were out of sight and mind. If he thought that he was wrong. What he was trying to get out of, I do not remember, but I fined him £2000.

Some time later, I was talking with Ridsdale and asked him if Dacourt had paid his fine. His reply was a story that we owed Dacourt money. 'It wouldn't be the same amount as the fine?' I asked. It proved to be the case, and that example highlighted one of the issues the club faced: I believed the chief executive wanted to be one of the boys. He had found a way so that Dacourt did not have to be punished for his actions. I felt that sort of response not only diminished team discipline, it undermined my position.

We played in fits and starts; we'd have a good run, then a terrible one. It was my job to get it together and I did not. I could not pierce the negative attitude of a squad that was doing not much more than go through the motions. It was down to me as manager and coach, though I am tempted to credit Ridsdale with assists, as he deserves nothing less for that sort of intervention in team matters. It is of great regret that nothing I did – and I did not operate as I normally would be expected to – had much effect on the team or at least on the majority of the players.

Ridsdale was concerned about the future of Leeds, I accept that, but he was now focused more on keeping the bankers happy than in keeping the team going. In my time there, we made just one signing, bringing in Nick Barmby for £2.75 million; otherwise the traffic was all one way. In January, we were forced to sell more players, with Robbie Fowler joining Manchester City in a £6 million deal, half payable on reaching a certain number of appearances.

I was told that Robbie's departure meant we would not have to sell Jonathan Woodgate, as to lose him at that stage of the season when we were struggling was crass stupidity. He was a central defender with the experience and quality I needed in the team. You cannot flog your top players and hope to win matches. However, Ridsdale was talking to Newcastle in London after we had played at Chelsea. The next day he flew to the North East and Woodgate was sold on 31 January. The line had been crossed. It was desperate for the club and fatal for me.

I feared Ridsdale would try to get me out without recognising my contract. If he manoeuvred me into saying I wanted out, I would get no compensation, so I told him the decision was his and that I wanted to stay on and had even put a £2000 deposit on a house we had decided to buy. He did not want me settling down, so that clinched it. Leeds United honoured my contract and I was free.

I don't want to waste time or expend any degree of energy talking about Ridsdale, but his attitude infuriated me. In 2007, long after he too had left the club, he produced an autobiography which struck me as a self-regarding litany of complaint. Everybody else at Leeds was wrong: David O'Leary was wrong, the board was wrong, his successor as chairman, Professor Roy McKenzie, had been groomed to take over from him.

As for me – I was the worst ever. The criticisms he made of me in his book were offensive in the extreme. He wrote: 'It was agreed unanimously to terminate his contract … It had all gone wrong under Terry … confused feedback from the players … constantly adjusting tactics for every match … chopping and changing … after a mini good run I was applauding the man I couldn't wait to remove … Leeds United had gone into reverse under his stewardship.' And so on. To be criticised by him for my coaching, when I was struggling against the constant changes enforced by losing so many key players, is ridiculous.

Sadly, the club has still not recovered from those turbulent times when the debts mounted and so many excellent players were sold off. I believe Leeds United will be successful again and that someone will find the formula, but it may not happen for a while yet.

# 18

# ENGLAND – YOU
# CAN'T SAY NO

THE FIRST MISTAKE Steve McClaren made early in our relationship was to ask me to warm up the England squad on the
pitch before our first match, a friendly against Greece at Old
Trafford. I joined up with Steve, at his request, to help him with my
experience; but warming up the team was not one of the roles I
envisaged he had in mind for me. The thought had never entered
my head. It is simply not a job for a former England manager, and
although I will not call his request offensive I considered it disrespectful. It was the most unfortunate of starts and it got worse.
Next he wanted me to wear 'civvy' clothes at matches and I
wouldn't have to sit on the bench, would I? As it happens I thought
I would. There are a lot of things to worry you when managing
England without concerning yourself with where I sat and what I
wore. I began to feel that Steve wanted my knowledge but did not
want me to be seen, perhaps fearing that some might wonder who

was in charge. He knew I was angry about these things, and came back to me and apologised, so we moved on.

You only properly learn about a person's character when you work with them. Steve had come across to me as an upfront, in your face, confident, maybe too confident, type. That was to be expected. He had gained a considerable reputation as Sir Alex Ferguson's number two at Manchester United, and you do not survive in that job unless you are better than average. He would also have learned a lot as England manager Sven-Göran Eriksson's assistant, which gave him experience of the international scene.

Steve was appointed in the role of England boss ahead of the 2006 World Cup finals, taking up the position in August. He decided he wanted me to play a part in running the national side, because he had read my earlier autobiography and was intrigued enough to ask further questions. He wanted me to explain how I had gone about changing the way England played; he was keen to know the ins and outs of the system we had used to beat the Dutch. He wanted to exchange views about numerous tactical issues and anything else I could inform him about that was worth exploring and developing. I was never certain in truth whether it was a good idea or a bad one for me to be involved, but it was clear Steve wanted me to untangle some niggles in his own mind.

I knew him only by reputation and the start between us was anything but promising. I was shocked by his 'warm up' suggestion. Initially, I thought he was talking about doing this on the training pitch from time to time, which I would also have said no to, but he actually meant before matches – on the pitch. I could think of many ambitious young coaches who would be more than happy to do it. I was furious that he should have put me in a position where I would say no, but there was no public argument about it. I just took it as a sign of his inexperience and his naivety. I tried to imagine him asking Sir Alex to be his warm-up man. I may be wrong but

I think that would be a job for the hair drier. I am not comparing myself to the former Old Trafford manager, but we are of the same age group and I suspect similar mindsets.

I have to say these early issues were quickly resolved without damaging our relationship in the long term or impinging on my job, which was to help England qualify for the Euros. I quickly realised that being an assistant at this stage of my life did not come naturally to me and was going to take some getting used to. There is no malice in Steve, but he was prone to making some decisions that I occasionally found bewildering, and in short time I was asking myself what I had let myself in for.

He wanted my experience, that's how he explained it to me. I knew I was not joining the staff as a coach, Steve would be in charge of that and he also had Steve Round for that side of his operation. I was there to offer advice. I did sit on the bench and I would make my contributions during matches and at half time, and afterwards when we would discuss the match in detail. If I was to be 'hidden', fine. I could live with anonymity after years in the front line.

We will never be close friends, but I admired Steve's courage under fire and the fact he was a better man, calm and controlled, when the critics and the fans were out to finish him for failing with England. When you face criticism at that level, life is hell but never once in my presence did Steve moan about results or disappointing performances or being pilloried by the media. I liked that. I liked the fact he was prepared to appoint Steve Round, one of our brightest young coaches, to work alongside him. It proved he was confident enough about his own ability to have the best close to him. I liked it when he asked me if I would be interested in advising him, as an old England head, on certain technical matters as his England assistant. I would never turn down the opportunity to work on behalf of my country. And I particularly admired his be-damned attitude when he shrugged off the 'Wally with the Brolly' embarrassment.

None of the characteristics I like about Steve stopped him failing, when we should have qualified comfortably for the 2008 European Championship finals. That was a blow to all of us involved and the blame should be shared. Steve was a very good coach, but if he lacked one essential attribute in this campaign it is the one all managers need to be on nodding terms with – luck. You can argue you make your own luck, but his misfortune was relentless and fatal. How do you explain away two England goalkeepers giving away howlers in separate games, with a renowned full-back scoring a freak own goal? What do you say when you are ordered to play a crucial international match on an artificial surface – one of the first – when a year later it is considered inappropriate and ripped up and laid with grass for a Champions League final?

Do not tell me we simply made the wrong selections for the wrong systems. When you plan to change the way you play – the basic reason I was brought in by Steve – and the key player in that system calls off on the day you are boarding the plane for the tie, is it anything other than bad luck? That also happened to Steve. He received no respite.

Like most people, I was surprised when he was named as England manager. His reputation as a coach was high, but he was relatively inexperienced. I thought the FA had got it wrong, that they should have waited a few years when his appointment might have been unarguable. At least when Sven-Göran Eriksson said he was standing down, the job went to an Englishman. Alan Curbishley had been mentioned in dispatches as had big Sam Allardyce and they would have had the support of the country, too, I am sure. But it was another big man, the Brazilian Luiz Felipe Scolari, who was offered the job only to turn it down the next day. What a humiliating experience for the FA. Guus Hiddink, the coach whose Dutch side was taken apart by my England team in the Euro 96 finals, was another foreigner also in the frame. Steve was not helped by coming in to the role as the FA's second or third choice.

I saw it as part of my role to accelerate the learning process every new England manager goes through. There were occasions when I felt he did not hear what I said, but there was nothing specific I could point to. We were confident we would make it to the finals, to be co-hosted by Austria and Switzerland, though we knew it would be tough. Group E included Croatia and Russia, who might or might not play to their potential, plus Macedonia, Israel, Estonia and Andorra, with two sides due to go to the finals.

Steve was very enthusiastic. I liked that about him, and it was obvious watching him with the players that he was a good coach who enjoyed working with them and the players enjoyed working with. After those initial misunderstandings about my role, we worked out exactly where I could help. We would have daily meetings, and I would react to whatever came up or made suggestions myself. Steve Round would then put across the manager's ideas on the training pitch.

One aspect of the job that nothing can really prepare you for is the national manager's role working with the press. I told him to remember they were not his friends as a group and never could be; they had a job to do and, no matter how close he thought they were to him and how much he felt they understood his problems, they would still criticise him if they had to. I am not convinced Steve ever acted on that advice. At one stage, aided by the FA's press office, he wanted to take four or five football reporters out for dinner, be hospitable, feed them angles for stories, and let them know what was on his mind. I told him that would be absolutely wrong. It would be good for the hand-picked newspapermen, but what about the ones left out in the cold? They would not be happy;

enemies might be made and anyway even his 'friends' from Fleet Street would not hold back and defend him if his team under-achieved. I explained that the only way to secure a good press was to keep on winning and to tell them the truth. Never try to manip-ulate them.

Steve was interested to learn how we had used different systems in our performances in Euro 96. For example, we talked about going with three at the back, with two attacking wing-backs. You can then have three in the heart of midfield, which can and should produce attacking football. He wanted to know how and when it could be done to maximum effect, but although we talked about it, he did not make any move to try to play that system until we took on Croatia, our key rivals, five games into his reign.

He had made a good start with a decisive victory (4-0) against Greece in a friendly at Old Trafford in August. It was then straight into the Group E matches that initially went to form with an easy win against Andorra (5-0). Four days later, we were happy to leave Macedonia with three points after a 1-0 success, but it was there we realised just how difficult a campaign this could be. When we drew 0-0 with them at Old Trafford in the return a month later – this was in the period Wembley was being rebuilt – I had that depressing thought confirmed.

We had lost Rio Ferdinand through injury before the match and then Steven Gerrard picked up a yellow card that kept him out of the next tie, four days later in Croatia. You have to expect this as part of the normal ups and downs you cater for without knowing exactly when they will happen. The media coverage was critical, rather than outright hostile, after the Macedonia game, and I could not argue with their assessment: we had to do better.

We knew that this next game was going to be one of the tough-est of the group, and Steve had decided he wanted to play three at the back from the start, plus Gary Neville and Ashley Cole as wing-backs, changing our formation from the usual back four. He wondered if we could change our set-up and surprise their manager, former West Ham star Slaven Bilić, with our formation. As he had played for such a long time in England, Bilić would have been expecting us to play with a flat back four, but time was against us. I pointed out I had spent two years working with the players prior to Euro 96, developing a range of tactical options, so it was a bit of a risk.

In England, when you talk about playing three at the back, people immediately assume you are talking about a sweeper system, but that's not necessarily the case. The players were receptive to the idea and understood what we wanted and how to make it work. With John Terry and a fit-again Rio Ferdinand, we had players who were adept at coping with change, and I had no worries about Neville and Cole. I was confident they would all slip into it effortlessly. The key to it all was Ledley King, who played exactly that role for Tottenham. He knew it inside out and was comfortable with it, and it had looked really good in training. Watching them prepare gave me a lot of confidence in our chances. He was such an outstanding footballer, like Paul McGrath before him; the sort who, because of persistent injury, wouldn't be able to train but would always be the best player on the day.

The plan was ruined when Ledley reported in with a recurrence of his knee problem. The doctor gave Ledley a complete thumbs down, which was heartbreaking. I felt as if fortune was not treating us with respect. He had been exceptional in the goalless draw against Macedonia, but was so badly injured it was decided he should not even travel to Zagreb. It was such a shame his career was stricken by injury. The world game never had the chance to fully appreciate his ability. It was also too late to revert to a back four, so Jamie Carragher came in to replace him. Carragher was mostly a full-back but he could play in the centre and I liked players who were adaptable. In my time with England, if I had Tony Adams in the centre I could play Stuart Pearce on the left of him and Gareth Southgate on the right. These players had the advantage that they were used to working on their side of the field, whereas if you play three out-and-out centre-halves, they can sometimes be all over the place if they have to go wide.

In addition to all this, there was an undercurrent to the qualifier, with sinister warnings about racist and fascist chanting against our players. It was an unfortunate build-up. In the match itself, Croatia took the lead with a looping header, which our defenders had not dealt with properly. But just after that there came an incident you would not consider as a possibility when Gary Neville rolled a pass back to Paul Robinson. The ball bobbled and as Paul went to clear, he kicked only thin air and was horrified, like the rest of us, as he turned to see the ball trundle on and over the line. We were 2-0 down and, with 20 minutes to go, we were unable to come back.

It was a far worse result than anticipated and, coming after that goalless draw against Macedonia, it was badly received. The England supporters, who had been kept behind at the end waiting to be herded back to their transport, were letting us have it with their vitriol. I recall talk in some quarters that Steve should stand down after just five matches. Lunacy!

We never played that formation again, but that doesn't mean it was a bad system. I had used it in Euro 96 and it had worked. He decided not to use it again, because I think he just wasn't comfortable with it and was not used to it. Was it wrong on the day? Well, if it does not work it is wrong, end of story. As Steve's assistant, I could argue the case for why we had used it, but that would not placate the supporters or the media, who quite rightly were interested only in the result – and the result that day in Zagreb was sickeningly disappointing.

It is after a bad result like this that the manager has to come into his own, and influence all around him with his positive attitude. I knew Steve would rally the team, and in the meantime he carried the blame for defeat, as managers should. The criticism he got was intensive and cruel, but he did not run for cover and instead faced the slaggings on the back pages, which I thought he did with good grace.

We then went on to play a couple of friendlies, getting a good 1-1 draw with Holland in Amsterdam and then losing 1-0 to Spain and an Andres Iniesta strike at Old Trafford. That result was hardly a disaster, as they were then on an unbeaten run of matches, including a terrific draw against Brazil back at Wembley, and they would go on to win the European Championships in the summer of 2008. Those games were followed by three more qualifiers, all away from home. We had a disappointing 0-0 draw in Israel, then beat Andorra 3-0 and Estonia also by 3-0.

With five games left to play, we were in fourth place, but just three points behind the group leaders Croatia. Meanwhile, Steve's team was developing and the players looked happy to play in London at the new Wembley. The goals started going in, which was a bonus, with three 3-0 wins in succession against Israel, Russia and Estonia. We had two games left to play, one in Moscow against Russia and then back to Wembley to take on Croatia, with qualification now in our own hands.

Sadly, our final two qualifying matches were disastrous. We were forced by UEFA to play Russia on an artificial pitch at the Luzhniki Stadium. Synthetic surfaces were banned by UEFA, except where weather conditions made anything other than plastic unplayable, and that included Moscow, where the snow and freezing conditions can come early. There are other parts of Russia less prone to such extreme weather, but the Russians wanted to play in Moscow. The decision by UEFA to force us to play an international match on an artificial surface was a disgrace. Did the FA protest strongly enough,

or was it another of those submissions without a fight by the great
and good, not wishing to disturb what they perceived as our relationship with our masters in Switzerland?

I had helped introduce the plastic pitch at Queens Park Rangers,
so I knew all the arguments for and against playing on one.
However, there is no doubt that there are clear differences between
playing on the two surfaces, so having time to practise on one was
essential. Steve was left to find a plastic pitch for England to train
on prior to leaving for Russia. He found one outside Manchester,
and the England squad were grateful to train on a little school's private artificial pitch in Altrincham. It was hardly ideal.

Moscow was everything we thought it would be: bloody cold,
bloody miserable and bloody unfair. I do not know if it was their
manager, Guus Hiddink, who ordered the plastic to be heavily
watered just prior to the match. Somehow I don't think they did it
to help us. Despite that and a touch of trepidation, we started well.
Wayne Rooney gave us the lead in the first half with a volley,
despite the Russians' complaints that he was offside. It was close,
but my instant reaction was that Wayne had been smarter than his
marker.

Wayne then conceded a penalty which they equalised from. It
was a foul but no penalty as it took place outside the box, as the television replays proved. The referee that day had earned a
reputation for some controversial decisions, and of course match
officials can get it wrong and deserve our sympathy on occasions,
but what should concern UEFA and FIFA administrators is when
a referee is regularly being criticised for his errors. In those circumstances, they should act to remove an official from refereeing
vital games. Within a few minutes of them equalising, they hit the
winner. This was the most important major international match
played on a synthetic surface. Afterwards, UEFA ordered it to be
ripped out and relaid with grass for the Champions League final a

year later. I do find it odd that what they deemed good enough for a national side was not good enough for their elite clubs.

Qualification was then out of our hands, until the Russians opened the door for us when they were beaten in Israel. It left us needing only a draw in the final match against Croatia at Wembley to qualify, something which seemed well within England's capabilities. If only! Steve's plans were crippled yet again, this time by a stack of injuries. I remember at least five players missing for duty. We had often used Emile Heskey and Michael Owen up front together, as they combined well, but they were both injured and unavailable, as was Wayne Rooney. The list went on: John Terry and Ashley Cole both had to withdraw.

The team we ended up with was: Carson; Richards, Campbell, Lescott, Bridge; Wright-Phillips, Lampard, Gerrard, Barry, J. Cole; Crouch. Among the substitutes was David Beckham. He had quit as England's captain after the 2006 World Cup, when Sven-Göran Eriksson was manager. When Steve took charge, he announced it was time to leave Beckham out of his immediate plans. It made good sense, and soon after Beckham decided he would play his football in California, where he would have to prove it was of a high enough standard for him to resurrect his international career. His absence allowed Steve to try out some of the younger players available. He continued to monitor Beckham and said he would bring him back if needed.

Beckham returned to the England side a year later, when he started in the friendly we played against Brazil in June 2007, and he had played in three matches before this one. There were stories circulating that some of Steve's staff, including me, were less than happy at his recall. These probably originated from the same people who had claimed Beckham ran the show, or tried to, under Eriksson and had become too self-important. However, there was no animosity from me towards David. For a start, Steve selected the squad and not me. Of course, he would listen to input from me and others, but I have always considered it the duty of the national coach to pick the best players without bias. If Steve, having watched David play in the States, believed he was fit for this level, then he was entitled to select him.

When I was England manager I appreciated the quality of the young players coming out of Old Trafford, David being one of them. He was too young to be considered for my squads, but I would have considered him – with no guarantees – for the 1998 World Cup qualifying campaign had I continued in the job. That pleasure would be Glenn Hoddle's. Would I have had him in the squad? I think so, but as I've said there would be no guarantees. You must always consider what a player can do for you and your system of play. Who would he replace? Glenn used him in the World Cup finals and that had a very unfortunate ending. It was not going David's way and that showed against Argentina when he flicked out with his boot, which earned him red and cost his team. He learned from that, and the criticism he received afterwards, and handles himself very well. The way to behave, his actions, every-thing was drummed into him by his management team. He conducts himself like you want your son to behave.

His presence could be uplifting, and his experience vital. He was battle-hardened and has had an extraordinary career that transcended football. He might have had an entourage that was described as the Beckham Circus, and he had extensive (and I would have thought tiring) interests outside football, but he has always been a fitting ambassador for the English game and I had no worries about him being included. If he could find a spark to ignite England's performances, then his selection would be justified. There might have been some envy, but I think the players liked him. I saw him as an asset, not a one-trick pony as he has been called. They used to say that about the great Hungarian Ferenc

Puskas, which England discovered to their regret was so much nonsense. David's crossing of the ball and his free-kicks were exceptional. It was his 30-yard, superbly executed free-kick in the last minute against Greece which guaranteed England's place in the 2002 World Cup finals. If he could conjure up one of those at the right time in this campaign, it would be invaluable.

Steve was confident, as were the players, as we went into the crucial game. It is not an excuse to say the pitch was a joke, with the conditions atrocious – they were! An England team should consider Wembley an advantage, but how could it be when the pitch had been torn up by an American football match three weeks earlier and turned into something resembling a farmer's field by a two-day rain storm. It would cut up badly, which was to neither team's advantage when we should have been doing everything we could to make it to our benefit.

One of the most controversial selections had been to choose Scott Carson in goal, in place of Paul Robinson. He had been in goal for our friendly win in Austria a few days before, in preference to David James. James was the more experienced man, but there had been a difference of opinion between him and Ray Clemence about the selection policy as I remember it, and that would have swung the vote in favour of Scott. David is a very confident man who would have believed he should have been involved. Paul would consider himself dropped and Steve went with Scott, which was a brave decision. Nobody could have foreseen the drama about to reveal itself.

The scene was bleak when the Croats took a two-goal lead inside the first 15 minutes. Their first goal will be remembered as another goalkeeping error. When you witness such a catastrophic blunder, you are helpless even if you can understand the player's agony. It was almost unbelievable, a where-were-you-when-it-happened moment. Niko Kranjčar is acknowledged as a player with superb skill and he would go on to earn an FA Cup winner's medal with Portsmouth that season, but this wasn't a moment of brilliance from him. He hit a speculative shot from 30 yards, Scott stooped to collect it, but as he did so the ball bounced just in front of him and went over his hands. For this sort of error to happen once in a campaign is unusual enough, but for it to happen with different goalkeepers a year apart is extreme, cruel misfortune. It serves no purpose to look back on an incident like this and say the selection was wrong, that it was down to Carson's inexperience. The considerable experience of Robinson had not saved us from a similar loss in Zagreb. I would have preferred experience on a night when a draw would have seen us qualify.

Ivica Olić then scored their second a few minutes later to leave England with a huge task to turn round the game. The gods had deserted England too frequently when we needed a little help. It highlighted the misfortunes that Steve had to endure. He was unlucky at a time when he was getting things together and producing good performances. He deserved better, but nothing changed for the rest of the half.

At the interval he made two changes, bringing on Beckham for Shaun Wright-Phillips, while Jermain Defoe replaced Gareth Barry to give us more firepower up front. I made the point that they had 20 minutes to pull one goal back and then 25 minutes to find the equaliser, in other words there was plenty of time and we should not panic. For a few minutes a revival looked possible, when Frank Lampard scored a penalty after Defoe was brought down. Then Beckham crossed for Peter Crouch to equalise. Suddenly the temperature in the stadium rose, as did our hopes. But Croatia's substitute Mladen Petrić found space for a winner and England were beaten. We had failed to qualify. Steve paid for it with his job, and I left with him.

Maybe he just didn't click in the role. I've heard people say he was a bit too sure of himself, too cocky, super confident up front, if I can put it that way, in the way he presented himself publicly, but you must have something about you as England manager, so I wouldn't blame him for that. I certainly wouldn't see it as a reason to rubbish the man. I felt he could have done better than to refer to players by their nicknames, with 'Stevie G' as an example. I didn't think he had to do that to prove his closeness to the squad and, innocent though it was, it didn't go down well with the general public. It seemed a bit naïve. Given that most people in the game saw him as a strange appointment, and perhaps thought he had been over-promoted and was in need of a few more years as a club manager, he would have done well to have appeared slightly less cocky. In my experience, he was at his most difficult, a bit too self-possessed, when things were going well, which didn't help him when things went wrong.

He took a considerable amount of destructive criticism from the media. Considering his inexperience, I thought he took that full-on and courageously. I never heard him complain about a bad press, even when he was lambasted as the 'Wally with the Brolly', for standing under an umbrella during the Croatia match. I have to say it was as big misjudgement as any I can remember from a national coach in front of a bitter, disillusioned crowd and a worldwide audience. If it is wet, you get soaked. I was nonplussed when I saw him with the umbrella. I did not think he would use it, and wondered what the hell he was doing when I first saw him with it on the track. When he put it up while England fans were screaming for his sacking, it was seen as the final straw. However, the real cause of his downfall was not that umbrella, or the performances, but the results. If Steve had been winning he could have taken a deck chair and sat outside the bench smoking a cigar in dark sunglasses. Everybody would have said it was funny and isn't he a lad.

# 19

# MY FINEST

THERE ARE PLAYERS so talented and endowed with such quality you cannot argue about their status. These players are the giants of our game, not necessarily in stature but by contribution. They do what others cannot, and in a sport swamped by envy they are generally accepted as special and loved. I could not count the number of occasions I have sat with my fellow professionals and discussed in bars, hotel lobbies or restaurants who were the greatest players we had seen. It is an illuminating exercise when everyone can have an opinion and especially when someone mentions a player whose genius has been undervalued or even forgotten.

These are my selections, to be agreed with or argued against – I can imagine there will be plenty of that. They are not in order of greatness. I doubt there is one of the players I have named who does not deserve to be there. The problem, as always, remains those you cannot include in a limited list. I have named Bobby Moore in my World and British Top Ten, the only player who appears in both. I could not leave him out of either, though I have coupled his name with that of Kevin Keegan in the British section with an explanation. It was my intention to increase the numbers to include all those who made my professional life so complete during Euro 96. That was impossible, so no room other than in my memory for Teddy Sheringham, Alan Shearer, Steve McManaman, Darren Anderton, dazzling Gazza, Tony Adams, Paul Ince, Gary Neville, Stuart Pearce, Gareth Southgate, the big man in goal David Seaman and David Platt.

There is no room either for David Beckham, whom I talk about in the chapter dealing with me signing on as Steve McClaren's England assistant; no Wayne Rooney or Steven Gerrard who have performed so brilliantly and consistently for club and country. Sacrilege! I can understand the accusation; why so few modern stars? They are fitter, more sophisticated in their approach to the game and unarguably richer.

Why no Gazza or Shearer or Gary Neville or Ryan Giggs? Why have I ignored Duncan Edwards, one of my earliest heroes, or Jimmy Greaves, a genius of a former team-mate, or the great Sir Tom Finney, who died at the beginning of 2014? Why? Because it is my choice and the players I have chosen were of extra-special significance to me. Bobby Moore was an old and wonderful friend, and if it was a choice between him and Tony Adams, great player though he was for me and England, then Bobby has my vote. I could name players from each of the six eras I have lived through who I loved to watch, but none were better than Messi or Ronaldo. This is not meant to start an argument. Each of the players I have named has made a massive impression on me and I am certain on everyone who loves the game.

## WORLD TOP TEN

DIEGO MARADONA – The most thrilling of players. On the ball he had a combination of bull-like strength and the grace of a dancer. He scored great goals and won major competitions on his own. There are very few players who have achieved that and I would hazard a guess none have done it with such impact. We know about his addictions and are shocked by them. Should we be? As a role model, of course yes, but we should also have sympathy for a human being who has been under the most intense of spotlights since he was a prodigiously talented teenager. Even then, he was considered to be the greatest of his generation, by some distance. Diego is arguably *the* greatest, and one of the biggest regrets of my career was that I was never able to play him at Barcelona because his money problems meant he needed to be transferred to recharge his bank account. I would love to have worked with the man.

LIONEL MESSI – Messi specialises in the impossible. You wonder what he is going to do and then he produces something astounding. It is one of my great pleasures to watch him if a Barcelona match coincides with my return to the city. Great players make you want to be there. Television is fine, and a great alternative, but to study Messi live is a different experience every time. What is it about Argentina that produces players of his unique ability? It is a combination of genes, the circumstances that produce hungry fighters, traditional role models and his country's obsession with football. I am not convinced luck is a factor. Players like Messi have a natural talent, but they have to work relentlessly to perfect it. He looks fragile, like a naughty schoolboy compared with the statuesque Cristiano Ronaldo, but he is strong and will run 60 yards with the ball and have the strength to keep going, shoot and probably score. Players who can do that are uncommonly strong.

CRISTIANO RONALDO – In my world list I have considered players from all eras and Ronaldo is indisputably a front runner, toe-to-toe with Messi. Does that rivalry drive them to higher and higher standards? Do they see it as a personal challenge in every match to do something that sets them apart? They will study what the other does, determined that when their careers are over they can look back and say: 'I was the best.' Cristiano has the self-confidence and belief never to be overshadowed by Lionel. Who would have thought the current era would have produced two players of such extraordinary talent and that we would be able to admire them both in competition with one another? Cristiano has his failings. He can irritate with his constant demand for protection from match officials, which is not always justified, but when he is on the ball you cannot avert your eyes. We enjoyed his presence at Old Trafford for a few years. I hope he will come back to grace the English game.

PELÉ – The first of the superstars? His talent was awesome, and he has remained untainted by any sort of public scandal. He played with free expression and a new style, quite unlike anything I had watched even from the most talented of European footballers. He was so full of joy, it seemed to me. He was relaxed, almost shy, in winning the World Cup for Brazil against Sweden in the 1958 final. I was transfixed as I watched him live on a small black and white telly. He was just 17 at the time, only a couple of years older than me, and that somehow confirmed the enormity of his performance. Even so, you could not say then he would be quite the icon he became. He made me more determined to earn my living from the game and eventually proud to be a professional. There was nothing he could not do with a ball and, like Maradona, he possessed a grace which had to withstand physical, often violent, tackles. Pelé could and did look after himself – very few were able to kick him out of the game – but relentless and cowardly marking did from time to time bring him to his knees, as against Bulgaria in the 1966 finals. He didn't dribble like Maradona, but devastated opponents with his sheer athleticism. I have spent time in his company, notably at an Umbro seminar in South Carolina, and remember him as a delightful man.

JOHAN CRUYFF – Not just a wonderful player but a great thinker. He was the leader of what became known as Total Football, working in conjunction with the coaching of Rinus Michels. The two of them developed the Dutch style of play we recognise as very special. They stretched each other for the good of their game. You cannot mention one without the other; the classic imaginative football produced by Johan and the innovative common-sense, clever coaching of Rinus. They learned from each other, the master footballer and the master coach. Johan comes into the greatest category because of his skill and fearlessness when it came to trying something new. He had the soaring confidence to let it all hang out when under intense pressure. Johan created an aura that all the greats possess.

BOBBY MOORE – Bobby was classic. For me, as a player and a man, he would be top of the tree. It has been said so many times, but we accept he was not the fastest on the ground but his mind was razor sharp, his positioning perfect. There was a majesty about his game, and leadership came naturally to him. When all about him was chaos, Bob would be cool and calm. If I do have a regret about not joining West Ham as a youngster, it would be not playing in the same team as Bobby. Bobby was a true great on the field and off it.

FRANZ BECKENBAUER – I played against him when I was with Chelsea prior to the World Cup in 1966. The Doc took us to Germany for a friendly match against the West German national side that could have been condemned as helping them out, though that would have been unfair. In that match I played directly against Franz and we beat them. He played football like he looked, coolly elegant. He was what would best be described as officer material. I bracket him with Bobby Moore and there were plenty of similarities between them. You think of one, you think of the other. If only Bobby could have been given the opportunity to do for England what Franz did for German football, as ambassador and national manager.

GERD MÜLLER – He is the one name people tend to forget, yet he was supreme at what he did: scoring goals. His record is phenomenal, and he has to be one of the top strikers of all time. I would suggest that, when you consider the strength of the Bundesliga, he could claim to be the best. He was a small figure, but lethal in front of goal. I do not usually make a great study of statistics, but I know his record is staggering: 'Der Bomber' scored 68 goals in 62 matches for Germany, 365 Bundesliga goals for Bayern Munich in 427 appearances, and 66 goals in 74 European club matches. We knew he was deadly, and it was his extra-time goal that knocked England out of the Mexico World Cup in 1970. In that tournament, considered the greatest finals of all time, he scored ten goals. I bumped into him in a bar in Germany when we were both still playing. I can testify that not only could he score goals like a champion, he could also drink like one. He is now a coach at Bayern Munich after winning his battle with alcohol.

MARCO VAN BASTEN – For a big man, he played with elegance and beauty, which is how I would describe the goals I have seen him score. His strike against Russia in the 1988 European Championship final in Germany came from what most assumed was an impossible angle, far too acute to score from. It is one of those goals I can remember frame by frame because it was so spectacular, a masterstroke. Marco is another who progressed under the influence of Cruyff and Michels.

ALFREDO DI STEFANO – We all remember him for the game in Glasgow in 1960 when his Real Madrid side, dressed all in white, destroyed the Germans of Eintracht Frankfurt 7-3. It stands as an example of how football should be played. Alfredo scored three goals and Ferenc Puskas four in what turned out to be a magnificent rout against an excellent Eintracht side. I remember how it was a record crowd at Hampden of 135,000, and like Pelé in the 1958 World Cup, I was able to watch it live on television and be astonished by the brilliance of the occasion. Di Stefano had an upright stance, and looked peerless, always in control, so impressive. He was an early hero of mine and has remained a player I recall with pleasure. We met when I was at Barcelona and the great man was manager of Valencia. At the end of the match, which we won, he came over to shake my hand, congratulated me on our win and wished me well as we set out to win the title – it was a special gesture from a man so closely associated with Barcelona's biggest rivals.

## BRITISH TOP TEN

PAUL MCGRATH – An unusual choice, I hear some say, but he was a wonderful player, and I tried to sign him for Queens Park Rangers, but in the end his wife stopped him from coming even though he wanted to. She worried there would be too much attention on him in London when in fact it would have been the reverse. You can hide in London and have your privacy. He could have walked down Bond Street unnoticed, but would have been swamped if he tried the same thing in any city street in the centre of Manchester, Birmingham or Liverpool. Despite his battle with drink, Paul was a hugely gifted defender. He also suffered fearful injuries and that meant he could not train, yet he would not only play brilliantly on match-day but often be the game's outstanding player. I hope he is sustained by the knowledge that he will be remembered as one of the all-time greats by people like me who so admired him.

GEORGE BEST – It is sad that George never played in the finals of a World Cup. He deserved to be compared on the field to the world's finest. We knew him for what he was: the possessor of a talent that was mesmeric. He learned to look after himself and, like Pelé, he shirked nothing. George's best defences against those who tried to cut him down were his skill and speed. He was as much a part of the Swinging Sixties as the Beatles and Carnaby Street, British football's first pop star and very much the man of his time. But that is all irrelevant to the contribution he made to our game. When I think of George's ability, it was no less than breathtaking. I said how disappointing it must have been for him never able to have the chance to compare himself with other greats, but the real sadness is that such a wonderful talent and charming man should kill himself with alcohol.

DENIS LAW – If you want a man for all seasons, then Denis comes in at number one. If you want a player who would fight and battle for the cause, then again he would be my number one. Denis was a warrior who would score goals on any surface. Like all great players, he would astound you with what he could do when all seemed lost. He was world-class, and I do not think there was a match I either played against him or watched him when he didn't come up with something quite different in his game. I have heard Scots (those based in Scotland, that is) contriving to diminish his ability, but I think they should recognise how lucky they were to have had someone of his talent play for them.

BOBBY MOORE – I have already stated my claim for Bobby, but also wanted to recognise the debt the English game owes to Kevin Keegan. For a number of years in the 1970s and early 1980s, Kevin was a playing sensation, a one-man band who stood out as someone who, through hard work and a force of energy that could light up a city, became one of Europe's elite footballers. He was an honest player and likewise as a manager.

DAVE MACKAY – He was a great hero of mine when I was watching football as a youngster and working to be a professional. To see Mackay and Danny Blanchflower play together was to see the perfect balance between two players. They complemented each other. It is important for young aspiring players to be influenced by the greats. Dave inspired me, and in time we played in the same Tottenham team.

BOBBY CHARLTON – Bobby had an incredible surge of speed. He was the quickest player off a standing start and it was even worse when he ran at you. You just knew that if he went past you then your goalkeeper would be tested. Bobby's ability to shoot from distance with power and accuracy was astounding in an era when the ball would be three times the weight it is today. A good man – he deserves his place in the history of our game.

BRYAN ROBSON – A wonderful team player, Bryan was a midfielder who wanted to score goals. He saw it as part of his job. I would marvel at his ability to score when not all midfield players, even the good ones, would attempt to. It was a vital part of his game whether with West Brom or Manchester United or England.

He played for me when I was England Under-21 coach; he was on the bench with me for Euro 96 and we worked together at Middlesbrough. His commitment to his team has always been total. He has my respect and the respect of all those he has worked with as a player, coach and manager.

KENNY DALGLISH – They said it was impossible to replace Kevin Keegan, but Liverpool did that when they signed Kenny from Celtic. He proved himself to be as valuable, if not more valuable, as Kevin. It was yet another example of brilliant Anfield husbandry by manager Bob Paisley. Kenny is all football brain. He could see in advance what to do and where to be for maximum effect. He was an astoundingly intelligent player. He produced great goals and scored great goals. I cannot name a player who has contributed more for his team. He is among the last of the truly great footballers to come out of Scotland.

JOHN CHARLES – John was a heroic almost mythical figure. Everything you read about him – his performances for Leeds and Wales and then the marvellous career he made in Italy – was the sort of thing that makes for a boyhood hero. He was extraordinary, and you cannot compare John to any other player. He could play centre-forward or centre-half and be equally good in either role. He would score a couple of goals and then, if the team was up against it, go back to protect the lead he had given them. He looked like a god and was treated like one in Italy, where he played for Juventus. John never received the recognition he should have done from the game. He is immortal.

CLIFF JONES – He was a master winger. Fast! No player could accelerate like Cliff. He was extraordinary. Not only would he go past you on either side, he would do it with the ball under control.

That is doubly remarkable. I loved to watch him play and when I played against him I guess watching is what I did a lot of, too. Cliff was an early hero of mine and it was a pleasure to sign for Tottenham when he was in the squad. He was no giant, about five foot seven, and lean like a whippet. And despite his height he was lethal in the air. If a cross came over from the right, he would zip in from the left and, as the defenders were poised to deal with it, too late – he would get there first. He was a hugely talented footballer and wonderful company. Cliff was a true great of the British game and justifiably rated in his prime as the best left winger in the world.

# 20

# ENGLAND FOR THE ENGLISH

No more svens and Fabios – only Englishmen managing England. The Football Association wouldn't have to put it in writing, simply select their man when the time comes and like all the other major football nations choose one of their own.

I have never been able to relate to those who rubbish England and English football. It is particularly difficult for me to accept that there are people out there involved in the great game who cannot grasp the value of international football, the passion it generates, the pride that stems from victory and the utter depression that follows defeat in major competition. I was brought up to believe in Queen and country. It is the way we were, as I have explained more fully elsewhere. Like most, I welcomed the influx of foreign players and coaches to the Premiership so I am no flag-waving xenophobe, no little Englander.

Arsène Wenger and Jose Mourinho are two foreign coaches who have added knowledge and colour to our club game and helped make ours the most watched and wealthiest league in world club football. But it would surely be unbecoming of us to let other countries believe there is such a dearth of coaching talent in England that we would ever again hand 'outsiders' the keys to the England national team as we have done twice since 2001.

Sven-Göran Eriksson and Fabio Capello were brought in at great expense to repair a run of failure (apart from two semi-finals, in the 1990 World Cup and the 1996 European Championships) since Sir Alf led us to the summit in 1966. Neither Sven nor Fabio resolved the problem. Sven stumbled in the quarter-finals against Brazil after a bright start to the 2002 World Cup in Japan, and in the quarter-finals again when they lost to Portugal on penalties in Euro 2004. It was the Portuguese who did for us again in Germany in 2006. His record is respectable but still below expectations given the players at his disposal.

Fabio's appointment was regarded as a triumph, but in reality it turned out to be another disappointment. His team qualified for the 2010 World Cup only to be hammered by the Germans 4-1. They had failed to make the quarter-finals and in the worst way possible. They rebounded from that to qualify without defeat for Euro 2012 prior to his resignation. Fabio had good and bad times, but England always appeared tense and never relaxed to me.

We are the only major power that has sanctioned a foreign coach, however talented, to take charge of our national side. Can you imagine Italy being managed by anybody other than an Italian? Or Brazil not being led by a Brazilian? It would be preposterous, not even a consideration. They haven't always been able to find a great innovative coach every time, but that's how it goes. They still want a countryman to look after their country. We have exposed ourselves to look desperate and there is no reason to be. When a foreign coach moves in to a job you are hiring a professional, someone who for the right money will do a job for the club or should do.

Life as an international coach is significantly different. When you are in charge of England, as I learned, it is about the values your parents and grandparents instilled into you. You were working for yourself and your team, but in essence you were doing it for the country, not just the supporters of a club. It is a heavy responsibility, and no matter how Sven and Fabio took to the job I do not believe they could possibly have had the same passion for and belief in succeeding as an Englishman. They would have the same determination to win, but that would be the demand of their professionalism.

It is nonsense to say we did not have coaches of our own who could not have done the job, maybe even more successfully than our imported Swede and Italian. Not all of them would have the backing of everybody, but so what? I could reel off a list of managers and coaches that were available to the Football Association and may have been considered but have been rejected since we went for Sven in 2001: Ron Atkinson, Sam Allardyce, Alan Curbishley, Alan Pardew (can he remain a contender after his 'face-to-face' with Hull's David Meyler? I doubt the FA would ever consider him now), Brian Kidd, Steve Bruce, Steve Coppell and Peter Taylor, who like Stuart Pearce stood in for one match. There are other names, England men such as Peter Reid who have to be considered. I had Bryan Robson on my staff for Euro 96 on the understanding that he was being groomed for the job, but an ideal man has been lost to England since his return to an ambassadorial role at Old Trafford.

Each of them is highly experienced, though I am not saying all would want the job or be suitable for it. The modern coach not only has to be a good teacher but a diplomat able to deal with FA bosses, his own staff, the players and the media. I was impressed with Steve Round, who was Steve McClaren's England coach when we worked together. He has packed a lot of experience into a relatively young age (43) and now that he is assistant to David Moyes at

Manchester United his CV is even more impressive. Of the other modern young coaches with international playing experience, Tony Adams and Gareth Southgate have the drive to make the breakthrough. Gareth is already involved with the FA as manager of the Under-21s, having already managed Middlesbrough. Tony has travelled into Europe and beyond to study and practise coaching. He is preparing himself for a big job and he would deserve the chance after a brilliant career for Arsenal and England. I would like to see him fixed up soon, the sooner the better. I remember another player with high potential as a manager or coach, Bobby Moore, who was never given the opportunity to achieve what I thought he was capable of. I could argue both Tony and Gareth need more experience and the wisdom that comes with age, but they are enlightened and intelligent. With men like these, and those impressing in the Championship such as Leicester's Nigel Pearson and Sean Dyche of Barnsley, the FA should never need to look elsewhere for new coaches.

There will always be problems connected to England. The supply of international-class footballers is one major hurdle to be negotiated and to achieve that we need more high-calibre teachers. Our coaching staffing levels nationwide are low when you compare them with the Germans, the French and smaller countries like the Dutch. We need thousands more coaches to influence our youngsters before bad habits become ingrained and impossible to rectify.

There are modern-day moans about how the England manager in recent years has fewer and fewer players to select from, owing to the numbers of foreigners operating in the Premier League. I don't think it has changed much, whether you were Sir Alf or Don Revie or Ron Greenwood. A friend told me how he was phoned by Alf way back when he was England manager. Alf asked him if he could possibly oblige him by checking in the *Rothmans Football Yearbook* how many players he could reasonably expect to have available. My friend did just that and phoned Alf back.

'How many?' Alf asked.

'Thirty-five,' my friend replied.

'That's very interesting,' Alf said. 'It is three more than I thought.'

Roy Hodgson would have been no better or worse when he selects his squad for the finals in Brazil. In those days the English leagues were packed with Scots, Welsh and Northern Irish, now it is French and Africans and just about every other nationality.

Alf was never recognised as the greatest of coaches in the teaching sense, but he was the first England manager to talk tactics. He walked into the bar area of the team hotel prior to 1966 and offered the press a drink. He then explained he had something to say of great importance, it being that England would use a 4-3-3 formation in future. It was dismissed by some as 'the numbers game' and not taken seriously. That was just six months before the World Cup finals.

It could be we have just too many foreign managers in the Premier League. Englishmen have found and will continue to find that their own country is a restricted market for them. That is something only the clubs can deal with. A new foreign manager will bring in his own backroom team, which again blocks the way for our coaching talent to work in the top league. And with more and more owners coming from overseas and investing their millions into our clubs, it is a trend that must be monitored by the Premier League.

The doors must be much more difficult to enter through, ideally open only to the very best foreign coaches. There can be little objection to someone like my pal Louis van Gaal operating in the Premiership, provided he was willing to give young English coaches an opportunity to develop at the top.

Van Gaal has a reputation for being arrogant, and I can confirm he does not hang about when it comes to speaking his mind, and he has an ego that is something to behold – and not without justification, as he is one of the great coaches of the modern era. I have grown to like the man and what he stands for, as he knows the business like few others.

I first got to know Louis when I spent a week with him, Pelé and other international coaches and administrators in South Carolina at an event organised by Umbro to look at the future of the game after Euro 96. He had recently won the European Cup with Ajax, and was full of confidence and bravado, so I kept winding him up as he told stories of how he had nutmegged Pelé when they had played against each other. When we were taken round Charleston on an open-topped carriage ride, he jumped down from his seat to greet two fans wearing Dutch shirts. I told him it was the first time I'd seen the star recognise the fan.

We were treated to some wonderful Southern-style hospitality, but it wasn't all to his taste: he didn't like the wonderful barbecue that was laid on one day, and nor would he join in on the country and western dancing. The next evening, we were invited to a black-tie function in a magnificent old mansion house, which was much more to his taste. Our host from Umbro made a speech at the end and, recognising that van Gaal had not been happy the evening before, he added: 'And Louis, I hope the food was good for you?'

'It was beautiful – absolutely,' replied the Dutchman, seemingly having finally learned some diplomatic skills. But then he ruined it by adding: 'But last night was shit.' He was out of order on this occasion, but he was saying it as he saw it, and we could do with more of the straight-talking Dutch attitude.

One thing I can be certain of is the ambition of the players to represent England. In my day it was easy to call them in. There were always one or two who did not have the requisite desire for the job, but the majority would be highly responsive. These were the ones who wanted to play. There were side issues that made it profitable for them, marketing and branding could produce big pay-days. But I can only speak from my own experience as a player who would happily volunteer to walk through a brick wall to play for his country. As a manager, I selected players with a similar attitude – it was never a problem.

Having spent some months looking back on my career and trying to put a human face on a business that increasingly revolves around money, I have now looked to the future, concentrating solely on the international scene where too many in the administrative side live for the money our game generates. If that keeps flowing from television and sponsors, they are happy, these men who know the price of everything and the value of nothing.

There is a ruthlessness there that can take or leave the traditions that made the game great and it is my fear that one day we will wake up and find that international football as we know it will have been sacrificed, reduced in importance at best, to suit the major club sides run by businessmen, not football men. Any undermining of international football would be opposed by the governing body FIFA, who will fight to the last man to retain their sophisticated and highly profitable World Cup tournaments, with the finals generating bucket-loads of cash. UEFA live off the money that comes from the Champions League, but their four-yearly European Championships are very healthy earners as part of the international circus.

Some years ago, before I was appointed manager of England in 1994, I was advised of a well-known and highly respected football man who had seriously suggested at a meeting of European clubs that international football could be played out each year in one month, say in June or July. The argument was that a country could complete all its friendlies in one month, a whole World Cup or

European Championship qualifying campaign in a month with the finals a year later. It is all too possible.

Why? In order to give Europe's top clubs – Real Madrid, Barcelona, Bayern Munich, Juventus, AC and Inter Milan, Paris St Germain, Manchester United, Manchester City, Arsenal and Chelsea – more time without interference to make even more money than they already do. The rest of the European game would continue as before, picking the bones left by the big boys. The point being made was that international football was something of an irrelevance. It chilled me then, not because I felt such a change was imminent but that a so-called football man thought so little about the international game, he saw radical surgery as a real possibility for the future.

It would have been all too possible. Thankfully, UEFA averted that absurdity when it was agreed in March 2014 to set up the UEFA Nations League involving the national sides of the 54 member nations. The devil is in the detail of how it can be achieved between tight club schedules and season breaks. I would be more convinced about the long-term success of what will be four international leagues involved in promotion and relegation, from the best to the weakest, if it was truly to maintain the importance of international football and improve competition and not only as a potential money-spinner for UEFA. It is infinitely better than reducing the importance and vitality of the international game to a sideshow.

# POSTSCRIPT

IT IS 7 JANUARY 2013 and we have disembarked at Valparaiso for the flight home. The trip was worthwhile in so many ways, one of the most important being the opportunity it has given me to reflect at leisure on my career. You never think you have achieved enough in life, and there are times I know when, but for my impetuosity, it would have been more advantageous to accept my fate, to stay put rather than move on, to be less restless in my approach to just about everything. But then you realise that all the controversies, the rows, the accusations and counter-accusations, the criticisms, the anger, the search for revenge, matter little. At the time these things caused severe irritation to me and to those around me, but such problems have never stopped me enjoying a loving family, or the company of friends.

The constant throughout my entire career is my love of the game and my amazement at its grip on the lives of people from every nationality, every creed, every colour, every section of society, the very rich and the very poor. Football is a phenomenon and the people have made it that. Why? It is beautiful and demands beauty from those who represent it. You do not have to be big or small to play, and these days you do not even need to be a boy to succeed, as the women's game continues to grow. All that matters is that you can do with your feet what other sports accomplish far less artistically with their hands. The clue is in the name.

It is the skill which astonishes. It grips you at a young age, whether it was the game I grew up with, played in heavy boots that covered the ankles, or the modern game, performed in carpet slippers. The best players, the truly exceptional ones, inspire you to try to emulate them. Few manage that, but the wonderment of watching outstanding skill remains my obsession. I still have the urge to coach and would do so tomorrow if a national job was made available. It would not be about the money, but just about the opportunity.

While football has given me a wealth of wonderful memories, it has not made me a wealthy man. I have accumulated more from outside of football than from in it, though the game is the catalyst that attracted the interest in me. I am able to devote time to projects that satisfy me, like my community club interest in the Welsh village my mother came from. I am involved in a European Union-backed scheme for youngsters, open to all throughout the member states, where we house them and will offer football coaching allied to educational facilities. I have benefited from property investment and now own a boutique hotel – La Escondida, which translates as 'The Hideaway' – in the stunning countryside inland between Alicante and Valencia in Spain, which I am currently renovating and will be ready for the summer of 2014. In the hills I have this ancient tower which was used as a lookout to warn when the Moors were about to attack centuries ago. There are plans made – stalled by the recession – for a major development in the area on the other ground I own in Spain to include at least one major hotel plus private housing.

I have my weekly *Sun* column during the season, plus my work with Al-Jazeera's Duncan Walkinshaw of beIN Sports channel as a football analyst, which means flying out to Qatar on a regular basis. I have rarely been soured by football or with players and my fellow coaches and managers. It is the humility of the many great football people I have worked with, as friend or rival, not the arrogance, bitterness and selfishness of the few, which has been enlightening. I have never lost my enthusiasm for the 'Beautiful Game'. It has given me the time of my life, and I hope that is conveyed in this memoir.

# ACKNOWLEDGEMENTS

THERE ARE OCCASIONS you thank folks for just being there. They jog the memory and you need that for a project as extensive as this. My grateful thanks to Ian Marshall of Simon & Schuster whose advice was there for me at all times and to Jonathan Harris, my literary agent. My thanks to my business partner Joe Pawlikowski and my PA Zoci Kuzmancevic; to Dan King for running a very critical eye over the chapters and whose opinions were clear and to the point; to Ian Doran for reading the initial manuscript and pointing out errors only a Fleet Street man would immediately spot; and to Ashley Price of APA Secretarial for transcribing a huge supply of taped interviews.

My lawyer and friend Nick Trainer was there as always to assure me of my rights. My former clubs refreshed the important dates in my career and pointed out events and incidents my memory needed prodding to recover: Tony Incenzo at Queens Park Rangers; Simon Felstein and Andy Porter of Tottenham Hotspur; Crystal Palace's Ian King and Middlesbrough's Graham Bell all looked up their records on my behalf. David Barber's memory of all things to do with the Football Association was invaluable. But for them, this would have been so much more difficult to compile.

I read a number of books on a refresher course of my life, some of which I enjoyed. Graham Hunter's tome on Barcelona, *Barça:*

*The Making of the Greatest Team in the World*, brought back memories of my time as part of a great club. I was also able to recall my days at QPR through Gordon Macey's comprehensive history of the club. On the internet, Statto, Soccerbase and Englandstats were there when needed.

And finally my thanks to Alex Montgomery for helping me put this all together. To all, once again, my thanks.

# INDEX